ENHANCING
GOVERNMENT

ENHANCING GOVERNMENT

FEDERALISM FOR THE 21ST CENTURY

Erwin Chemerinsky

STANFORD LAW BOOKS
An Imprint of Stanford University Press
Stanford, California

Stanford University Press
Stanford, California

©2008 by the Board of Trustees of the Leland Stanford Junior
University. All rights reserved.

Printed in the United States of America on acid-free,
archival-quality paper

Library of Congress Cataloging-in-Publication Data

Chemerinsky, Erwin.
  Enhancing government : federalism for the 21st century / Erwin
Chemerinsky.
    p. cm.
  Includes bibliographical references and index.
  ISBN 978-0-8047-5198-8 (cloth : alk. paper) — ISBN
978-0-8047-5199-5 (pbk. : alk. paper)
    1. Federal government—United States. 2. Constitutional law—
United States. 3. United States. Supreme Court. I. Title.
  KF4600.C48 2008
  342.73′042—dc22

                                                  2008001960

Typeset by Newgen in 10/15 Sabon

For Catherine

Contents

Acknowledgments

THE THESIS FOR THIS BOOK, that federalism could be reinvented as being about empowering government at all levels, occurred to me over twenty years ago. Since then, the law of federalism has changed dramatically. I have no doubt that when constitutional historians look back at the Rehnquist Court they will say that its greatest changes in constitutional law were in the area of federalism. The Roberts Court likely will build on these decisions and impose even greater limits on federal power. My central thesis is that these decisions restricting federal power in the name of states' rights are terribly misguided and advance none of the underlying reasons for having a federalist structure of government.

Over the past two decades, as the law of federalism has changed, I have worked to create my alternative conception of federalism. I have written many articles in law reviews, working out various aspects of this thesis. But this book is my first effort to develop an overall argument for my approach to federalism.

Because I have been working on these ideas for so long, it is impossible to acknowledge all who helped me or all who read and commented on earlier parts of the manuscript. At the risk of omission, I especially want to thank Bill Marshall, Larry Simon, and Stephen Siegel. I am especially grateful to Neil Siegel for his detailed comments on the entire manuscript. Their contributions to my thinking is reflected throughout the book, although I have no doubt that each disagrees with some of what I have written.

Finally, and most significantly, I want to thank Catherine Fisk. More than anyone else, she has sharpened my thinking on this and all subjects. Her support, encouragement, and love made this book, and so much else, possible.

ENHANCING GOVERNMENT

Introduction

THE THESIS

IN THIS BOOK, I challenge the traditional conception of federalism as a limit on federal power very much followed by the Supreme Court over the past ten years. I argue for an alternative vision of federalism as empowerment of government at all levels. The federalism of the 1990s and the early twenty-first century—in both the Supreme Court and Congress—has been about restricting federal authority for the sake of protecting states' autonomy. The new Supreme Court, with Chief Justice John Roberts and Justice Samuel Alito, is likely to be even more aggressive in limiting federal power in the name of states' rights. This book strongly criticizes this approach as failing to serve the underlying goals of federalism and, more generally, of government. Federalism should be reconceived as being about equipping each level of government with expansive tools to enhance liberty and deal with social problems.

The genius of having multiple levels of government is that there are many different actors—federal, state, and local—that can advance freedom and respond to society's needs. Yet, the federalism decisions over the past decade have been striking in that they have ignored these values and have applied federalism principles in a highly formalistic fashion to invalidate desirable government actions.

In the 1990s, the Supreme Court used federalism as the justification for declaring unconstitutional federal laws requiring the cleanup of nuclear waste[1] and background checks for people seeking to own firearms,[2] prohibiting guns near schools,[3] and allowing victims of gender-motivated violence to sue in federal court.[4] All of these are unquestionably socially beneficial laws. Few in our society would argue against containing radioactive material or in favor of having guns near schools and permitting criminals unrestricted access to firearms. Yet, the Supreme Court's rulings in each of these cases expressly ignored the social benefits of the laws and instead relied on a highly formalistic approach to federalism as the basis for limiting federal authority and striking down these statutes.[5]

During the same time, the Supreme Court also has used federalism to dramatically limit the scope of Congress's power to enforce the post–Civil War, or Reconstruction, amendments, which authorize the federal government to act to prevent and remedy civil rights violations by the states. For example, the Court used federalism as the basis for invalidating the Religious Freedom Restoration Act, a federal law significantly expanding religious freedom.[6] Although the act was adopted by an almost unanimous vote in both houses of Congress, the Court declared it unconstitutional without even considering the benefit of the law in advancing a crucial aspect of liberty. Once more, the Court's reasoning was highly formalistic, and federalism was used entirely as a limit on federal power. Subsequently, in the past decade, the Court has relied on this decision to limit Congress's power to authorize suits against state governments when states infringe patents and when they discriminate in the workplace based on age and disability.[7]

Ironically, at the same time, a Court that professes commitment to states' rights has repeatedly found state laws preempted by federal law. For example, in one case, the Supreme Court found preemption of product liability under state law despite a provision in federal law expressly preserving all other causes of action.[8] In another decision, the Court held that a state could not refuse to contract with companies doing business in Burma, thus denying states a basic choice as to how to spend taxpayers' money.[9] In another, the Court found that federal law preempted state regulation of outdoor billboards and signs in stores advertising cigarettes, even though there was no indication that the federal law had anything to do with the placement of advertisements.[10]

In this book, I argue for a very different approach to federalism. In dealing with federalism, the Supreme Court's decisions should be based on open and express attention, and where necessary, the balancing of how to best advance liberty while enhancing effective governance. Generally, this will mean abandoning the use of federalism as a judicial limit on federal or state authority and instead employing it to uphold the power of each level of government to deal with social problems.

More specifically, seeing federalism in terms of empowerment rather than limits will profoundly reorient constitutional law in three major ways. First, it will mean a broad conception of congressional power unconstrained by concerns of federalism. Congress's authority under provisions such as the commerce clause and Section 5 of the Fourteenth Amendment[11] should be expansively interpreted, limited primarily by the political process and judicial protection of other parts of the Constitution, such as separation of powers and individual rights. The Tenth Amendment should not be interpreted as an independent basis for invalidating federal laws.[12] This, of course, is not a radical change in the law; it is a return to the approach to federalism followed from 1937 to 1995.

Second, viewing federalism as empowerment will mean significant expansion in the availability of federal courts to hear federal claims. Since the end of the Earl Warren Court, the Supreme Court has repeatedly and significantly narrowed the scope of federal jurisdiction in the name of federalism. This has occurred through the Court's restrictions on who has standing to sue in federal court;[13] its expansion of states' Eleventh Amendment immunity,[14] which bars suits against states in federal court; its creation of new abstention doctrines;[15] and its great narrowing in the availability of federal courts to grant habeas corpus petitions.[16] In particular, I am very critical of the unprecedented expansion of sovereign immunity in which the Court has invented a principle found nowhere in the Constitution and has made it supreme over the enforcement of the Constitution and all federal laws. These rulings neither advance liberty nor enhance effective government. Rather than using federalism to limit federal court authority, a better view would be to use federalism to more broadly open the doors to both federal and state courts to those asserting federal claims, and especially, those federal claims that are constitutional.

Third, reorienting federalism as being about empowerment and not limits also would mean an enhancement in state and local power. Actions by these levels of government are repeatedly limited in the name of federalism by preemption. Removing the shackles of federalism would mean a much more limited preemption doctrine, with courts finding for preemption based only on an express congressional declaration of a need to serve an important governing interest, or in cases where federal law and state law are mutually exclusive. It is important to recognize that seeing federalism as empowerment is not about aggrandizing federal authority; it is empowering government at all levels, including at the state and local levels, to deal with society's urgent needs.

The central idea is that federalism should not be a highly formalistic doctrine used to limit the ability of government to deal with important problems. Instead, federalism should be reconceived as a functional analysis of how to best equip each level of government with the authority that it needs to respond to the serious problems facing American society.[17]

My primary focus in this book is on the approach to federalism that should be followed by the Supreme Court in interpreting the Constitution. I analyze and criticize the approach to federalism that the Court has followed throughout the twentieth century and particularly in recent years. This book is descriptive of the constitutional doctrines that have been developed, normative in its criticism of them, and prescriptive in offering an alternative approach to constitutional federalism. Additionally, I argue that Congress should approach federalism in a functional way and be guided by the underlying values of federalism—including efficiency, participation, concern for externalities, and fostering community—in deciding the scope of federal law.

THE POLITICAL CONTEXT

No area of constitutional law has changed more dramatically in the past fifteen years than federalism. In 1995, for the first time in sixty years, the Supreme Court declared a federal law unconstitutional as exceeding the scope of Congress's commerce clause power.[18] For only the second and third times in sixty years, the Court invalidated a federal law for violating the Tenth Amendment, and the first case had been expressly overruled.[19] At the same time, the Court has used federalism to enlarge the states' immunity to sue in federal court for violations of federal statutes.[20] These decisions have spawned literally hundreds of lower court decisions concerning federalism and ensure that federalism will be a constant issue before the Supreme Court for years to come. Although it is unclear how far the Court will extend these rulings, the cases signal a major change in constitutional law and American government. There is no mistaking the Court's ardent desire to use federalism to limit the powers of Congress and the federal courts.

At the same time, federalism was often invoked in the Republican-controlled Congress of the 1990s. Soon after the Republican triumph in the 1994 election, the new congressional leaders, Bob Dole and Newt Gingrich, held a press conference at which they displayed a large poster containing the words of the Tenth Amendment and proclaimed a return to the principles of federalism.[21] In fact, one of the first laws adopted by the new Congress was the "unfunded mandates law," which prohibits Congress from enacting statutes that impose substantial costs on state and local governments.[22] Another example of a law with important federalism implications is the Antiterrorism and Effective Death Penalty Act of 1996, which greatly restricts the ability of federal courts to grant habeas corpus relief to those convicted in state courts.[23]

Not surprisingly, these changes have occurred at times when conservatives were in control of both the Supreme Court and Congress. In the Supreme Court, recent federalism rulings usually have been decided by a 5–4 margin, with the majority comprised of the five most conservative Justices: Chief Justice William Rehnquist and Justices Sandra Day O'Connor, Antonin Scalia, Anthony Kennedy, and Clarence Thomas.[24] The shift from Justice O'Connor to the more conservative Justice Alito offers the likelihood of even greater limits imposed by the Supreme Court based on federalism. In Congress, of course, it has been the conservatives that have invoked federalism in a wide variety of areas, such as in arguing for the radical changes in welfare law enacted in 1996.[25]

At the time that this book is going to press, Democrats control both houses of Congress. There have not been any major federalism decisions in the first two years of the Roberts Court. Yet, analysis of the issue at this time is no less important. The future political composition of Congress, of course, is uncertain, but there is no doubt that the Supreme Court will be quite conservative for many years to come. The first two years of the Roberts Court have shown a Court significantly more conservative than its predecessor,[26] and there is no doubt that soon it will turn its attention to federalism.

Conservative use of federalism is nothing new in American history. Since the country's earliest days, federalism has been used as a political argument primarily in support of conservative causes. During the early nineteenth century, John Calhoun argued that states had independent sovereignty and could interpose their authority between the federal government and the people to nullify federal actions restricting slavery.[27] During Reconstruction, Southern states claimed that the federal military presence was incompatible with state sovereignty and federalism.

In the early twentieth century, federalism was successfully used as the basis for challenging federal laws regulating child labor, imposing the minimum wage, and protecting consumers.[28] During the depression, conservatives objected to President Franklin Roosevelt's proposals, such as Social Security, on the grounds that they usurped functions properly left to state governments.[29]

During the 1950s and 1960s, objections to federal civil rights efforts were phrased primarily in terms of federalism. Southerners challenged Supreme Court decisions mandating desegregation and objected to proposed federal civil rights legislation by resurrecting the arguments of John Calhoun.[30] Segregation and discrimination were defended less on the grounds that they were desirable practices and more in terms of the states' rights to choose their own laws concerning race relations.

In the 1980s, President Ronald Reagan proclaimed a "new federalism" as the basis for attempting to dismantle federal social welfare programs. In his first presidential inaugural address, President Reagan said that he sought to "restore the balance between levels of government."[31] Federalism was thus employed as the basis for cutting back on countless federal programs.

Hindsight reveals that federalism has been primarily a conservative argument used to resist progressive federal efforts, especially in the areas of civil rights and social welfare. There is, of course, nothing inherent to federalism that makes it conservative. In the relatively recent past, prominent liberals, such as Justice William Brennan, have argued that there should be more use of state constitutions to protect individual liberties.[32] But the federalism of the 1990s and the early twenty-first century, like federalism throughout much of American history, has been mostly a tool employed by conservatives to champion conservative goals.

FEDERALISM AS A BASIS FOR LIMITING GOVERNMENT

More specifically, and more subtly, throughout American history, and especially in the 1990s, federalism has been used by conservatives as a way of trying to limit government power.[33] In other words, conservatives have used federalism as a procedural way of blocking substantive reforms with which they disagree. During the first third of this century, a conservative Supreme Court used federalism to limit Congress's power and to strike down many federal laws. Since 1970, the conservative Warren Burger and William Rehnquist Courts used federalism as a basis for limiting federal court jurisdiction, especially in suits against state governments and in reviewing state court decisions.

Over the last ten years of the Rehnquist Court, again federalism was used to limit Congress's power by restricting the scope of the commerce clause, limiting authority under Section 5 of the Fourteenth Amendment, reviving the Tenth Amendment as a constraint on federal power, and greatly restricting Congress's ability to authorize suits against state governments. In each instance, a conservative Court has employed federalism to invalidate progressive legislation, such as gun control efforts and the expansion of religious freedoms. Simultaneously, federalism was used by the conservative Congress of the 1990s in a similar fashion, such as in greatly restricting access by prisoners to federal court in the Prison Litigation Reform Act and the Antiterrorism and Effective Death Penalty Act. In other words, conservatives use federalism as a tool to limit the power of the federal government, whether out of true concern for protecting state governments or as a way of blocking federal actions opposed on other grounds.

It is striking that the Court's use of federalism as a limit on government power has little to do with the values that it has identified as being served by federalism.[34] The values traditionally invoked to justify federalism—states are closer to the people, states serve as a barrier to tyranny by the federal government, states are laboratories for experimentation—have virtually nothing to do with the Court's decisions and, on reflection, are of little use in constitutional decision making. For example, it is difficult to see how preventing Congress from requiring states to clean up their nuclear waste lessens the likelihood of government tyranny or enhances desirable experimentation. These frequently mentioned values of federalism are little more than slogans invoked to explain the benefits of having multiple levels of government. They have essentially no relationship to any of the Court's federalism decisions.

Moreover, these values, and the Court's use of them, focus on only an aspect of federalism: protecting state governments. Although the phrase "dual sovereignty" has always been invoked as a basis for protecting the states, the other half of *dual* is the federal government and its interests under the Constitution. Federalism also is about safeguarding the federal government and the supremacy of federal law. Yet, the federalism decisions of the 1990s have given no weight, or even mention, to this consideration. For example, in expanding the Eleventh Amendment's bar on federal court jurisdiction, the Court did not even discuss whether this jeopardizes the successful enforcement and implementation of federal laws.

AN ALTERNATIVE VISION

The conservative conception of federalism as a way of limiting federal power, on examination, is highly formalistic and should be replaced by a functional analysis of how to equip each level of government with the authority to deal with social problems and enhance liberty. While the traditional approach to federalism has been about limiting federal power, an alternative conception would be to see federalism as a basis for empowering each level of government to deal with social problems. The benefit of having three levels of government is that there are multiple power centers capable of action. Federal and state courts, from this view, both should be available to protect constitutional rights. Federal, state, and local legislatures should have the authority to deal with social problems, such as guns near schools, criminals owning firearms, and the disposal of nuclear waste.

Constitutional doctrines about federalism should focus on how to empower each level of government with the necessary authority to deal with the complex problems of the twenty-first century. Viewing federalism as empowerment, not limits, would have major implications for areas of constitutional law, such as the scope of Congress's power, federal court jurisdiction, and preemption doctrines.

THE ORGANIZATION OF THIS BOOK

I develop this thesis in six chapters. Chapter 1 focuses on the paradox of post-1937 federalism. It seeks to answer the questions: How did constitutional law get here? and Where is it going?

From 1937 to 1992, the Supreme Court aggressively used federalism as the basis for limiting federal *judicial* power. At the same time, the Court almost completely refused to employ federalism as the grounds for limiting federal *legislative* power. This approach to federalism persisted almost unchanged for those 55 years, with only one federal statute being declared unconstitutional on federalism grounds, and that case— *National League of Cities v. Usery*[35]—was later expressly overruled. The Court's frequent use of federalism as the basis for limiting federal judicial authority was reflected in decisions that included the requiring of abstention, the expanding the scope of the Eleventh Amendment and state immunity to federal court litigation, and the limiting the availability of federal habeas corpus review.

Chapter 1 explores this paradox and argues that the inconsistent approach rested primarily on two premises. One is that judicial enforcement of federalism as a limit on Congress is unnecessary because the political process will adequately protect state government interests. In contrast, the emphasis on federalism as a limit on federal judicial power is based on the premise that comity—respect for state governments—is a crucial value in the two-tiered system of government created by the Constitution. At a minimum, these premises do not explain the paradox because each assumption can be applied equally in analyzing the power of Congress and the authority of the federal courts. More importantly, each assumption is dubious; it is highly questionable whether the interests of states are adequately protected through the national political process and it is doubtful whether comity should be regarded as a decisive constitutional value.

The chapter concludes by showing how the Supreme Court's federalism decisions over the past ten years have ended the paradox of post-1937 federalism. Federalism is now used as a significant limit both on the federal judicial and the federal legislative powers. I then look to the future and suggest that based on their past writings and judicial opinions, the two newest justices, Roberts and Alito, are likely to consistently vote to limit federal power in the name of states' rights. Chapter 2 examines the formalistic nature of the federalism decisions during the 1990s, and hence federalism's failure. The Supreme Court's formalism can be seen in rulings that have been reasoned deductively from largely unjustified major premises to conclusions, without consideration of what would be the most desirable allocation of power between the federal and state governments.

I then argue that federalism decisions must be based on a functional, not formal, analysis. In part, this is because it is not possible to identify any clear premises for reasoning with regard to federalism issues. The text of the Constitution says virtually nothing about the allocation of power between the federal and state governments. The framers were largely silent about this issue and their views are of limited relevance given that the government is now so vastly different from what they envisioned. There has been no consistent tradition in Supreme Court decisions that deal with federalism; quite the contrary, the rulings have been remarkably inconsistent.

Analysis must be functional because ultimately the issue of federalism is about what allocation of power provides the best governance with the least chances of abuse. Federalism is about how power should be divided between federal and state governments, and this must be based on a functional analysis of what provides for best governance in each context. Functional analysis is preferable to formalism in analyzing federalism, because it considers both the interests of the federal and the state governments and because it sees federalism as a means to effective government and not an end in itself. For example, in determining the meaning of the Eleventh Amendment, the Court must balance the benefits of state accountability with the desirability of state immunity. Yet, such functional analysis is completely absent from the Eleventh Amendment decisions of the 1990s.

Chapter 3 begins analysis of the content of a functional approach to federalism by considering the values served by federalism. Initially, I argue that the values traditionally identified as underlying federalism are of little use in a functional analysis. From time to time, the Court alludes to the underlying benefits of federalism: limiting tyranny by the federal government; enhancing democracy by providing governance that is closer to the people; providing laboratories for experimentation; and enhancing liberty. But these values are seldom more than just conclusions as to why states are important and why a federalist structure of government is desirable. Rarely, if ever, is there any explanation as to how these particular values are compromised by particular federal laws.

Initially in Chapter 3, I consider these values and especially the Court's treatment of them. I suggest that neither aspect of the paradox of post-1937 federalism has any relationship to the traditionally identified values of federalism. More significantly, the Supreme Court's decisions in the 1990s that have been highly protective of states' institutional interests have little relation to the underlying values of federalism.

I then consider the values served by the existence of both federal and state governments. The ultimate goals for government are enhancing liberty and effectively meeting society's needs. Federalism accomplishes both by securing multiple actors that can protect freedom and respond to social problems.

Moreover, federalism has other benefits: efficiency, as sometimes it is more efficient to have action at the national level and sometimes at the local; participation, as sometimes national action better engages involvement and other times localism does so; community empowerment, which is sometimes a benefit of decentralization; and economic gains, as sometimes national action is needed to deal with externalities for the sake of the economy. I suggest that these are the values that Congress should consider in deciding when national action is needed and when it is preferable to leave matters to state and local actors.

Chapter 4 suggests that federalism can be reinvented primarily in terms of empowerment, not limits.[36] The chapter begins by describing the extent to which federalism doctrines have been about limiting government power. Not only has this manifested itself as limits on federal authority but also as decisions in areas such as preemption, which have used federalism to limit state and local power.

I then outline the alternative conception of federalism. Reconceiving federalism in terms of empowerment is the best way to achieve the underlying goals of advancing liberty and enhancing effective government: having multiple levels of government means that there are several different actors capable of dealing with society's needs.[37]

Reorienting federalism in this way would mean a dramatic change in the scope of Congress's authority. Congress's power under the commerce clause and Section 5 of the Fourteenth Amendment, as well as its spending power, would be broadly defined.

Several examples are used and discussed in detail to illustrate how my proposed functional approach to federalism would be different than the Rehnquist Court's rulings. For instance, in light of the historical failure of many states to provide an adequate remedy for women who are victims of gender-motivated violence, it was appropriate and desirable for Congress to decide as it did in the Violence Against Women Act. From a functional perspective, this law very much advanced liberty and provided more effective government. The law is a paradigm illustration of how if one level of government is failing, as many states were, it is beneficial for another level of government to act. Another example discussed in detail to help showcase functionalism's benefits, and explain how functionalism differs from formalism, is the Rehnquist Court's many decisions concerning state sovereign immunity. I argue that the Court's decisions in this area have been misguided and have wrongly sacrificed government accountability; an express balancing of the goals of federalism leads to exactly the opposite conclusions reached by the majority on the Supreme Court.

Chapter 5 develops what it would mean to reconceptualize federalism in terms of empowering federal court jurisdiction. For decades, courts and scholars have focused on whether there is parity between federal and state courts in their willingness to uphold constitutional rights in defining the scope of federal jurisdiction. I argue that this is misguided in that there is no meaningful way of assessing the comparative virtues of two levels of courts. The goal in defining federal court jurisdiction should be this: allowing litigants with constitutional claims to choose the forum that they believe is most likely to vindicate their claims. For example, such an approach would mean much narrower abstention doctrines and much greater availability of federal habeas corpus relief.

Chapter 6 looks at federalism as empowerment in terms of preemption. In recent years, the Supreme Court has broadly defined preemption doctrines, frequently finding progressive state and local regulations to be preempted by federal law. I argue for a much narrower approach to preemption that would leave more authority to state and local governments. Under this approach, preemption should be found only if a federal law expressly preempts state and local action, or if there is a direct conflict with federal law.

WHY

The challenge for the twenty-first century is to reinvent American government so that it can effectively deal with the enormous, enduring social problems and the growing threats to personal freedom. Increasing the chains on government—as the Court and Congress are now doing in the name of federalism—is exactly the wrong way to enter the new millennium. Today, government is often perceived as unresponsive to or incapable of addressing society's most pressing problems. The possibility of effective government is maximized by having three levels of legislative power capable of action, and two levels of judicial power capable of protecting rights. In this book, I want to challenge the currently dominant conception of federalism as limiting government and argue for a new, empowering vision.

This alternative approach is actually more protective of states. By basing federalism not on formalism but on advancing the underlying values, the interests of all levels of government can be advanced. State and local governments, as much as the federal government, can benefit from the increased authority that comes from a vision of federalism as empowerment.

Contrary to the current Court's approach, the structure of government should not be regarded as an end in itself. Government at all levels exists to advance human freedom and to meet the needs of society. In this book, I seek to offer an alternative conception of federalism that is consciously oriented to achieving these goals.

The Paradox of Post-1937 Federalism: How Did We Get Here and Where Are We Going?

AS A TEACHER, DURING the 1980s and early 1990s I often was struck by the seeming inconsistency in the cases I taught in both my Federal Courts and Constitutional Law courses. Many mornings across many semesters, in Constitutional Law, I taught cases like *United States v. Darby*[1] and *Garcia v. San Antonio Metropolitan Transit Authority*[2] that eschew any use of federalism considerations as a limit on federal legislative power. Then, in the afternoon, I taught Federal Courts and looked at cases like *Younger v. Harris* that proclaim the importance of "Our Federalism" as a major limit on federal judicial authority.[3]

Indeed, I believe that this paradox was at the core of the Supreme Court's handling of federalism issues from 1937 until the 1990s. Federalism was not used by the judiciary as a limit on federal legislative power, but federalism was used by the judiciary as a limit on federal judicial power.[4]

In this chapter, I first describe the seeming inconsistency in the cases concerning federal legislative and federal judicial power. Then I suggest that the Court's premises do not justify the difference in approach; the justifications for the *absence* of federalism as a limit on federal power apply as much to the federal judiciary as to Congress, and the justifications for the *use* of federalism as a limit apply as much to Congress as to the courts. More importantly, the decisions in each area rest on premises that are highly questionable.

I then suggest that the decisions of the Rehnquist Court bring an end to this paradox by reviving the Tenth Amendment as a constraint on congressional actions and by creating judicially enforced limits on the scope of Congress's commerce clause power, which allows the legislature to regulate commerce with foreign nations and Indian tribes as well as among the states. This tendency toward restraining congressional authority is reflected most notably in the following cases: *New York v. United States*; *United States v. Lopez*; *Seminole Tribe of Florida v. Florida*; *City of Boerne v. Flores*; *Printz v. United States*; *Florida Prepaid Postsecondary Education Expense Board v. College Savings Bank*; *Alden v. Maine*; and *United States v. Morrison*. I review these cases in some detail, both to show that they mark an end to the paradox described in the first part of the chapter and to provide a basis for criticizing them in subsequent chapters.

Interestingly, in the first few years of the twenty-first century, the Supreme Court's federalism decisions have come down in favor of federal power and against the states' rights position.[5] I suggest that these decisions do not mark a reversal of a trend; the Court has not overruled earlier decisions, but neither has it extended them. I conclude by suggesting that these past few years are likely to represent a pause in aggressive judicial protection of federalism. Based on all that is known about Chief Justice John Roberts and Justice Samuel Alito, the Supreme Court will no doubt significantly expand the protection of federalism and limit federal power in the years ahead. This means the Court will intensify efforts to limit both federal legislative power and federal judicial power in the name of states' rights and federalism.

The focus of this chapter is thus descriptive, seeking to explain where the law is and how it got there. Subsequent chapters are critical of this approach to federalism, and the final chapters in the book offer an alternative vision of federalism.

THE PARADOX DESCRIBED: FEDERALISM LIMITS ON JUDICIAL POWER, BUT NOT LEGISLATIVE POWER

The paradox described above manifested itself early in the emergence of modern, post-1937 constitutional law.[6] In *National Labor Relations Board v. Jones & Laughlin Steel Corp.*,[7] *United States v. Darby*,[8] and *Wickard v. Filburn*,[9] the Supreme Court made it clear that federalism would not be used as a limit on congressional power. The Court rejected the core notion of dual federalism that there is a zone of activities that is left exclusively to the states for regulation and control.[10]

From the late nineteenth century until 1937, the Supreme Court used this notion of dual federalism both to construe narrowly the scope of congressional power under Article I of the Constitution and to invalidate laws as violating the Tenth Amendment (which provides that all powers not granted to the United States are reserved to the states and the people, respectively). For example, the Court restrictively defined the meaning of "commerce" to exclude mining, manufacture, and production from the scope of congressional regulatory power.[11] Additionally, the Court held that federal laws regulating aspects of business such as production violated the Tenth Amendment. The Tenth Amendment, the Court expressly declared, reserves a zone of activities to the states and thus invalidated federal laws that limit the use of child labor,[12] that provide subsidies to agriculture,[13] and that require a minimum wage[14] on the grounds that they interfered with state sovereignty and violated the amendment.

But *National Labor Relations Board v. Jones & Laughlin Steel Corp.*, *United States v. Darby*, and *Wickard v. Filburn* ended the doctrine of dual federalism. No longer were considerations of federalism used as the basis for narrowly defining Congress's power. No longer was the Tenth Amendment a restraint on federal legislative authority. *Darby* declared that the Tenth Amendment is "but a truism," that all power not granted to Congress are reserved to the states.[15] In *Darby*, the Supreme Court upheld the federal law providing for the minimum wage. In other words, the Tenth Amendment simply was a reminder that Congress could legislate only if it had express or implied authority. The Tenth Amendment did not reserve to the states a zone of activities for their exclusive control.

Almost simultaneous with the demise of federalism as a limit on congressional authority, the Court proclaimed the importance of federalism as a limit on federal judicial power. *Erie Railroad Co. v. Tompkins* held that the use of federal common law in diversity cases was an unconstitutional usurpation of state power.[16] At the same time that the Court was rejecting the Tenth Amendment as a limit on Congress, the Court apparently was relying on it to explain that federal common law had "invaded rights which . . . are reserved by the Constitution to the several states."[17]

There was a striking tension between *Erie*'s reliance on the Tenth Amendment and *Darby*'s almost simultaneous proclamation that the Tenth Amendment is but a truism. Even so, the analysis of the Tenth Amendment in either case was not merely rhetorical or superfluous to the result. Each case set the paradigm for the Supreme Court's use of federalism for at least the next half century. The ruling in *Erie*, that dramatically changed litigation in the United States, was very much based on the Tenth Amendment. The Court gave three reasons for overruling *Swift v. Tyson* (which had provided that federal courts were to develop federal common law) and holding that federal courts should apply state law in diversity cases. On examination, though, it is clear that only the Tenth Amendment explains the decision.

First, the Court said that new historical research cast doubt on the validity of the holding in *Swift v. Tyson*. Specifically, Justice Louis Brandeis, writing for the majority, cited the research of Charles Warren.[18] Warren said that he found an earlier handwritten draft of the Judiciary Act of 1789.[19] But this argument, by itself, clearly did not justify overruling *Swift v. Tyson*.[20] *Swift* interpreted a federal statute, the Rules of Decision Act, which provided that federal courts were to use state law as their basis for decisions in the absence of federal law. Congress, of course, could amend the law if it disagreed with the Court's decision, such as if Congress was persuaded by Warren's research. Judge Henry Friendly explained: "If ever Congress' reenactment of a statute or failure to alter it could be fairly taken as approving a prior judicial interpretation, the unchanged existence of section 34 for a century after Story's construction was such a case."[21]

Second, *Swift v. Tyson* was overruled because "[e]xperience in applying [it] . . . had revealed its defects, political and social; and the benefits expected to flow from the rule did not accrue. Persistence of state courts in their own opinions on questions of common law prevented uniformity; and the impossibility of discovering a satisfactory line of demarcation between the province of general law and that of local law developed a new well of uncertainties."[22] Without a doubt, the strongest argument for overruling *Swift* was its pernicious effects on the fair administration of civil justice. *Swift* encouraged forum shopping, and it was unjust that the results in a case depended on the citizenship of the parties. However, again, this argument did not justify the *Court* overruling *Swift*. The ill effects of using federal common law in diversity cases could have been demonstrated to Congress and it was for *Congress* to decide whether to revise the federal statute.

Indeed, Justice Brandeis expressly admitted the inadequacy of the first two arguments to justify overruling *Swift*. Justice Brandeis declared: "If only a question of statutory construction were involved, we would not be prepared to abandon a doctrine so widely applied through nearly a century. But the unconstitutionality of the course pursued has now been made clear and compels us to do so."[23] In other words, the ruling in *Erie* was based on the third argument: that applying federal common law in diversity cases violated the Tenth Amendment. Justice Brandeis quoted Justice Oliver Wendell Holmes, indicating that *Swift v. Tyson* represented an "unconstitutional usurpation of powers by courts of the United States."[24] There was surprisingly little explanation in the opinion as to why *Swift v. Tyson* usurped states' rights, but it is clear that the *Erie* very much rested on this conclusion. *Erie*'s use of federalism as a limit on federal judicial power reflected an approach that is followed to this day.

The importance of the decision cannot be overstated. *Erie* substantially changed the nature of law practice. A huge body of federal common law was simply wiped from the books. Attorneys' choice of forum decisions was radically altered as was federal and state relations. Unless there is a federal constitutional, treaty, or statutory provision, state law controls in all transactions and in all courts in the country. As *Erie* proclaimed, "There is no general federal common law."[25] *Erie* made clear that federalism provides a crucial limit on the scope of federal judicial power.

United States v. Darby, decided just three years later, is no less significant in defining a paradigm for federalism, especially when looked at together with *National Labor Relations Board v. Jones & Laughlin Steel Corp.*, which preceded *Erie* by a year, and *Wickard v. Filburn*, which succeeded *Darby* by a year.

Jones & Laughlin Steel involved a constitutional challenge to the National Labor Relations Act, which gave employees the right to bargain collectively, prohibited unfair labor practices—such as discrimination against union members—and established the National Labor Relations Board to enforce the law.[26] The law contained detailed findings on the relationship between labor activity and commerce. The act applied when there was an effect on commerce and, in fact, it expressly defined "affecting commerce" as meaning "in commerce, or burdening or obstructing commerce or the free flow of commerce, or having led or tending to lead to a labor dispute burdening or obstructing commerce or the free flow of commerce."[27]

The Court initially explained how the Jones & Laughlin Steel Corporation was clearly a part of interstate commerce. It was the fourth largest producer of steel, with factories in Pennsylvania; mines in Pennsylvania, Minnesota, Michigan, and West Virginia; steel fabricating plants in Louisiana and New York; warehouses in Illinois, Michigan, Tennessee, and Ohio; and steamships operating on the Great Lakes.[28] The Court noted that overall the steel industry employed 33,000 and 44,000 individuals to mine ore and coal, respectively; 4,000 to quarry limestone; 16,000 and 343,000 to manufacture coke and steel, respectively; and 83,000 to transport its products.

In light of these findings, *Jones & Laughlin Steel* does not at first seem to be a radical departure from the earlier decisions. The Court explained how the steel business was part of the stream of commerce and how labor relations within it had a direct effect on this commerce. However, there was no doubt that the decision marked a major shift in the law. The Court flatly declared that "the fact that the employees . . . were engaged in production is not determinative."[29] The decision spoke broadly of Congress's commerce power: "The fundamental principle is that the power to regulate commerce is the power to enact 'all appropriate legislation' for 'its protection and advancement,' 'to adopt measures' to 'promote its growth and insure its safety,' 'to foster, protect, control, and restrain.' That power is plenary and may be exerted to protect interstate commerce no matter what the source of the dangers which threaten it."[30]

Although the Court's holding in *Jones & Laughlin* might be squared with the decisions of the earlier era, the Court clearly signaled a major change in direction.[31] In fact, in a companion case, which has received much less attention, the Court upheld the application of the National Labor Relations Act to a relatively small clothing manufacturer.[32]

The radical nature of the Court's shift was apparent in the 1941 decision, *United States v. Darby*.[33] *Darby* involved a challenge to the constitutionality of the Fair Labor Standards Act of 1938. This act prohibited the shipment in interstate commerce of goods made by employees who were paid less than the prescribed minimum wage (25 cents per hour at that time). In upholding the act, the Court departed from all aspects of the pre-1937 commerce clause doctrines.

The Court rejected the view that production was left entirely to state regulation, explaining that Congress may control production by regulating shipments in interstate commerce. The decision said: "While manufacture is not of itself interstate commerce, the shipment of manufactured goods interstate is such commerce and the prohibition of such shipment by Congress is indubitably a regulation of commerce."[34] The Court spoke repeatedly of "the plenary power conferred on Congress by the commerce clause."[35]

Perhaps most significantly, the Court expressly overruled *Hammer v. Dagenhart* and emphatically rejected the view that the Tenth Amendment limits Congress's power. In its most famous words, the Court declared that "[t]he amendment states but a truism that all is retained which has not been surrendered."[36] This means that a law is constitutional so long as it is within the scope of Congress's power; the Tenth Amendment would not be used by the judiciary as a basis for invalidating federal laws.

The third major decision, *Wickard v. Filburn* left no doubt that the pre-1937 commerce clause doctrines had been completely abandoned.[37] Under the Agricultural Adjustment Act, the secretary of agriculture set a quota for wheat production in which each farmer was given an allotment. Farmer Filburn owned a small dairy farm in Ohio and grew wheat primarily for home consumption and to feed his livestock. His allotment for 1941 was 222 bushels of wheat, but he grew 461 bushels and was fined $117. He claimed that federal law could not constitutionally be applied to him because the wheat that he grew for home consumption was not a part of interstate commerce.

Justice Robert Jackson wrote an opinion that upheld the application of federal law and ruled against farmer Filburn. The limits on commerce power that were enforced in the earlier era were flatly rejected. The Court stated: "[Q]uestions of the power of Congress are not to be decided by reference to any formula which would give controlling force to nomenclature such as 'production' and 'indirect' and foreclose consideration of the actual effects of the activity in question upon interstate commerce." [38] In other words, the distinctions that were crucial in the earlier era—between commerce and production, and between direct and indirect effects on commerce—no longer were followed. The Court declared: "Once an economic measure of the reach of the power granted to Congress in the Commerce Clause is accepted, questions of federal power cannot be decided simply by finding the activity in question to be 'production,' nor can consideration of its economic effects be foreclosed by calling them 'indirect.' " [39]

The application of the Agricultural Adjustment Act to homegrown wheat was upheld because of the cumulative effect of that wheat on the national market. The Court explained that homegrown wheat was the single most variable factor in the wheat market and that it could account for more than 20 percent of production.[40] Therefore, even though Filburn's wheat only had a negligible impact on interstate commerce, Congress could regulate his production because cumulatively homegrown wheat had a substantial effect on interstate commerce. The Court noted that even though Filburn's "own contribution to the demand for wheat may be trivial by itself, [it] is not enough to remove him from the scope of federal regulation where, as here, his contribution, taken together with that of many others similarly situated, is far from trivial." [41]

These decisions, *Erie, Jones & Laughlin Steel Corp., Wickard,* and *Darby,* are reviewed at length because they defined the paradigm for the Supreme Court's federalism analysis for over a half century. This approach to federalism—the Court's refusal to both limit congressional power through state sovereignty and restrain federal judicial authority—continued, almost without exception, from 1937 until at least 1992.

Professor Laurence Tribe, in his seminal 1987 text, remarks that "[f]or almost four decades after 1937, the conventional wisdom was that federalism in general—and the rights of states in particular—provided no judicially enforceable limits on congressional power." [42] In 1976, the Court appeared to revive federalism as a limit on congressional power in *National League of Cities v. Usery*, in which a federal law that required state and local governments to pay their employees a minimum wage was invalidated.[43] The Supreme Court held that Congress could not regulate states in areas of "traditional" or "integral" state responsibility.[44] But just nine years later, in *Garcia v. San Antonio Metropolitan Transit Authority*, the Court expressly overruled *National League of Cities*.[45]

Justice Harry Blackmun, writing in *Garcia*, unequivocally declared that it was not for the federal courts to enforce the Tenth Amendment. He explained that it had proven impossible to define what activities are so "integral" to state governments that Congress cannot regulate them. He expressly relied on Columbia Law professor Herbert Wechsler's landmark article from 1954, *The Political Safeguards of Federalism: The Role of the States in the Composition and Selection of the National Government*, and concluded that the national political process provided sufficient safeguards to protect state government interests.[46] *Garcia* was thus a strong reaffirmation of the post-1937 judicial deference to Congress and of the Court's unwillingness to even consider federalism challenges to federal legislation.

The Supreme Court's emphasis on federalism as a limit on federal judicial power also remained almost unchanged for over a half century. *Erie*, of course, stands as a cornerstone of the law since 1938. Additionally, the Court developed several abstention doctrines that were expressly based on the need for federal judicial deference to state courts. For example, *Railroad Commission of Texas v. Pullman Co.*[47] held that federal courts must abstain in constitutional cases if state law is unclear and a state court's clarification of its law can make a federal constitutional ruling unnecessary. *Pullman* decided that the federal district court erred in declaring unconstitutional a Texas regulation that was blatant race discrimination. The Railroad Commission of Texas issued a regulation preventing the operation of sleeping cars unless there was not only a porter but also a conductor present. In Texas, at this time, conductors were white and porters were black.

The Court said that it was unclear under Texas law whether the commission had authority to issue the rule. The Court further stated that the federal court should have abstained from deciding the case until the state court had the chance to clarify the state law. If the state court ruled in favor of the plaintiffs, holding that the commission acted improperly in promulgating the regulation, then the matter would be resolved. However, if the state court upheld the regulation, then the matter could return to federal court for a determination of the constitutional issue. In other words, the Supreme Court held that where state law is uncertain and a clarification of state law might make a federal court's determination of a constitutional question unnecessary, the federal court should abstain until the state court has had an opportunity to resolve the uncertainty as to state law.

The Supreme Court emphasized federalism and the need for state courts. It said that abstention avoided friction between federal and state courts. Justice Felix Frankfurter, writing for the Court, stated that "[f]ew public interests have a higher claim upon the discretion of a federal chancellor than the avoidance of needless friction with state policies." [48]

Moreover, the *Pullman* Court explained that abstention is desirable on federalism grounds because it reduces the likelihood of erroneous interpretations of state law. State courts are the authoritative voice as to the meaning of state laws. Apart from the tensions caused by mistakes in construing state law, there is an independent value in the correct interpretation of the law and in avoiding situations where the federal court's view of state law is later overruled by the state court. [49] Thus, it is argued that it is preferable to allow state courts to interpret state law, rather than have federal courts guess as to how state courts would do so. [50]

The *Pullman* abstention, like other abstention doctrines, is illustrative of the Supreme Court's use of federalism as a limit on federal judicial power during the same era that it was eschewing the use of federalism as a limit on congressional authority. [51] Although these decisions have been followed throughout the post-1937 era, the Earl Warren Court moved away from concerns about states' rights as a limit on federal court authority especially in decisions expanding the scope of federal habeas corpus review.[52] But the Warren Burger and Rehnquist Courts consistently relied on federalism as the basis for narrowing the scope of federal judicial power.[53] For example, the Court, even prior to the 1990s, ruled that the Eleventh Amendment broadly bars suits against state governments in federal courts.[54] Likewise, the Court frequently invoked concerns about state sovereignty and autonomy as justifications for restricting the scope of federal habeas corpus review.[55] As mentioned earlier, the Supreme Court expressly relied on federalism concerns to require that federal courts avoid interfering with pending state court proceedings.[56] Indeed, *Rizzo v. Goode* held that considerations of federalism limited the ability of federal courts to hear allegations of abusive practices by a local police department.[57]

There is a striking difference between the Court's reaffirmation in *Garcia* of *Darby*'s holding that the Tenth Amendment is but a truism and its statement in *Younger v. Harris* that " 'Our Federalism' . . . occupies a highly important place in our Nation's history and its future." [58] The difference reflects how the Court's treatment of federalism varied depending on whether the issue is a limit on the power of Congress or on that of the federal courts.

THE ASSUMPTIONS OF THE PARADOX

The paradox of Supreme Court use of federalism as a limit on federal judicial power, but not federal legislative power, rested primarily on two premises. One is that judicial enforcement of federalism as a limit on Congress is unnecessary because the political process will adequately protect state government interests. This is implicit throughout the post-1937 period and explicit in the Court's decision in *Garcia*.[59] Professor Herbert Wechsler's *Political Safeguards of Federalism*[60] provides the intellectual foundation for this approach. Wechsler argues that the interests of the states are represented in the national political process and that the nature of that process provides sufficient protection of state sovereignty, thus making it unnecessary for the courts to enforce federalism as a limit on Congress.[61]

In contrast, the emphasis on federalism as a limit on federal judicial power is based on the premise that comity—respect for state governments—is a crucial value in the two-tiered system of government created by the Constitution. In *Younger v. Harris*, for example, the Court explicitly invoked the notion of comity and emphasized that an injunction halting state judicial proceedings would be an undue "negative reflection" on the competence of state courts and a disruption likely to cause friction between the court systems.[62] Similarly, in *Fair Assessment in Real Estate Association Inc. v. McNary*, the Court refused to allow the federal court to decide a section 1983 challenge to the constitutionality of a state's tax collection practices, because "such a determination would be fully as intrusive as the equitable actions that are barred by principles of comity."[63]

In holding that state court decisions should have preclusive effect in federal section 1983 actions, the Court emphasized that "comity between state and federal courts" is a "bulwark of the federal system" and that the dignity of the state courts necessitates federal judicial respect for state court judgments.[64] Similarly, in limiting the scope of federal habeas corpus review, the Court frequently emphasized that "[f]ederal habeas review creates friction between our state and federal courts, as state judges—however able and thorough—know that their judgments may be set aside by a single federal judge, years after it was entered and affirmed on direct appeal."[65]

Interestingly, each premise is very much confined to its own sphere. The Supreme Court did not speak of the importance of comity in the relationship between Congress and the states. Nor did the Court discuss whether the federal judiciary is sufficiently sensitive to the interests of the states as to make enforcement of federalism as a limit unnecessary.

But neither premise logically is confined to just its own sphere. Moreover, each premise is based on factual assumptions that are, at the very least, unsupported and indeed highly questionable.

The Court's refusal to use federalism as a limit on Congress was based on the assumption that the states' interests are adequately represented in the national political process. Yet why aren't those interests also adequately represented in the judicial process? Advocates before a court certainly can argue the importance of states' interests as a consideration for judicial decision making. The judiciary can give weight to federalism as a value in deciding jurisdictional doctrines, such as the scope of habeas corpus and state sovereign immunity. One of the problems with Supreme Court discussions of federalism in decisions concerning federal jurisdiction is that the Court has made it seem that federalism dictates the result, rather than that federalism is one of the important values to be weighed and considered. For example, in decisions about the scope of the Eleventh Amendment, there never really is any discussion about the proper balance between the desire for state immunity and the need for state accountability.[66]

Perhaps more to the point, the assumption that states' interests are adequately represented in the national political process seems highly questionable.[67] At the time the Constitution was written, states chose senators and thus were directly represented in Congress. But now, with the popular election of senators, why believe that the states' interests as states are adequately protected in Congress?[68] The assumption must be that the voters, in choosing representatives and senators, weigh heavily the extent to which the individual legislator's votes reflect the interests of the state as an entity. Yet, simple observation of congressional elections shows that the deciding issues are usually basic ones; for example, the economy, health care, and the personalities of the candidates. The interests of the voters are the focus of attention, not the institutional interests of state and local governments. Certainly, it could well be that the "primary constituencies of the national representatives may . . . be precisely those that advocate an extension of the federal power to the disadvantage of the states."[69] Modern political analysis suggests that elected representatives respond to the pressure of interest groups, especially interest groups that contribute money to campaigns.[70] From this perspective, states are unlikely to be a particularly powerful interest group.

I am not making the "strong" claim that Herbert Wechsler is wrong and that Congress inadequately protects state governments' interests. Rather, I am suggesting a "weaker" claim that Wechsler's thesis depends on factual assumptions about congressional behavior that are not proven and not intuitively obvious, either. In all likelihood, the reality is that

Congress is sometimes sensitive to the interests of states and sometimes not, depending on the issue and the times and the composition of Congress. At the very least, there is no reason to believe that Congress will be more sensitive to the interests of states than will be the courts. Judicial concern about federalism as a constitutional principle is likely to cause courts to give at least as much attention to the needs of states as Congress in light of a political process in which states are a relatively weak interest group.

Correspondingly, the value of comity that is so important in the area of judicial federalism has no logical limit to just that area. The notion of comity of nations—respect for the government of another sovereign—could apply equally forcefully in evaluating congressional legislation regulating state and local government conduct. In fact, virtually every federal law regulating state and local government actions could be objected to as being inconsistent with comity. The Court has said that federal court actions, such as federal injunctions of state proceedings, imply an inferiority of state courts and inappropriately assume that state courts will not adequately protect federal rights.[71] But the same could be said about federal legislative mandates to the states, that they imply an inferiority of state legislatures and an assumption that states will not act on their own to deal with social problems. For instance, federal commands to the states to clean up nuclear waste or to check backgrounds before issuing firearm permits could be seen as implying the same lack of confidence in state governments as the Court finds in federal habeas corpus review or in federal injunctions of state court proceedings.

Comity simply seems a highly questionable basis for judicial decision making. The very existence of a federal government and particularly the federal courts is based on a judgment about the inadequacy of state governments acting alone and a distrust of state courts. Diversity jurisdiction, for example, exists because of a fear that state courts will be parochial and protect their own citizens at the expense of out-of-staters.[72] Removal jurisdiction, especially in the civil rights removal context, reflects a distrust of state courts.[73] General federal question jurisdiction was created in 1875 for fear of state court hostility to federal claims.[74] In fact, the framers, such as James Madison, who argued for the existence of federal courts, did so because of doubts about the state courts, especially in cases involving federal law and out-of-state citizens.[75]

Therefore, because the existence of federal courts and federal jurisdiction is, in itself, an implicit insult to the state courts, it does not make much sense to say that jurisdictional principles must be defined to avoid offending the dignity of state courts. In light of the insult to state courts represented by the very existence of federal jurisdiction, it is not clear how much additional affront there is in allowing federal courts to enjoin unconstitutional state court proceedings or in expanding federal habeas corpus jurisdiction.

Moreover, at most, comity is one value. But the questions must be more specific: how are particular federal actions incompatible with comity and what types of federal justifications warrant disregarding comity?[76] The concept of comity itself, of course, cannot answer these questions. Nor has the Supreme Court addressed these basic issues when it has invoked comity as a basis for decisions. Ultimately, the value of comity must be balanced against other values, most notably the need to ensure the supremacy of federal law and to effectuate the acts of the federal government. Because there is no reason why comity should trump these values, analysis must be based on a weighing of the competing concerns.

Again, I am not making the "strong" claim that comity is irrelevant. Rather, I am arguing that comity as a basis for deciding cases rests on assumptions that are, at the very least, highly questionable. Moreover, comity alone provides no guidance as to when federalism should be used as a limit on federal power because it must be weighed against the competing interests of the federal government. In reality, in some areas trust in state governments is appropriate and in some areas it is misguided; analysis of comity must be contextual and empirical, not universal and assumed. Yet, the Supreme Court uses comity as if it were a deciding principle without careful attention as to how it should be balanced against the need for a federal forum to vindicate federal rights.

In other words, both aspects of the post-1937 paradox in judicial treatment of federalism rest on premises that do not justify the Court's seeming inconsistency. An argument might be made that the difference in approaches is justified by the judgment that federal judicial power is a greater threat to the states than federal legislative power. Federal courts can award money damages that literally have the effect of removing dollars from state treasuries.[77] The Eleventh Amendment was a response to such a judgment and obviously meant to protect the states from such federal encroachments. Perhaps the paradox of post-1937 federalism can be explained based on the Court's unstated sense that states needed more protection from the federal courts than from Congress.

On examination, though, this argument, too, fails to justify the difference in approaches. First, most of the Supreme Court decisions restricting federal court jurisdiction did not involve claims for money damages against the states. *Erie*, for instance, did not involve a suit against the state but rather concerned the law to be applied in litigation between private parties. *Younger v. Harris*, which proclaimed the importance of "Our Federalism," limited the ability of the federal courts to issue injunctions. In fact, subsequent cases make it questionable whether *Younger* applies at all when the claim is for money damages.[78]

Second, Congress, too, can impose enormous costs on state governments. *National League of Cities v. Usery* was based on the Court's expressed concern about the fiscal impact of requiring state governments to pay the minimum wage. More generally, federal unfunded mandates can place great financial burdens on state governments.[79] It thus seems highly questionable that if states need protection from the federal government, that they would need more safeguards from the federal judiciary than from Congress.[80]

In reality, the Court's treatment of federalism between 1937 and the 1990s probably has much less to do with its expressly stated premises of trusting the political process and respecting state judiciaries, and much more to do with judicial value judgments that are not reflected in these premises.

The Court's refusal to enforce federalism as a limit on Congress is very much a reaction to the earlier invalidation of New Deal programs. President Franklin Roosevelt appointed justices that he could trust to affirm federal regulatory efforts, and these justices—many of whom had been architects of New Deal programs—crafted legal doctrines that upheld federal power without any judicially enforced federalism limits. These doctrines survived largely because of stare decisis, the generally recognized need for federal regulatory legislation, but also because of a perceived inability to define meaningful limits based on federalism.

In contrast, the emphasis on federalism as a limit on federal judicial power, especially in the Burger and Rehnquist Courts, exhibits value choices not reflected in the rhetoric about comity. The Burger and Rehnquist Courts generally restricted the scope of individual liberties, and especially the rights of criminal defendants.[81] The Supreme Courts have perceived that state courts would be less likely to vindicate federal rights, and thus have limited federal jurisdiction as a way to achieve substantive goals. For example, Professor Burt Neuborne explains that the Supreme Court's restrictions of federal court jurisdiction based on its stated belief that there is parity between federal and state courts may be a "pretext for funneling federal constitutional decision-making into state courts precisely because they are less likely to be receptive to vigorous enforcement of federal constitutional doctrine."[82] In other words, one way in which the Burger and Rehnquist Courts have ruled against individual rights claims is by denying them access to the federal courts.

Yet, neither of these likely actual grounds for decisions is ever explored in the Supreme Court decisions. The result is decisions that are based on premises that are unsupported and dubious.

THE END OF THE PARADOX:
THE DECISIONS OF THE REHNQUIST COURT

For more than a half century, the paradox described above dominated Supreme Court decisions concerning federalism. Now, however, the paradox would seem to have ended, as federalism has been reborn as a limit on congressional power.[83] In a very short dissent in *Garcia*, Justice William Rehnquist (the jurist was not yet chief) proclaimed that federalism should represent a limit on Congress's power, and said: "I do not think it incumbent on those of us in dissent to spell out further the fine points of a principle that will, I am confident, in time again command the support of a majority of the Court."[84] Rehnquist's prophecy proved accurate and it took less than a decade for it to come true.

The first indication of this revival of federalism occurred in *Gregory v. Ashcroft* in 1991.[85] State court judges in Missouri challenged the state's mandatory retirement age for judges as being invalid because it violated the federal Age Discrimination in Employment Act. The Supreme Court held that a federal law will be applied to important state government activities only if there is a clear statement from Congress that the law was meant to apply. The Court did not use the Tenth Amendment to invalidate the federal law on its face or as applied. Instead, the Court used the Tenth Amendment and federalism considerations as a rule of construction. It ruled that a federal law that imposes a substantial burden on a state government will be applied only if Congress clearly indicated that it wanted the law to apply. The Age Discrimination in Employment Act lacks such a clear statement and hence the Court refused to apply it to preempt the Missouri mandatory retirement age. Justice Sandra Day O'Connor, writing for the Court, discussed the importance of autonomous state governments as a check on possible federal tyranny and stressed the significance of the Tenth Amendment as a constitutional protector of state sovereignty.

A year later, in *New York v. United States*, the Court—for only the second time in fifty-five years and the first since the overruled *National League of Cities* decision—invalidated a federal law as violating the Tenth Amendment.[86] The federal law, the 1985 Low-Level Radioactive Waste Policy Amendments Act,[87] created a statutory duty for states to provide for the safe disposal of radioactive waste generated within their borders. The act provided monetary incentives for compliance, and allowed states to impose a surcharge on waste received from other states. Additionally, and most controversially, to ensure effective state government action, the law provided that states would "take title" to any waste within their borders that was not properly disposed of by January 1, 1996, and then would "be liable for all damages directly or indirectly incurred."

The Supreme Court ruled that Congress, pursuant to its authority under the commerce clause, could regulate the disposal of radioactive waste. However, by a 6–3 margin, the Court held that the "take title" provision of the law is unconstitutional because it gives state governments the choice between "either accepting ownership of waste or regulating according to the instructions of Congress." Justice O'Connor said that it was impermissible for Congress to impose either option on the states. Forcing states to accept ownership of radioactive waste would impermissibly "commandeer" state governments, and requiring state compliance with federal regulatory statutes would impermissibly impose on states a requirement to implement federal legislation. The Court concluded that it was "clear" that because of the Tenth Amendment, "[t]he Federal Government may not compel the States to enact or administer a federal regulatory program." [88]

Although the Court said that it was not "revisit[ing]" the holdings of earlier cases, such as *Garcia*, it clearly rejected *Garcia*'s conclusion that the federal judiciary would not use the Tenth Amendment to invalidate federal laws.[89] Indeed, it appears that if a federal law compels state legislative or regulatory activity, the statute is unconstitutional even if there is a compelling need for the federal action. After *New York v. United States*, the Tenth Amendment is a basis for lawyers to use in challenging federal laws that regulate state governments, either by forcing state administrative or state legislative action. In particular, federal energy and environmental laws, which often rely on state government implementation, are potentially vulnerable.

The extent to which *New York v. United States* rejects the approach to federalism that had been in place for the prior fifty years is illustrated by the Court's statement that its decision was based on both the limits that exist on congressional power under Article I and under the Tenth Amendment.[90] Justice O'Connor's opinion presented these two arguments as if they were completely indistinct.

The claims, however, are quite different. One focuses on whether Congress has authority under Article I of the Constitution to act; the other considers whether there is a constraint on this power. Justice O'Connor's approach conflates these two issues. There is no doubt under post-1937 constitutional law that Congress has the authority under the commerce clause to regulate the disposal of nuclear waste. Justice O'Connor's majority opinion expressly recognized this.[91] Therefore, Justice O'Connor must be saying that entirely apart from the Tenth Amendment, state sovereignty creates a limit on congressional power.

This is very similar to the Court's approach to the Eleventh Amendment, which sees state sovereignty in terms of limiting federal court subject-matter jurisdiction, even apart from the text of the amendment. The text of the Eleventh Amendment disallows suits against states by citizens of other states and foreign countries. But the Court has also found that a state cannot be sued by its own citizens because of a broader principle of state sovereign immunity, of which the Eleventh Amendment is a part.[92] *New York v. United States* takes a similar approach to Congress's power, finding a limit entirely separate from the Tenth Amendment, and thus firmly indicates that the paradox described above has disappeared.

Yet, in both instances, in analyzing the use of federalism as a limit on Congress and on the federal courts, there is the question of why this non-textual value should be given so much weight. Indeed, for a justice who emphasizes text as the central focus of constitutional analysis, these conclusions should be especially troubling. As discussed in Chapter 2, the Tenth Amendment's text says only that Congress may act when it has constitutional authority, but states may act unless there is a constitutional prohibition. The Eleventh Amendment's text indicates just that a state cannot be sued by citizens of other states or of foreign countries. Where the Constitution wanted state sovereignty to be constitutionally protected, the text provides such protection as in barring suits against states by citizens from other states. But in other areas, it is questionable as to why the justices most committed to following text allow a non-textual value to trump textual constitutional protections.

More generally, the key question is why protecting states is so important that it should be seen as limiting the very definition of congressional powers under Article I. If the Court is serious that state sovereignty restricts the scope of Article I, entirely apart from Tenth Amendment considerations, then *New York v. United States* has even broader implications than generally recognized. As discussed below, with a new, more conservative Court, in which Justice Alito has replaced Justice O'Connor, the case could portend a return to pre-1937 constitutional jurisprudence where the Court also used considerations of state sovereignty to narrowly define the scope of federal power. Although it is unlikely that the particular distinctions of the pre-1937 era will reemerge, other distinctions imposing limits on federal power could be manifested in the future.

New York v. United States marked the return of federalism as a basis for declaring federal laws unconstitutional. The subsequent decision in *United States v. Lopez* means the revival of federalism as a basis for limiting the scope of congressional authority.[93] From 1936 until April 26, 1995, the Supreme Court did not declare unconstitutional even one federal law as exceeding the scope of Congress's power under the commerce clause. For almost sixty years, it has been clear that Congress has broad authority to legislate pursuant to Article I, Section 8, of the Constitution, which empowers it to regulate commerce among the states. So long as Congress does not violate another constitutional provision, such as the First Amendment, legislation adopted under the commerce power would be upheld because almost any activity has some reasonable relationship to interstate commerce. A vast array of social and economic regulations were adopted under this power, ranging from civil rights laws to environmental protection statutes, from criminal laws to statutes creating most federal regulatory agencies.

However, in *United States v. Lopez*, by a 5–4 margin, the Supreme Court declared unconstitutional the Gun-Free School Zones Act of 1990, which made it a federal crime to have a gun within one thousand feet of a school.[94] Splitting along ideological lines, the Court ruled that the relationship to interstate commerce was too tangential and uncertain to uphold the law as a valid exercise of Congress's commerce power. Chief Justice Rehnquist wrote the opinion and was joined by Justices O'Connor, Anthony Kennedy, Antonin Scalia, and Clarence Thomas. Justices John Paul Stevens, David Souter, Ruth Bader Ginsburg, and Stephen Breyer dissented.

Alfonso Lopez was a twelfth-grade student at Edison High School in San Antonio, Texas, in 1992, when he was arrested for carrying a concealed .38-caliber handgun and five bullets. He was charged with and convicted of violating the Gun-Free School Zones Act and sentenced to six months' imprisonment and two years of supervised release.

Lopez appealed on the grounds that the act was an unconstitutional exercise of Congress's commerce power. The United States Supreme

Court agreed and concluded that the law was unconstitutional because it was not substantially related to interstate commerce.

Chief Justice Rehnquist's opinion began by emphasizing that the Constitution creates a national government of enumerated power.[95] That is, Congress can legislate only if there is express or implied power provided in the Constitution. The basis for this can be found not only in junior high school civics but through a strong belief that federalism requires defining congressional power so that there are real and meaningful limits as to its scope. Although it is a classic statement, its commitment to using federalism as a limit on the federal legislative power reflects a return to the pre-1937 approach and the clear demise of the paradigm of federalism that had controlled for almost sixty years.

After reviewing the history of decisions under the commerce clause, the Court identified three types of activities that Congress can regulate under this power. First, Congress can "regulate the use of the channels of interstate commerce."[96] *Heart of Atlanta Motel Inc. v. United States* upheld the federal law prohibiting discrimination by hotels and restaurants as an example of protecting the channels of interstate commerce.[97]

Second, Congress may legislate "to regulate and protect the instrumentalities of interstate commerce" and to regulate persons and things in interstate commerce.[98] The Court here cited several cases upholding congressional authority to regulate the railroads under its commerce power.[99]

Finally, the Court said that Congress may "regulate those activities having a substantial relation to interstate commerce."[100] Chief Justice Rehnquist said that the law was uncertain as to whether an activity must "affect" or "substantially affect" interstate commerce to be regulated under this approach. Chief Justice Rehnquist concluded that the more restrictive interpretation of congressional power is preferable and that "the proper test requires an analysis of whether the regulated activity 'substantially affects' interstate commerce."[101]

The Court concluded that the presence of a gun near a school did not substantially affect interstate commerce and that therefore the federal law was unconstitutional. Chief Justice Rehnquist noted that nothing in the act limited its application to instances where there was proof of an effect on interstate commerce. The Court specifically rejected the federal government's claim that regulation was justified under the commerce clause because possession of a gun near a school may result in violent crime that can adversely affect the economy.

The key difference between the majority and the dissent was over whether a "substantial" effect was necessary in order for Congress to regulate and whether that was present in this case. Justices Stevens, Souter, and Breyer wrote dissenting opinions. Justice Breyer's dissent was the most thorough and was joined by the other dissenting justices—Stevens, Souter, and Ginsburg. The dissent criticized the majority for engaging in undue judicial activism; for abandoning almost sixty years of precedent; and for invalidating an important federal statute. Justice Breyer argued that the judiciary should uphold a federal law as a valid exercise of the commerce power, so long as there is a "rational basis" that an activity affects interstate commerce.[102] Justice Breyer then explained why guns inherently are a part of interstate commerce and why guns near schools have an economic impact that justifies federal regulation under the commerce power. The majority's disagreement with this reflects its desire to limit Congress's authority and thus marks a clear return to the pre-1937 view of judicially enforced limits on federal legislative power. *Lopez* shows that the post-1937 paradox has truly ended.

In fact, this is made even clearer by the concurring opinions, which were written by Justice Thomas and also by Justice Kennedy, whose opinion was joined by Justice O'Connor. Justice Thomas's opinion was notable because it urged a much narrower view of congressional power than was adopted by the majority.[103] Under Justice Thomas's view, Congress should not be able to regulate activities that have a substantial effect on interstate commerce. In other words, Thomas would use federalism as a limit on Congress even more than the limit was employed during the first third of this century. Thomas's opinion was truly radical in its scope; countless federal laws would be unconstitutional had his opinion been the majority view of the Court. Justices Kennedy and O'Connor stressed federalism and the relationship between limiting Congress's authority and protecting state prerogatives.

In *Lopez*, the five most conservative justices—one appointed by

President Richard Nixon, three by President Ronald Reagan, and one by President George W. Bush—invalidated an unquestionably popular federal statute. Although these justices are most commonly associated with advocating judicial restraint, in *Lopez* they abandoned decades of deference to the legislature under the commerce clause. The narrow definition of Congress's power gives the Court a basis for striking down countless federal laws.

For example, many federal drug laws might be vulnerable because they regulate activities that are only tangentially related to interstate commerce.[104] Innumerable federal criminal laws were adopted under Congress's commerce clause authority. Similarly, a vast array of civil laws, ranging from environmental statutes like the Endangered Species Act to discrimination laws like the Americans with Disabilities Act might be challenged based on *Lopez*.[105]

The impact of *Lopez* and the extent to which it will radically change Congress's power and constitutional law will not be known until the Roberts Court has had the chance to decide cases concerning the scope of commerce power. The majority opinion in *Lopez* did little to explain what "substantially affects" interstate commerce actually means. No criteria were articulated to be used by lower courts or by the Supreme Court in the future. The *Lopez* decision opened a door to constitutional challenges that were previously closed.

A year after *Lopez*, in *Seminole Tribe of Florida v. Florida*, the Supreme Court imposed another limit on Congress's power based on federalism.[106] The Supreme Court held that Congress may abrogate the Eleventh Amendment only when acting under its Section 5 powers and not under any other constitutional authority. This overruled a series of case decided in the late 1980s in which the Supreme Court held that Congress may authorize suits when acting pursuant to other constitutional powers, so long as the federal law, in its text, clearly and expressly permits federal court jurisdiction over state governments. In *Pennsylvania v. Union Gas Co.*, in 1989, the Supreme Court held that Congress could authorize suits against states in federal court provided the law, in its text, was clear in authorizing such litigation.[107] *Union Gas* also was a 5–4 decision, and the five justices in the majority were William Brennan,

Byron White, Thurgood Marshall, Blackmun, and Stevens. By 1996, four of these five justices had left the High Court. In contrast, the four dissenters in *Union Gas*—Rehnquist, O'Connor, Scalia, and Kennedy—remained. They were joined by Justice Thomas, who created the majority needed to overrule a decision that was only seven years old.

Thus, in *Seminole Tribe* in 1996, the Supreme Court, with exactly the same ideological division as in *United States v. Lopez*, declared the authorization for suits against states in violation of the Eleventh Amendment. *Seminole Tribe* involved a suit under the Indian Gaming Regulatory Act, which required that states negotiate with Indian tribes to form compacts that would allow gambling on Native American land. The act specifically authorized suits against states in federal court as an enforcement mechanism.

The Supreme Court held that the federal statute authorizing suits against states in federal court was unconstitutional. Congress may authorize suits against states only when acting pursuant to Section 5 of the Fourteenth Amendment and not pursuant to other federal power, such as the Indian commerce clause. Chief Justice Rehnquist, writing for the majority in the 5–4 decision, emphasized that *Pennsylvania v. Union Gas Co.* was a plurality opinion. Chief Justice Rehnquist declared that "[t]he plurality's rationale . . . deviated sharply from our established federalism jurisprudence and essentially eviscerated our decision in *Hans*." [108] The Court concluded: "Reconsidering the decision in *Union Gas*, we conclude that none of the policies underlying stare decisis require our continuing adherence of its holding." [109]

Seminole Tribe thus uses federalism as a limit on congressional power to authorize suits against state governments in federal court. It, too, makes clear that the paradox described above is no more.

A year after *Seminole Tribe*, in *Printz v. United States*,[110] the Court applied and extended *New York v. United States*. *Printz* involved a challenge to the federal Brady Handgun Violence Prevention Act.[111] The law required that the "chief law enforcement officer" of each local jurisdiction conduct background checks before issuing permits for firearms. The Court, in a 5–4 decision, split exactly as in *Lopez* and in *Seminole Tribe*, and found that the law violated the Tenth Amendment.

THE PARADOX OF POST-1937 FEDERALISM

Justice Scalia wrote for the majority and revived the phrase "dual sovereignty" to explain the structure of American government.[112] After reviewing early American history, which he said was devoid of authority for federal mandates to state governments, Scalia declared that "[i]t is incontestable that the Constitution established a system of dual sovereignty."[113] He concluded that "[t]he power of the Federal Government would be augmented immeasurably if it were able to impress into its service—and at no cost to itself—the police officers of the 50 states."[114]

Justice Scalia then presented another, quite novel, argument for why the Brady Bill is unconstitutional: it violates separation of powers because it delegates executive power to state governments. Article II vests in the president the authority to execute federal laws. Scalia said that delegating executive power to state governments would undermine presidential authority and prevent there being a unitary executive with all such power vested in one official. He wrote: "The Brady Act effectively transfers this responsibility to thousands of CLEOs [Councils of Local Elected Officials] in the 50 states, who are left to implement the program without meaningful Presidential control. . . . That unity would be shattered, and the power of the President would be subject to reduction, if Congress could act as effectively without the President as with him, by simply requiring state officers to execute its laws."[115]

Although a critique of *Printz*, and the other recent decisions, is left to Chapter 2, it should be noted that requiring the federal executive to conduct background checks before any handgun is issued in the United States would be far more of an intrusion on the executive power than delegating this task to the states. Indeed, the Brady Bill's strong support by the president makes the claim of intrusion into executive prerogatives highly suspect. As argued in Chapter 2, the focus on presidential power, like other aspects of *Printz* and the 1990s federalism decisions, is highly formalistic and avoids any functional analysis of the actual impact on presidential power of the assignment of this task to state and local governments.

Printz v. United States makes it clear that there are significant judicially enforced limits on federal legislative power so as to protect state governments. Justice Scalia's conclusion to the majority opinion is unequivocal in this regard:

We held in *New York* that Congress cannot compel the States to enact or enforce a federal regulatory program. Today we hold that Congress cannot circumvent that prohibition by conscripting State officers directly. The Federal Government may neither issue directives requiring the States to address particular problems, nor command the States' officers or those if their political subdivisions, to administer or enforce a federal regulatory program. It matters not whether policy-making is involved, and no case-by-case weighing of burdens or benefits is necessary, such commands are fundamentally incompatible with our constitutional system of dual sovereignty.[116]

The Court could not have been clearer that federalism is very much a judicially enforced limit on federal judicial power.

The Court also used federalism to limit congressional power in *City of Boerne v. Flores*, where the Court dramatically restricted the scope of Congress's authority under Section 5 of the Fourteenth Amendment.[117] In 1990, in *Employment Division v. Smith*,[118] the Supreme Court substantially narrowed the protections of the establishment clause of the First Amendment. *Smith* held that the free exercise clause is not violated by a neutral law of general applicability. The Supreme Court rejected a challenge by Native Americans to a law prohibiting consumption of peyote, despite the claim that their religion requires its use. The Court explained that the law was neutral, in that it was not motivated by a desire to interfere with religion, and was generally applicable, in that it applied to everyone. Such neutral laws of general applicability, said the Court, do not violate the free exercise clause even if they substantially burden religious practices.

In 1993, Congress enacted, and President Bill Clinton signed, the Religious Freedom Restoration Act, which sought to overrule *Smith*.[119] More precisely, Congress sought by statute to restore religious freedom to what it had previously been under the First Amendment. The Religious Freedom Restoration Act required that courts use strict scrutiny in evaluating free exercise clause challenges, even to neutral laws of general applicability that burden religion. In *City of Boerne v. Flores*, the Supreme Court declared the act unconstitutional. The Court, relying heavily on federalism concerns, held that the law exceeds the scope of Congress's power under Section 5 of the Fourteenth Amendment. The case involved a church that could not alter the structure of its building because it had been classified as a historic landmark. The church sued under the Religious Freedom Restoration Act, and the city argued that the law was unconstitutional.

Section 5 is brief and states: "The Congress shall have power to enforce, by appropriate legislation, the provisions of this article." The issue in *City of Boerne v. Flores* concerned the meaning of this provision; may Congress use it to expand the scope of rights? More specifically, is Congress limited to providing remedies for violations of constitutional rights recognized by the Supreme Court; or may Congress use its power under these amendments to adopt an independent interpretation of the Constitution, even overruling Supreme Court decisions?

The Court answered these questions to limit federal power and ostensibly advance federalism. Justice Kennedy, writing for the majority, stated: "Congress's power under §5, however, extends only to 'enforc[ing]' the provisions of the Fourteenth Amendment. . . . The design of the Fourteenth Amendment and the text of §5 are inconsistent with the suggestion that Congress has the power to decree the substance of the Fourteenth Amendment's restrictions on the states. *Legislation which alters the meaning of the Free Exercise Clause cannot be said to be enforcing the Clause. Congress does not enforce a constitutional right by changing what the right is.*" [120] Justice Kennedy expressly invoked federalism and the need to protect states as a key justification for his opinion.

The Court chose a very narrow definition of Congress's Section 5 power and as a result declared the Religious Freedom Restoration Act unconstitutional. Justice Kennedy explained that this was done, in large part, based on federalism concerns and the need to constrain congressional power and to leave governance to the states. The Court imposed a significant limit on congressional authority and explicitly saw this as benefiting state governments.

One more major Rehnquist Court decision limiting Congress's power is especially notable. *United States v. Morrison*, in 2000, presented the question as to whether the civil damages provision of the federal Violence Against Women Act is constitutional.[121] The provision authorizes victims of gender-motivated violence to sue for money damages. Congress enacted the Violence Against Women Act based on detailed findings of the inadequacy of state laws in protected women who are victims of domestic violence and sexual assaults. For example, Congress found that gender-motivated violence costs the American economy billions of dollars a year and is a substantial constraint on freedom of travel by women throughout the country.

The case was brought by Christy Brzonkala, who allegedly was raped by football players while a freshman at Virginia Polytechnic Institute. The players were not criminally prosecuted and ultimately avoided even sanctions by the university. Brzonkala filed suit against her assailants and the university under the civil damages provision of the Violence Against Women Act.

The issue before the Supreme Court was whether the civil damages provision of the act could be upheld, either as an exercise of Congress's commerce clause authority or as permissible under Congress's power pursuant to Section 5 of the Fourteenth Amendment. In a 5–4 decision, the Court held that Congress lacked the authority to adopt the provision under either of these powers. The split was the same as in all of the recent federalism rulings: Chief Justice Rehnquist wrote the opinion, joined by Justices O'Connor, Scalia, Kennedy, and Thomas. Justices Stevens, Souter, Ginsburg, and Breyer dissented.

In *Morrison*, the Court reaffirmed the three-part test for Congress's commerce clause authority that was articulated in *United States v. Lopez*. Congress may regulate a) the channels of interstate commerce, b) the instrumentalities of and persons or things in interstate commerce, and c) the activities that have a substantial effect on interstate commerce. The United States government and the plaintiff, Christy Brzonkala, defended the law based on the third part of the test, on the grounds that violence against women has a substantial effect on the national economy. There was a lengthy legislative history of the Violence Against Women Act in which Congress found that assaults against women, when looked at cumulatively across the country, have a substantial effect on interstate commerce. The Supreme Court expressly rejected this argument as insufficient to sustain the law. Chief Justice Rehnquist emphasized that Congress was regulating noneconomic activity that has traditionally been dealt with by state laws. He wrote: "Gender-motivated crimes of violence are not, in any sense of the phrase, economic activity. While we need not adopt a categorical rule against aggregating the effects of any noneconomic activity in order to decide these cases, thus far in our Nation's history our cases have upheld Commerce Clause regulation of intrastate activity only where that activity is economic in nature." [122]

The Supreme Court decided Congress's findings of impact on the economy were inadequate to sustain the law under the commerce clause. Chief Justice Rehnquist declared: "But the existence of congressional findings is not sufficient, by itself, to sustain the constitutionality of commerce clause legislation. As we stated in Lopez, '[S] imply because Congress may conclude that a particular activity substantially affects interstate commerce does not necessarily make it so.'" [123] Congress, according to the Court, was relying on a "but-for causal chain from the initial occurrence of violent crime . . . to every attenuated effect upon interstate commerce." [124] The Supreme Court stated that "[i]f accepted, petitioners' reasoning would allow Congress to regulate any crime as long as the nationwide, aggregated impact of that crime has substantial effects on employment, production, transit or consumption." [125] By this reasoning, the Court explained, Congress could regulate all violent crimes in the United States. The High Court thus concluded: "We accordingly reject the argument that Congress may regulate noneconomic, violent criminal conduct based solely on that conduct's aggregated effect on interstate commerce. The Constitution requires a distinction between what is truly national and what is truly local." [126]

Justice Clarence Thomas wrote a concurring opinion in which he again objected, as in *Lopez*, to the "substantial effects" test as a way of justifying congressional action under the commerce. He wrote:

[T]he very notion of a "substantial effects" test under the Commerce Clause is inconsistent with the original understanding of Congress' powers and with this Court's early Commerce Clause cases. By continuing to apply this rootless and malleable standard, however circumscribed, the Court has encouraged the Federal Government to persist in its view that the Commerce Clause has virtually no limits. Until this Court replaces its existing Commerce Clause jurisprudence with a standard more consistent with the original understanding, we will continue to see Congress appropriating state police powers under the guise of regulating commerce.[127]

That is to say, Justice Thomas would go significantly further than the majority in limiting the scope of Congress's commerce power; the majority in *Morrison* would allow Congress to regulate economic activities based on their cumulative impact on the economy, but Justice Thomas would not allow Congress such maneuverability.

Justice Souter wrote a dissenting opinion, joined by Justices Stevens, Ginsburg, and Souter. Justice Souter stressed the need for judicial deference to congressional fact-finding:

Congress has the power to legislate with regard to activity that, in the aggregate, has a substantial effect on interstate commerce. The fact of such a substantial effect is not an issue for the courts in the first instance, but for the Congress, whose institutional capacity for gathering evidence and taking testimony far exceeds ours. By passing legislation, Congress indicates its conclusion, whether explicitly or not, that facts support its exercise of the commerce power. The business of the courts is to review the congressional assessment, not for soundness but simply for the rationality of concluding that a jurisdictional basis exists in fact.[128]

Justice Souter stressed that Congress had conducted voluminous hearings and found that violence against women has an enormous effect on the American economy. He wrote: "But the sufficiency of the evidence before Congress to provide a rational basis for the finding cannot seriously be questioned. Indeed, the legislative record here is far more voluminous than the record compiled by Congress and found sufficient in two prior cases upholding Title II of the Civil Rights Act of 1964 against Commerce Clause challenges." [129]

Thus, *Morrison* goes further than *Lopez* in limiting the scope of

Congress's commerce power by narrowing the ability of Congress to regulate based on findings of substantial effects on interstate commerce. At least in areas that the Court regards as traditionally regulated by the states, Congress cannot regulate noneconomic activity based on a cumulative substantial effect on interstate commerce.

All of these cases demonstrate that the Supreme Court rejected the post-1937 view that federalism is not a limit on Congress's power. At the same time, the Court very much continued to use federalism as a limit on judicial power. This was most evident in the cases concerning sovereign immunity. Based on *Seminole Tribe*, the Court held that specific federal statutes could not be used to sue state governments. In *Florida Prepaid Postsecondary Education Expense Board v. College Savings Bank*,[130] *Kimel v. Florida Board of Regents*,[131] and *University of Alabama v. Garrett*[132] the Court, in 5–4 decisions, found that laws adopted by Congress exceeded the scope of Congress's Section 5 power and thus could not be used to sue state governments.

Florida Prepaid held that a federal law authorizing suits against states for patent infringement exceeded the scope of Congress's Section 5 authority. The Court said that the law was not "proportionate" or "congruent" because of the absence of proof of a pattern of such violations by state governments. *Kimel* ruled that state governments could not be sued for violating the Age Discrimination in Employment Act. The Court held that the law prohibits much more than the Constitution, since age discrimination receives only rational basis review, and that the legislative record did not document a pattern of unconstitutional age discrimination by state governments. *Garrett* decided that state governments cannot be sued for violating Title I of the Americans with Disabilities Act, which prohibits employment discrimination based on disability and requires that employers make reasonable accommodations for disabilities. As in *Kimel*, the Court found that the law prohibits much that would not violate the Constitution, because disability discrimination receives only rational basis review under equal protection. The Court said that the legislative record did not sufficiently document unconstitutional discrimination by state governments against the disabled in employment to make the law "proportionate" or "congruent" to the problem.

In fact, the Court went even further in using federalism as a limit on judicial power, concluding that sovereign immunity means that state governments cannot be sued in state courts or in federal agencies. *Alden v. Maine* declared that state governments cannot be sued in state court without state consent.[133] Probation officers in Maine sued, claiming that they were owed overtime pay under the federal Fair Labor Standards Act. The suit was initially filed in federal court but was dismissed based on the Eleventh Amendment. The probation officers then sued in Maine state court. The Supreme Court, in a 5–4 decision, ruled that the state had sovereign immunity and could not be sued in state court, even on a federal claim, without state consent. Justice Kennedy wrote the opinion and acknowledged that the Constitution and its framers were silent about the ability to sue state governments in state courts. Justice Kennedy said, though, that it was unthinkable that the states would have ratified the Constitution had they thought that it made them subject to suit without their consent. The Court declared: "We hold that the powers delegated to Congress under Article I of the United States Constitution do not include the power to subject nonconsenting States to private suits for damages in state courts." [134]

Subsequently, in *Federal Maritime Commission v. South Carolina State Port Authority*,[135] the Supreme Court maintained that states cannot be named as defendants in federal administrative agency proceedings. A cruise ship company brought a claim against a state agency in the Federal Maritime Commission, claiming that it had been discriminated against in violation of federal maritime law. In a 5–4 decision, it was determined that such actions are barred by sovereign immunity. Bolstering the opinion was *Alden v. Maine*'s conclusion that sovereign immunity is broader than the protections of the Eleventh Amendment. The Court said that the "preeminent purpose" of sovereign immunity is to protect the "dignity" of state governments and that such dignity would be impermissibly offended by allowing states to be named as defendants in agency proceedings without state consent.[136]

THE CONTENT OF 1990S FEDERALISM

Taken together, these cases represent a dramatic change in post-1937 constitutional law. Yet, it is uncertain how far the Supreme Court will go in applying and extending these limits. After all, there were many predictions about the likely impact of *National League of Cities v. Usery*, and virtually none of these came true.[137] But even with this caution in mind, the cases described above are a major change in the law. For fifty-five years, with the brief exception of *National League of Cities*, the Court had ruled that the Tenth Amendment does not limit congressional power. For sixty years, the scope of commerce power was maintained without limits. For decades, Congress's authority under Section 5 of the Fourteenth Amendment had been defined expansively. Now, federalism and the Tenth Amendment again represent a restraint on federal legislative power.

The Federalism Revolution in the Rehnquist Court

Four aspects of the Rehnquist Court's federalism revolution are apparent. First, the Supreme Court will enforce limits on Congress's power under the commerce clause and under Section 5 of the Fourteenth Amendment. Influenced by federalism concerns, the Court will narrow the scope of Congress's authority and see itself as limiting more areas of governance to state and local governments. Congress may act only to regulate the channels of interstate commerce, the instrumentalities of and persons or things in interstate commerce, and the activities that have a substantial effect on interstate commerce. It is unclear how "substantial effect" will be defined, and the constitutionality of scores of federal laws will turn on this issue. It also is unclear as to what will be sufficient to demonstrate that a person or thing is in interstate commerce. At the same time, the Court says that Congress cannot expand the scope of rights when acting under Section 5 of the Fourteenth Amendment but rather can only provide remedies for rights recognized by the courts.

Second, the Tenth Amendment limits Congress's power to regulate state governments. Federal laws that compel state legislative or regulatory activity are unconstitutional. This is the holding of *New York v.*

United States and *United States v. Printz*, and it now seems clear that federal laws will be invalidated if they "commandeer" state governments to regulate or legislate.

Garcia's conclusion that the protection of states is left to the political process obviously has been overruled. The decisions of the 1990s are all about judicial protection of federalism. In fact, it appears that *National League of Cities* again is good law; once more, there would be a basis for finding unconstitutional a requirement that states pay their employees a minimum wage. As *National League of Cities* argued, state and local governments can pay the minimum wage only by raising taxes or cutting other social programs. Either, of course, is federal compulsion of state and local expenditures and of legislative activity.

The more recent cases go much further than *National League of Cities* in limiting congressional authority. *National League of Cities* said that Congress could not regulate states in areas of "traditional" or "integral" state government activity. *New York v. United States* and *Printz v. United States* have no such limiting language. Under these recent rulings, any compulsion of the states is unconstitutional.

Thus far, the Court has not indicated that the Tenth Amendment will be used as a limit on federal laws regulating *private* conduct, such as it did during the earlier era of dual federalism. Then, the Tenth Amendment was used to invalidate federal regulation of private employment relations, such as in the Child Labor Act and in declaring a federal minimum wage unconstitutional.[138] But the cases thus far do not suggest that the Supreme Court will use the Tenth Amendment as a restriction on federal regulation of the private sector. However, federal regulation of private activity can be challenged as exceeding the scope of Congress's commerce clause authority as in *United States v. Lopez*.

According to the third aspect of the federalism revolution, the scope of other congressional powers and the extent to which they are limited by federalism principles is uncertain. It is unclear whether the Court will use the Tenth Amendment as a limit on Congress's ability to induce states to behave in particular ways through strings on federal grants. *South Dakota v. Dole*, in 1987, expressly held that even though grants often have the effect of coercing state behavior, Congress may properly place the choice before state governments.[139] *New York v. United States* indicated that Congress can induce states to clean up low level nuclear waste so long as Congress does this as a condition for receipt of federal funds. The Court has said only that the conditions must relate to the purpose of the grant and that the conditions must be expressly stated.[140]

The reality, of course, is that strings on grants can be as coercive as any direct requirement. Therefore, it is possible that they, too, might be limited in the future on federalism grounds. The Supreme Court might do this by express use of the Tenth Amendment as a restraint on Congress's spending power or by strictly enforcing the requirement that conditions relate to the purposes of the grant. Also, the argument in *Printz v. United States* that commands to state governments violate separation of powers is a basis for challenging strings on grants to state and local governments. As discussed above, the Court in *Printz* said that requiring state and local governments to enforce federal laws violated the constitutional requirement that there be a unitary executive with all enforcement authority residing in the president. This limit would seem to apply whether Congress is acting under its commerce power or its spending authority. For instance, if Congress required that states conduct background checks before issuing firearm permits as a condition for receiving federal law enforcement funds, this would seem to take away power from the president in the same way that the Court found objectionable in *Printz*.

According to the fourth aspect of the revolution, federalism will continue to be used as a limit on federal judicial power in areas such as habeas corpus review, abstention, and the Eleventh Amendment. For example, the Court continues to strictly enforce the preclusion of federal courts hearing claims of new rights on habeas corpus[141] and to use federalism as a limit on the scope of habeas corpus review. Additionally, the Court strongly insists that federal courts not decide unclear issues of state law but rather use state laws that allow certification of issues to state courts.[142] Also, the Court expands the Eleventh Amendment's protection of states from being sued in federal court.[143]

The bottom line of all of these cases is that the paradox of post-1937 federalism is clearly at an end. Federalism will be used by the Supreme Court as a limit on federal legislative and judicial powers.

IS THE FEDERALISM REVOLUTION OVER?

All of the above accurately describes the developments in federalism from early in the twentieth century until about 2002. In the last few years of the Rehnquist Court, though, every federalism case was decided against the states' rights position and in favor of federal power. To have a complete picture of the law, it is important to add these cases to the description. Then, based on all of what has happened, it is possible to assess where the Roberts Court is likely to go.

Most notably, between 2002 and 2005, the Supreme Court rejected challenges to the scope of Congress's authority, allowed federal laws to be used to sue state governments, and created a new exception to sovereign immunity. First, the Court upheld several challenges in the face of federalism challenges. The two most recent commerce clause cases, as of this writing, both refused to extend limits on Congress's power and upheld the federal statutes. *Pierce County, Washington v. Guillen*[144] unanimously reaffirmed broad authority for Congress to legislate concerning road safety as part of its power to regulate the channels of interstate commerce. A federal statute provides that if a local government does a traffic study as part of applying for federal funds, that study is not discoverable. Congress's concern was that local governments would refrain from conducting such investigations if theses studies could be used as evidence against local entities in suits arising from automobile accidents.

Guillen involved two separate accidents at intersections in the state of Washington, and the local governments had recently conducted studies of traffic conditions at both locations. The plaintiffs sued the local governments and sought access to the traffic studies. The Washington Supreme Court declared unconstitutional the federal law that exempted these studies from discovery. The United States Supreme Court, in an opinion by Justice Clarence Thomas, unanimously reversed and upheld the federal law. Justice Thomas explained that "[i]t is well established that the Commerce Clause gives Congress authority to regulate the use of the channels of interstate commerce. . . . [The statutes] can be viewed as legislation aimed at improving safety in the channels of interstate commerce and increasing protection for the instrumentalities of inter-state commerce. As such, they fall within Congress' Commerce Clause power." [145]

More dramatically, *Gonzales v. Raich* [146] held that Congress consti-tutionally may use its power to regulate commerce among the states to prohibit the cultivation and possession of small amounts of marijuana for medicinal purposes. Although California has created an exemption to its state marijuana laws for medical uses, no such exemption exists to the federal law. In a 6–3 decision, with the majority opinion written by Justice John Paul Stevens, the federal law was upheld. Justices Kennedy, Souter, Ginsburg, and Breyer joined the majority opinion, and Justice Antonin Scalia concurred in the judgment. Justice Stevens explained that for almost seventy years, Congress has had the authority to regulate ac-tivities that have a substantial effect on interstate commerce. The Court concluded that marijuana, looked at cumulatively, including that grown for medical purposes, has a substantial effect on interstate commerce. Justice Stevens's opinion relied on a precedent from over sixty years ago: *Wickard v. Filburn*, discussed above, which maintained that Congress may regulate the amount of wheat that farmers grow for their own home consumption.

How does *Gonzales v. Raich* fit into the Court's recent commerce clause jurisprudence? The Court did not change the test for the com-merce clause that it has followed since *Lopez* in 1995. Nor did the Court revisit its holding in *Morrison* that in regulating non-economic activi-ties, substantial effect cannot be based on cumulative impact. Instead, *Gonzales v. Raich* stands for the proposition that intrastate production of a commodity sold in interstate commerce is economic activity and thus substantial effect can be based on cumulative impact. Justice Sca-lia, concurred in the judgment and emphasized that Congress, pursuant to the necessary and proper clause, has the authority to control intra-state production of goods that are of a type that end up in interstate commerce.

Also, the Court rejected a federalism challenge to a law adopted un-der Congress's spending power. *Sabri v. United States* [147] unanimously upheld the constitutionality of a federal law that prohibits bribery of state, local, and tribal officials of entities that receive at least $10,000 in federal funds.[148] An individual convicted under this law argued that his activities had nothing to do with the area of local government that received federal funds and that Congress exceeded the scope of its spending power. The claim was that Congress could prohibit bribery only as to those state, local, and tribal activities that actually got federal money.

The Supreme Court expressly rejected this argument. In an opinion by Justice David Souter, the Court explained: "Money is fungible, bribed officials are untrustworthy stewards of federal funds, and corrupt contractors do not deliver dollar-for-dollar value."[149] The Court firmly rejected the federalism challenge to the law and concluded that the criminal law was constitutional because Congress has the "power to bring federal power directly to bear on individuals who convert public spending into unearned private gain, not a means for bringing federal economic might to bear on a State's own choices of public policy."[150]

This trend toward judicial opinions that favor federal power can also be seen in the Court allowing states to be sued by finding laws to be valid enactments under Section 5 of the Fourteenth Amendment. In *Nevada Department of Human Resources v. Hibbs*, the Supreme Court held that state governments could be sued under the family leave provisions of the Family and Medical Leave Act.[151] In a 6–3 decision, with the majority opinion written by Chief Justice William Rehnquist, the stated intention of the law was to prevent gender discrimination. Congress was concerned that due to social roles women would suffer more than men in the workplace from a lack of family leave. Since gender discrimination, unlike age or disability discrimination, receives heightened scrutiny under equal protection, the Court decided that Congress had greater authority to legislate under Section 5, and the law thus could be used to sue the state government.

Similarly, *Tennessee v. Lane* held that state governments can be sued for discriminating against people with disabilities, pursuant to Title II of the Americans with Disabilities Act, with regard to the fundamental right of access to the courts.[152] Justice Stevens, writing for the Court, emphasized that there is a well established fundamental right of access to the courts and that Congress may enforce it by authorizing suits against state governments. However, the Court left open the issue of whether states may be sued for other violations of Title II, which prohibits state and local governments from discriminating against people with disabilities in government programs, services, and activities.

The initial cases of the Roberts Court continue this pattern. Most recently, *United States v. Georgia* decided that state governments may be sued, pursuant to federal statutes, for constitutional violations.[153] The Court allowed a suit under Title II of the Americans with Disabilities Act by a prisoner who was a paraplegic and in a wheelchair. The cell, including its toilet facilities, were not accessible to him, and he could not use the prison library or chapel. The unanimous decision written by Justice Scalia maintained that the suit could go forward because the prisoner was alleging a violation of his right to be free from cruel and unusual punishment, and Congress may authorize such suits.

In *Central Virginia Community College v. Katz*, the Court held that sovereign immunity does not apply in bankruptcy proceedings.[154] Congress may constitutionally authorize suits against state governments in such cases.

A RENEWED EMPHASIS ON THE LIMITING OF FEDERAL POWER

If one focuses on these recent cases, it is tempting to conclude that the federalism decisions of the 1990s were aberrational and that the Supreme Court has reverted to its post-1937 view of federalism. But there is every reason to believe that these recent examples represent just a pause in the Court's enforcement of federalism as a limit on congressional power. First, none of the recent cases repudiate or even undermine the Rehnquist Court's federalism decisions. It was just that the Court did not extend the principles, either.

Second, some of the recent cases were 5–4 decisions, with Justice Sandra Day O'Connor in the majority. For instance, *Tennessee v. Lane* and *Central Virginia Community College v. Katz* were both 5–4 decisions, with Justice O'Connor voting along with Justices Stevens, Souter, Ginsburg, and Breyer. With Justice O'Connor no longer on the Court, there is the prospect for dramatic change.

In fact, everything that is known about the two new justices—John Roberts and Samuel Alito—indicates the likelihood of a renewed emphasis on limiting federal power based on federalism. Most notably, Justice Alito seems much more likely to agree with the conservative bloc of Roberts, Scalia, Kennedy, and Thomas, whereas O'Connor often departed from this group. For example, as a judge on the United States Court of Appeals for the Third Circuit, Judge Alito dissented and would have invalidated a federal law banning the transfer or possession of machine guns.[155] Judge Alito argued that the law was unconstitutional as exceeding the scope of Congress's commerce power, even though six other circuits had upheld the law without a dissent.

The contrast to Justice O'Connor is even clearer in that she voted to allow states to be sued for violating the provisions of the Family and Medical Leave Act, while Judge Alito, on the Third Circuit, came to an opposite conclusion.[156] Judge Alito voted to bar such suits, whereas the Supreme Court in *Hibbs* subsequently allowed suits under the statute.

In their first year on the Supreme Court, Chief Justice Roberts and Justice Alito had little opportunity to rule on federalism cases. The only cases concerning federalism provided a clear indication that they are likely to join with Justices Scalia and Thomas. In *Central Virginia Community College v. Katz*, Chief Justice Roberts joined with Justices Scalia, Kennedy, and Thomas in dissenting to the holding that sovereign immunity does not apply in bankruptcy proceedings. In *United States v. Rapanos*, Chief Justice Roberts and Justice Alito joined with Justices Scalia and Thomas in a plurality opinion.[157] The issue in *Rapanos* was whether the federal Water Pollution Control Act could be applied to intrastate waters that connect with navigable waters through tributaries. Justice Scalia, joined by the other three conservatives, would have rejected this view and adopted a narrow definition of navigable waters. At the end of his majority opinion, he stressed the constitutional limits on congressional power.

Justice Kennedy concurred in the judgment and said that the Water Pollution Control Act can be applied to waters that have "substantial nexus" to navigable waters. This, from a practical perspective, is to be treated as the holding of the case. But what's crucial is that again Chief

Justice Roberts and Justice Alito were with Justices Scalia and Thomas in a case with important implications as to federalism.

If John Kerry had won the 2004 presidential election and had nominated the replacements for Chief Justice Rehnquist and Justice O'Connor, the Rehnquist Court's federalism revolution likely would have ended. Most of the decisions protecting states' rights would have been overruled, or at least limited. Now, however, with Chief Justice Roberts and Justice Alito, the Rehnquist Court's federalism rulings seem secure and are likely to be built upon in the years ahead. Indeed, there is every reason to believe that the five conservative Justices—Roberts, Scalia, Kennedy, Thomas, and Alito—will remain on the Court for many years to come and that they will use federalism as the Rehnquist Court did to limit congressional power and to expand the scope of state sovereign immunity.

Thus, it seems particularly important to analyze these opinions and decide whether they are desirable. This analysis begins in Chapter 2.

CHAPTER 2

The Formalism of the Federalism
Decisions and Its Failure

DURING THE 1980S, there was a flurry of Supreme Court decisions dealing with issues of separation of powers. Cases included *INS v. Chadha*,[1] which invalidated the legislative veto; *Northern Pipeline Construction Co. v. Marathon Pipe Line Co.*,[2] which declared the bankruptcy courts unconstitutional; and *Bowsher v. Synar*,[3] which invalidated the Graham-Rudman Deficit Reduction Act. It was widely noted that these decisions were highly formalistic and did not take a functional approach to separation of powers.[4] The decisions were formalistic in that they reasoned deductively from minimally justified premises and expressly eschewed consideration of what result would be best from a policy perspective.

In the past decade of the Rehnquist Court, as described in Chapter 1, there was a flurry of Supreme Court decisions dealing with federalism. In analyzing these cases, I argue that the Supreme Court's approach to federalism was formalistic, not functional. As the Court did with separation of powers in the 1980s, the federalism decisions of the 1990s and this decade have reasoned deductively from assumed major premises and have largely ignored functional considerations in allocating power between federal and state governments. Indeed, even the federalism decisions from the last years of the Rehnquist Court, which upheld federal power and rejected states' rights arguments, were highly formalistic.

I begin this chapter by identifying the assumptions behind the Rehnquist Court's decisions protecting federalism. In analyzing these cases, I first identify their premises and the extent to which the cases rested on assumptions that never were justified.

I then argue that the Rehnquist Court's federalism decisions were highly formalistic, reasoning from assumed premises deductively to conclusions. This also was true of the latter decisions of the Rehnquist Court that upheld federal laws in the face of states' rights challenges.

After describing the formalism of the federalism decisions from the last ten years of the Rehnquist Court, I explain why a formalistic approach to federalism is misguided.[5] The Constitution is silent about the allocation of power between federal and state governments. Nor can major premises be derived from the intent of the framers. Ultimately, the analysis must focus on what is the most desirable division of authority between federal and state governments; that is, what arrangement will best lead to effective government. This analysis, of necessity, is functional.

THE ASSUMPTIONS OF THE REHNQUIST COURT'S FEDERALISM DECISIONS

In examining the Rehnquist Court's federalism decisions, it is striking to note that they rest on fundamental assumptions that the Court never justified. In identifying these assumptions, it is apparent that each is crucial and none can be taken for granted. None, for example, can be derived from the text or the intent behind the provisions (even assuming the appropriateness of an originalist method of constitutional interpretation). At this point, I examine a list of six assumptions that came out of the Rehnquist Court. Although this list is not exhaustive, it certainly indicates some of the major assumptions made by the Rehnquist Court that were never justified.

1. *It is for the judiciary to impose limits on Congress in the name of protecting federalism and the authority of state governments; the political process, with minimal judicial review, is not adequate for this.*

As discussed in Chapter 1, in 1954, Professor Herbert Weschler wrote his famous *Political Safeguards* suggesting that judicial protection of states and of federalism was unnecessary because the political process adequately safeguards the interests of state governments.[6] Later, Professor Jesse Choper advanced a similar thesis and argued against judicial enforcement of federalism principles.[7]

In *Garcia v. San Antonio Metropolitan Transit Authority*, the Su-

preme Court expressly invoked and cited Wechsler and Choper in concluding that it was not for the federal judiciary to enforce limits on
Congress based on federalism.[8] In overruling *National League of Cities
v. Usery*,[9] the Court said that the political process adequately protected
the interests of state governments. Justice Harry Blackmun, writing for
the majority, stated:

> Apart from the limitation on federal authority inherent in the delegated nature
> of Congress' Article I powers, the principal means chosen by the Framers to
> ensure the role of the States in the federal system lies in the structure of the
> Federal Government itself. It is no novelty to observe that the composition of the
> Federal Government was designed in large part to protect the States from over-
> reaching by Congress. . . . In short, the Framers chose to rely on a federal system
> in which special restraints on federal power over the States inhered principally
> in the workings of the National Government itself, rather than in discrete limi-
> tations on the objects of federal authority. *State sovereign interests, then, are
> more properly protected by procedural safeguards inherent in the structure of
> the federal system than by judicially created limitations on federal power.* The
> effectiveness of the federal political process in preserving the States' interests is
> apparent even today in the course of federal legislation.[10]

The Rehnquist Court's federalism decisions obviously reject this view
that the political safeguards of federalism are adequate. For example,
the use of the Tenth Amendment as a limit on congressional power, such
as in *New York v. United States*[11] and *Printz v. United States*,[12] is based
on the assumption that the political process is inadequate to safeguard
state governments and the courts must do so. Limiting the ability of
Congress to authorize suits against state governments is also based on
this assumption.[13]

But never did the Rehnquist Court justify this crucial premise that
the political process is insufficient to protect the states and that it is
the judicial role to do so. Indeed, never did the Rehnquist Court even
acknowledge that it was rejecting the Court's express conclusion from
Garcia. Certainly, the assumption that states' interests are adequately
represented in the national political process is highly questionable, as

discussed in Chapter 1.[14] At the time the Constitution was written, states chose senators and thus were directly represented in Congress. But now, with popular election of senators, why believe that the states' interests as states are adequately protected in Congress?[15] The assumption must be that the voters, in choosing representatives and senators, weigh heavily the extent to which the individual legislator votes in a manner that serves the interests of the state as an entity. Yet, simple observation of congressional elections shows that the issues are usually basic ones about the economy, health care, and the personalities of the candidates. The interests of the voters are the focus of attention, not the institutional interests of state and local governments. Indeed, it may well be that the "primary constituencies of the national representatives may . . . be precisely those that advocate an extension of the federal power to the disadvantage of the states."[16]

But what is crucial is that the Rehnquist Court never made any of these arguments challenging the view that the political process would adequately protect the states. Instead, it simply assumed the inadequacy of the political process, even though the Court had said just the opposite in 1985 in *Garcia*.

2. *There is a meaningful and desirable distinction between economic and noneconomic activities in terms of Congress's authority to regulate commerce among the states.*

In *United States v. Morrison*,[17] the Supreme Court held that the civil damages provision of the Violence Against Women Act was unconstitutional, even though Congress had made detailed findings about the national economic consequences of violence against women. Chief Justice Rehnquist's majority opinion concluded that Congress could not regulate noneconomic activity, such as sexual assaults, based on the cumulative impact on commerce. The Court said that "[i]f accepted, petitioners' reasoning would allow Congress to regulate any crime as long as the nationwide, aggregated impact of that crime has substantial effects on employment, production, transit or consumption."[18] By this reasoning, the Court explained, Congress could regulate all violent crimes in the

United States. The Court thus concluded: "We accordingly reject the argument that Congress may regulate noneconomic, violent criminal conduct based solely on that conduct's aggregated effect on interstate commerce. The Constitution requires a distinction between what is truly national and what is truly local."[19]

The Court returned to this distinction more recently in *Gonzales v. Raich*.[20] There the Court held that Congress constitutionally may use its power to regulate commerce among the states to prohibit the cultivation and possession of small amounts of marijuana for medicinal purposes. Although California has created an exemption to its state marijuana laws for medical uses, no such exemption exists to the federal law. In a 6–3 decision, with the majority opinion written by Justice Stevens, the Court upheld the federal law. Justice John Paul Stevens explained that for almost seventy years Congress has had the authority to regulate activities that have a substantial effect on interstate commerce. The Court concluded that marijuana, looked at cumulatively, including that grown for medical purposes, has a substantial effect on interstate commerce. Justice Stevens opinion relied on a precedent from over sixty years ago: *Wickard v. Filburn*,[21] which held that Congress may regulate the amount of wheat that farmers grow for their own home consumption.

Gonzales v. Raich stands for the proposition that intrastate production of a commodity sold in interstate commerce is economic activity and thus substantial effect can be based on cumulative impact. Thus, the distinction between economic and noneconomic activities is crucial to the Rehnquist Court's commerce clause jurisprudence. But never was it justified by the Court. Certainly, the distinction can be questioned. For example, it is unclear what makes something economic as opposed to noneconomic. Almost everything has some economic consequences, so this inevitably seems to require an arbitrary line, perhaps between what has direct and indirect effects. Yet, such a distinction between direct and indirect effects had earlier been tried by the Court and was then expressly rejected.[22] Again, the key point is that the Rehnquist Court assumed, but did not justify, the distinction between economic and noneconomic effects that was crucial to its commerce clause jurisprudence.

3. *Federal laws that compel state and local governments to comply with federal mandates undermine accountability by confusing voters as to who to hold responsible.*

New York v. United States held that Congress may not commandeer states and force them to enact laws or adopt regulations.[23] Justice Sandra Day O'Connor's majority opinion expressly rested on the premise that such commandeering would undermine the accountability of state governments. The Court concluded that it was "clear" that because of the Tenth Amendment and limits on the scope of Congress's power under Article I, "[t]he Federal Government may not compel the States to enact or administer a federal regulatory program."[24] Allowing Congress to commandeer state governments, the Court explained, would undermine government accountability because Congress could make a decision, but the states would take the political heat and be held responsible for a decision that was not theirs.[25]

But this assumption is highly questionable. It is unclear why voters would be confused by federal mandates. They could be informed when a state was acting because of a federal command. Everyone is used to doing things, like paying taxes, because it is required by the federal government. The Court never justified why accountability could not be preserved by state and local officials simply by explaining to the voters when the state was acting pursuant to a federal mandate.

Nor did the Court ever justify why federal actions that frustrate state accountability violate the Tenth Amendment. The Court assumed that the Tenth Amendment includes such a protection, but it had never been articulated prior to *New York v. United States* and to this day never has been justified.

4. *Sovereign immunity is a constitutional principle, extending beyond the protections of the Eleventh Amendment, and it outweighs in importance government accountability as a constitutional principle.*

The Rehnquist Court has found that sovereign immunity, particularly for state governments, is a constitutional requirement. *Alden v. Maine* declared: "We hold that the powers delegated to Congress under Article I of the United States Constitution do not include the power to subject nonconsenting States to private suits for damages in state courts."[26] In *Federal Maritime Commission v. South Carolina State Port Authority*,[27] the Supreme Court further enlarged sovereign immunity by holding that private actions may not be brought against state governments in federal administrative agencies. Justice Clarence Thomas, writing the opinion in the case, said: "The preeminent purpose of state sovereign immunity is to accord States the dignity that is consistent with their status as sovereign entities."[28] The Court ruled that it would be impermissibly offend the "dignity" of state governments to allow them to be named as defendants in administrative agency proceedings. Justice Thomas explained: "Given both this interest in protecting States' dignity and the strong similarities between [Federal Maritime Commission] proceedings and civil litigation, we hold that state sovereign immunity bars the [Federal Maritime Commission] from adjudicating complaints filed by a private party against a nonconsenting state. Simply put, if the Framers thought it an impermissible affront to a State's dignity to be required to answer the complaints of private parties in federal courts, we cannot assume that they would have found it acceptable to compel a State to do exactly the same thing before the administrative tribunal of an agency."[29]

Sovereign immunity, as applied by the Rehnquist Court, is a right of state governments to be free from suit without their consent. Yet, the assumption of such a right is highly questionable because it is a right that cannot be found in the text or the framers' intent.

The text of the Constitution is silent about sovereign immunity. Not one clause of the first seven articles remotely even hints at the idea that the government has immunity from suits. No constitutional amendment has bestowed sovereign immunity on the federal government.

A claim might be made that the Eleventh Amendment provides sovereign immunity to state governments. Yet, if this is a textual argument, a careful reading of the text does not support the claim. The Eleventh Amendment states, "The Judicial power of the United States shall not be construed to extend to any suit in law or equity, commenced or prosecuted against one of the United States by Citizens of another State, or by Citizens or Subjects of any foreign state." Initially, it should be noted that the Eleventh Amendment applies only in federal court; it is a restriction solely on "the judicial power of the United States." In *Alden v. Maine*, the Court recognized this and based its holding entirely on the broad principle of state sovereign immunity and not in any way on the text of the Eleventh Amendment. Justice Anthony Kennedy, writing for the majority, stated: "[S]overeign immunity derives not from the Eleventh Amendment but from the structure of the original Constitution itself."[30]

Moreover, the text of the Eleventh Amendment restricts only those suits against states that are based on diversity of citizenship; it says that the federal judicial power does not extend to a suit against a state by a citizen of another state or of a foreign country. Nothing within it bars a suit against a state by its own citizens. The restriction on states being sued by their own citizens was the holding of *Hans v. Louisiana*, more than a century ago, but it certainly can't be based on a textual argument regarding the Eleventh Amendment.[31]

Nor can sovereign immunity be justified from an originalist perspective based on framers' intent. It is important to remember that originalists believe that when the text is silent, a right is protected under the Constitution only if the framers' intent is clear in justifying protection.[32] If the intent is unclear, the right is not constitutionally protected. At the very least, the framers' intent is completely ambiguous as to sovereign immunity.

There was not discussion of sovereign immunity at the Constitutional Convention in Philadelphia in 1787. The issue did arise in the state ratifying conventions. The dispute was over whether Article III authorized suits against non-consenting states in federal court. Two of the clauses of Article III, Section 2, specifically deal with suits against state governments. These provisions permit suits "between a State and Citizens of another state" and "between a State . . . and foreign . . . Citizens." The dispute was over whether the above-quoted language of Article III was meant to override the sovereign immunity that kept states from being sued in state courts. As Justice David Souter observed, "[T]he 1787 draft in fact said nothing on the subject and it was this very silence that occasioned some, though apparently not widespread, dispute among the framers and others over whether ratification of the Constitution would preclude a state sued in federal court from asserting sovereign immunity as it could have done on any nonfederal matter litigated in its own courts."[33] There is no record of any debate about this issue or these clauses at the Constitutional Convention.

Moreover, the Rehnquist Court's sovereign immunity decisions assumed that the states will voluntarily comply with federal law. In *Alden v. Maine*, Justice Kennedy expressly defended sovereign immunity based on this assumption. He wrote:

> The constitutional privilege of a State to assert its sovereign immunity in its own courts does not confer upon the State a concomitant right to disregard the Constitution or valid federal law. The States and their officers are bound by obligations imposed by the Constitution and by federal statutes that comport with the constitutional design. We are unwilling to assume the States will refuse to honor the Constitution or obey the binding laws of the United States. The good faith of the States thus provides an important assurance that "[t]his Constitution, and the Laws of the United States which shall be made in Pursuance thereof . . . shall be the supreme Law of the Land." (U.S.C., Article VI)[34]

What, then, is the assurance that state governments will comply with federal law?: trust in the good faith of state governments. Is it possible to imagine that thirty or forty years ago, at the height of the civil rights movement, the Supreme Court would have made such an assumption and issued such a statement that state governments simply could be trusted to voluntarily comply with federal law?

Put another way, the Rehnquist Court's sovereign immunity decisions assume that government immunity is more important than government accountability. Yet, this assumption is never justified or even acknowledged by the Court.

5. *The desire to protect the authority of state governments does not require a narrow preemption doctrine.*

One would expect that a Court concerned with federalism and states' rights also would be narrowing the scope of federal preemption of state laws. Narrowing the circumstances of federal preemption leaves more room for state and local governments to act. Quite the opposite, though, over the past several years, the Rehnquist Court repeatedly has found preemption of important state laws, even when federal law was silent about preemption or explicitly preserved state laws.[35]

For example, *Geier v. American Honda Motor Co. Inc.*[36] found preemption of a state products liability lawsuit for an unsafe vehicle notwithstanding a statutory provision which expressly provided that "[c]ompliance with" a federal safety standard does "not exempt any person from any liability under the common law."[37] The Court decided, in *Lorillard Tobacco Co. v. Reilly,*[38] that federal law preempted state regulation of outdoor billboards and signs in stores advertising cigarettes. *Crosby v. National Foreign Trade Council*[39] invalidated a Massachusetts law that restricted the ability of the state and its agency to purchase goods and services from companies that did business with Burma. Most recently, in *American Insurance Association v. Garamendi*, the Supreme Court held preemption of a California law requiring that insurance companies doing business in that state disclose Holocaust-era insurance policies.[40] The Court invalidated the California statute, despite the absence of any federal law expressing an intent to preempt state law, based on the "dormant foreign affairs power of the president."

At the very least, these and other cases like them are inconsistent with the Supreme Court's often-stated presumption against preemption. For example, the Court declared: "[B]ecause the States are independent sovereigns in our federal system, we have long presumed that Congress does not cavalierly preempt state-law causes of action. In all preemption cases, and particularly in those in which Congress has legislated in a field which the States have traditionally occupied, we 'start with the presumption' that 'the historic police powers of the States were not to be superseded by the Federal Act unless that was the clear and manifest purpose of Congress."[41] Yet, the recent Supreme Court preemption cases clearly put the presumption in favor of preemption.[42]

More importantly, the decisions assume that principles of federalism and the desire to protect states from federal power don't apply with regard to preemption. Again, this assumption is never acknowledged or justified by the Court.

6. *The social desirability of federal legislation does not matter in evaluating whether laws violate principles of federalism.*

In *New York v. United States*, Justice O'Connor's majority opinion expressly rejected any consideration of whether the federal law requiring cleaning up of nuclear waste was desirable or even based on a compelling need. Justice O'Connor declared: "No matter how powerful the federal interest involved, the Constitution simply does not give Congress the authority to require the States to regulate."[43]

Yet, this assumption, that the strength of the justification for the federal action is irrelevant, was never justified by the Court. Indeed, throughout the Rehnquist Court's federalism decisions, there was the implicit assumption that the desirability or need for the federal action was irrelevant in evaluating it from a federalism perspective. To me, what is most striking about the Rehnquist Court's federalism decisions is that they invalidated laws that unquestionably were socially important and even essential. Consider the cases discussed in Chapter 1. In *United States v. Lopez*, the Court struck down a federal law that prohibited guns within one thousand feet of schools. Would anyone want kids to have guns in school? *United States v. Morrison* invalidated a provision of the Violence Against Women Act, which allowed victims of gender-motivated violence to sue in federal court. Shouldn't such victims have the ability to sue, especially in light of Congress's findings that state courts often are hostile to such claims? In *New York v. United States*, the Court struck down a federal law that required states to clean up their low-level nuclear waste. Surely no one would argue that it is better to allow such waste to remain a danger to the public. *Printz v. United States* declared unconstitutional a federal law that required state and local law enforcement personnel to conduct background checks before issuing permits for firearms. Isn't it desirable to check out people before giving them gun permits?

Simply put, the Rehnquist Court's federalism decisions consistently assumed that the desirability of legislation is irrelevant in evaluating whether it violates the Tenth or Eleventh Amendments, or other principles of federalism. Yet, the more the rights of states are analogized to individual rights, the more questionable it becomes as to why they should not be treated the same in allowing compelling government interests to trump rights.

THE FORMALISTIC APPROACH OF THE FEDERALISM DECISIONS

These assumptions with respect to desirability are a key aspect of the federalism cases of recent years. The Court has reasoned deductively from largely unjustified major premises to conclusions, without consideration of what would be the most desirable allocation of power between the federal and state governments. In other words, each of the major federalism rulings of the 1990s—*New York v. United States, United States v. Lopez, Seminole Tribe of Florida v. Florida, Printz v. United States,* and *City of Boerne v. Flores*—has been highly formalistic and has expressly disavowed a functional analysis. Each decision warrants separate examination, and for each I want to show how the Court has reasoned deductively from minimally justified premises. This reasoning proceeded without consideration of what would be the most desirable allocation of power between the federal and state governments and eschewed any consideration of the functional benefits of federal laws. I then show that the same formalism is evident in the latter decisions of the Rehnquist Court, which rejected federalism challenges.

New York v. United States

As discussed in Chapter 1, in *New York v. United States,* in 1992, the Court declared unconstitutional a federal law on federalism grounds for only the second time since 1936.[44] The law pertained to the 1985 Low-Level Radioactive Waste Policy Amendments Act, which forced states to clean up their nuclear waste by 1996.

The Supreme Court ruled that Congress, pursuant to its authority under the commerce clause, could regulate the disposal of radioactive waste. However, by a 6–3 margin, the Court held that the "take title" provision of the law was unconstitutional because it gave state governments the choice between "either accepting ownership of waste or regulating according to the instructions of Congress."[45] Justice O'Connor, writing the opinion, said that it was impermissible for Congress to impose either option on the states. Forcing states to accept ownership of radioactive waste would impermissibly "commandeer" state governments, and requiring state compliance with federal regulatory statutes would impermissibly impose on states a requirement to implement federal legislation. The Court concluded that it was "clear" that because of the Tenth Amendment and limits on the scope of Congress's power under Article I, "[t]he Federal Government may not compel the States to enact or administer a federal regulatory program."[46]

The Court's explanation for why the law violated federalism was the epitome of formalistic reasoning. The decision can be summarized as a syllogism:

Major premise: Congress may not compel state governments to adopt laws or regulations.
Minor premise: The Low-Level Radioactive Waste Disposal Act compels state governments to adopt laws or regulations.
Conclusion: The Low-Level Radioactive Waste Disposal Act is unconstitutional.

The primary reason Justice O'Connor gave for why Congress cannot compel states to act is that it would frustrate democratic accountability because voters would not understand that the state was acting pursuant to a federal mandate. The Court explained that allowing Congress to commandeer state governments would undermine accountability because Congress could make a decision, but the states would take the political heat and be held responsible for a decision that was not theirs. Justice O'Connor wrote:

[W]here the federal government compels states to regulate, the accountability of both state and federal officials is diminished. . . . [W]here the federal government directs the States to regulate, it may be state officials who will bear the brunt of public disapproval, while the federal officials who devised the program may remain insulated from the electoral ramifications of their decision. Accountability is this diminished when, due to federal coercion, elected state officials cannot regulate in accordance with the views of the local electorate in matters not preempted by federal regulation.[47]

Justice O'Connor's reasoning here also can be summarized as a syllogism:

> *Major premise:* Democratic accountability requires that voters clearly understand which level of government is responsible for actions taken.
>
> *Minor premise:* Congress forcing state and local governments to enact legislation or regulation frustrates democratic accountability.
>
> *Conclusion:* Congress forcing state and local governments to enact legislation or regulation interferes with democratic accountability and is thus unconstitutional.

The major premise of the syllogism was simply asserted by the Court. Justice O'Connor offered no justification as to the constitutional basis for this premise of democratic accountability. Nothing in the Constitution's text supports this premise. Nor is it grounded in prior Supreme Court decisions. Perhaps it can be justified by political theory, but Justice O'Connor made no attempt to do so in her majority opinion.

Nor was the minor premise justified; there was no explanation as to why the voters could not understand when the state was acting pursuant to a federal mandate. Justice O'Connor assumed that if Congress forces the states to do something, voters will not hold Congress responsible but will blame the conduct on the primary actor, state governments. Voters, however, can surely comprehend when a state is acting because it is required to do so by federal law. Every person does many things that he or she otherwise would not because of federal mandates. Paying taxes is a simple example. Why then cannot people understand that a state government, too, might have to do something because of a federal mandate?

State government officials, of course, could explain to the voters that the federal government required the particular actions. Justice O'Connor never said why the federal government would not be held accountable under such circumstances. Perhaps most importantly, the rejection of a functional analysis is evidenced by Justice O'Connor's conclusion that a compelling government interest is not sufficient to permit a law that otherwise would violate the Tenth Amendment. Justice O'Connor wrote that "[n]o matter how powerful the federal interest involved, the Constitution simply does not give Congress the authority to require the States to regulate."[48] In fact, Justice O'Connor conceded that "[t]he result may appear 'formalistic' in a given case to partisans of the measure at issue, because such measures are typically the product of the era's perceived necessity."[49] The decision appears formalistic because it *is* formalistic: the Court reasoned deductively from premises that were minimally defended while disavowing any attention to functional considerations.

United States v. Lopez

Formalism also is evident in the second major federalism decision of the 1990s, *United States v. Lopez.*[50] In *Lopez,* as described in Chapter 1, the Supreme Court, by a 5–4 margin, declared unconstitutional the Gun-Free School Zones Act of 1990. This was the act that made it a federal crime to have a gun within one thousand feet of a school.[51] Splitting along ideological lines, the Court ruled that the relationship to interstate commerce was too tangential and uncertain to uphold the law as a valid exercise of Congress's commerce power. Also discussed in Chapter 1, the Court identified three circumstances in which Congress can act under its commerce clause authority: Congress can regulate the channels of interstate commerce, the instrumentalities of and persons or things in interstate commerce, and the activities that have a substantial effect on interstate commerce.

Chief Justice Rehnquist's opinion for the Court again can be summarized as a syllogism:

Major premise: Congress may use its commerce power in only three situations: to regulate the channels of interstate commerce, the instrumentalities of or persons or things in interstate commerce, and the activities that have a substantial effect on interstate commerce.

Minor premise: The Gun-Free School Zones Act does not fit into any of these three categories.

Conclusion: The Gun-Free School Zones Act is unconstitutional.

Chief Justice Rehnquist offered no justification for the major premise or why these are the only situations in which Congress can regulate under its commerce clause authority. Indeed, the decision was highly reminiscent of the opinion more than a decade earlier in *Northern Pipeline Construction Co. v. Marathon Pipe Line Co.,*[52] where the Court declared unconstitutional the federal bankruptcy courts. Justice William Brennan, writing for the plurality, identified four situations allowing Congress to create courts in which judges lack life tenure and get no protection against cuts in salary. No explanation or justification was provided as to why these four situations were exclusive. He then concluded that the bankruptcy courts were unconstitutional because they did not fit into these four categories.

The limits imposed in *Lopez* were not justified by the text of the Constitution, by the framers' intent, or by precedent. Moreover, the Court's opinion in *Lopez* was highly formalistic in that it gave no consideration to the functional desirability of having Congress prohibit guns near schools. Obviously, firearms near schools are bad and there is a national interest in law prohibiting this.

Seminole Tribe of Florida v. Florida

The third case in the 1990s concerning federalism was *Seminole Tribe of Florida v. Florida,* and it, too, shared the formalistic approach of the earlier two decisions.[53] Again, as covered in Chapter 1, the Indian Gaming Regulatory Act, enacted by Congress pursuant to the Indian commerce clause, permitted Indian tribes to conduct gambling only pursuant to a compact between a state and a tribe.[54] Under the act, states had a duty to negotiate in good faith with a tribe toward the formation of a compact. The law specifically provided that tribes could sue states in federal court to compel performance of this duty.[55]

The Supreme Court, with exactly the same ideological division as in *United States v. Lopez*, declared the authorization for suits against states unconstitutional on grounds that it violated the Eleventh Amendment. Chief Justice Rehnquist again wrote the opinion, joined by Justices O'Connor, Scalia, Kennedy, and Thomas; Justices Stevens, Souter, Ginsburg, and Breyer dissented.

Chief Justice Rehnquist's opinion for the Court again can be summarized as a syllogism:

Major premise: Subject matter jurisdiction cannot be authorized by Congress where not permitted by the Constitution.

Minor premise: The Eleventh Amendment is a constitutional bar to subject matter jurisdiction for suits against state governments, even when brought by their own citizens.

Conclusion: Congress cannot authorize subject matter jurisdiction for suits against state governments where barred by the Eleventh Amendment.

Although the major premise is an axiom of American law, the minor premise is far more controversial because, as explained above, the text of the Eleventh Amendment speaks only of suits against states brought by citizens of other states and citizens of foreign countries. Moreover, impressive historical research suggests that the Eleventh Amendment was intended only as a restriction on suits against states that were based solely on diversity jurisdiction.[56]

Nor can the decision be justified based on precedent. *Pennsylvania v. Union Gas Co.*, in 1989, held that Congress could authorize suits against states in federal court, so long as the law was textually clear in authorizing such litigation.[57] *Seminole Tribe* overruled *Union Gas*, even though it had been decided just seven years earlier. The four dissenters in *Union Gas*—Rehnquist, O'Connor, Scalia, and Kennedy—were joined by Thomas to create the new majority.

As described above, the Court in *Seminole Tribe* completely ignored functional considerations, such as the need to hold state governments accountable through actions in federal court. Chief Justice Rehnquist concluded his opinion for the Court by declaring:

In overruling *Union Gas* today, we reconfirm that the background principle of state sovereign immunity embodied in the Eleventh Amendment is not so ephemeral as to dissipate when the subject of the suit is an area, like the regulation of Indian commerce, that is under the exclusive control of the Federal government. Even when the Constitution gives Congress complete law-making authority over a particular area, the Eleventh Amendment prevents congressional authorization of suits by private parties against unconsenting states. The Eleventh Amendment restricts the judicial power under Article III, and Article I cannot be used to circumvent the constitutional limits placed upon federal jurisdiction.[58]

No weight whatsoever was given to the functional need to ensure state compliance with federal laws.

The Court, however, recognized that Congress could authorize suits against states when acting pursuant to its powers under Section 5 of the Fourteenth Amendment. Yet, this, too, seemed based entirely on formalistic considerations: the Fourteenth Amendment was adopted after the Eleventh Amendment, not like the commerce power that preceded the Eleventh Amendment. Chief Justice Rehnquist wrote: "*Fitzpatrick* [which held that Congress could authorize suits against states when acting pursuant to Section 5 of the Fourteenth Amendment] was based upon a rationale wholly inapplicable to the Interstate Commerce Clause, viz., that the Fourteenth Amendment, adopted well after the Eleventh Amendment and the ratification of the Constitution, operated to alter the pre-existing balance between state and federal power achieved by Article III and the Eleventh Amendment."[59]

In *Idaho v. Coeur d'Alene Tribe of Idaho*, Justice Kennedy, joined only by Chief Justice Rehnquist, urged a radical change as to when state officers may be sued in federal court.[60] Justice Kennedy urged a functional approach: federal courts would conduct case-by-case balancing and hear suits against state officers only when necessary to effectuate federal interests. Justice Kennedy outlined two instances in which the exercise of federal jurisdiction would be warranted: if state forums were unavailable or if there was a need for federal court interpretation of federal law.[61] Although, as discussed in subsequent chapters, I strongly disagree with this approach, its express functionality is dramatically different from other federalism opinions by conservative justices in the 1990s. However, seven Justices—O'Connor, Scalia, and Thomas in the majority, and Stevens, Souter, Ginsburg, and Breyer in dissent—rejected the Kennedy approach.

Printz v. United States

Another major federalism decision of the period was *Printz v. United States*,[62] which declared unconstitutional the Brady Handgun Violence Prevention Act.[63] As discussed in Chapter 1, the Court held that forcing state and local law enforcement personnel to conduct background checks before issuing permits for firearms violates the Tenth Amendment.

Justice Scalia, writing for the majority, made two major arguments. Each was highly formalistic. First, compelling state and local activity is inconsistent with dual sovereignty and the Tenth Amendment. This argument, like that in the other cases, was classic formalistic reasoning and can be summarized as a syllogism:

Major premise: The Tenth Amendment is violated by federal laws that compel state and local governments to act.
Minor premise: The Brady Bill compels state and local governments to conduct background checks before issuing permits for firearms.
Conclusion: The Brady Bill violates the Tenth Amendment.

The Court justified the major premise of the syllogism in three ways. First, Justice Scalia said that "[b]ecause there is no constitutional text speaking to this precise question, the answer . . . must be sought in historical understanding and practice, in the structure of the Constitution, and in the jurisprudence of the Court."[64] Justice Scalia reviewed the experience in early American history and found that there was no support for requiring states to participate in a federal regulatory scheme. As to history, Justice Scalia said that Congress, in the initial years of American history, did not compel state activity and since "early Congresses avoided use of this highly attractive power, we would have reason to believe that the power was thought not to exist."[65]

As Justice Souter points out in dissent, there is a strong argument that

Justice Scalia is incorrect in terms of the framers' intent.[66] Strong statements exist from James Madison and Alexander Hamilton that Congress could call upon states to execute federal laws. More to the point, it seems very dubious to rely on the absence of a practice in the first Congresses as a means to establishing a constitutional limit. There are any number of reasons why the federal government did not require state action at the time: it might not have considered the possibility; it might have thought the government's goals could best be achieved by direct federal action; it might have sought to establish the federal government's own authority to act; or political pressures at the time might have prevented specific mandates. To infer rejection of congressional power from inaction is to assume the truth of one explanation to the exclusion of all others. The absence of a particular practice at a specific time does not mean that those then in power thought it unconstitutional. There are many explanations for why a type of law was not used at a given moment.

Second, Justice Scalia justified the major premise in *Printz* by invoking the structure of the Constitution. He wrote that "[i]t is incontestable that the Constitution established a system of dual sovereignty."[67] Yet, this does not explain why federal mandates to states are inconsistent with dual sovereignty. The argument, as presented by Scalia, is entirely based on a definition of dual sovereignty and what it means in terms of the structure of American government. Indeed, the concept of dual sovereignty is purely descriptive of having both federal and state governments. There must be separate reasons, apart from the existence of dual sovereignty, as to why a federal law unduly intrudes state prerogatives. This requires a normative theory about federalism and the proper relationship of federal and state governments. Justice Scalia did not even allude to such a theory but just concluded that federal mandates to state governments violates dual sovereignty.

Finally, Justice Scalia said that the invalidation of the Brady Bill is supported by *New York v. United States*, which held that Congress may not compel state legislative or regulatory activity. But, as described above, this decision was highly formalistic and the Court in *Printz* offered no more of a functional analysis than was present in that case.

Justice Scalia also presented another reason, apart from the Tenth

Amendment, as to why the Brady Bill is unconstitutional: it violates separation of powers. Scalia argued that the executive power is solely vested in the president, and that the assignment of enforcement tasks to state and local governments is inconsistent with this authority.[68]

Although this argument is novel in federalism cases, it, too, is classic formalism that can be summarized as a syllogism:

Major premise: The president alone can possess federal executive authority, and therefore delegations of executive authority other than to the president are unconstitutional.

Minor premise: The Brady Bill delegates executive authority to state and local governments for the enforcement of a federal law.

Conclusion: The Brady Bill is unconstitutional.

Many aspects of this syllogism are unjustified and troubling. First, the Court never justified the premise that only the president can possess federal executive authority. Justice Scalia offered no explanation of authority, except for a citation to a then-recent law-review article taking the position that the Constitution creates a unitary executive.[69] In fact, there are many instances in which Congress grants executive power to entities, such as federal independent regulatory commissions, that are not directly accountable to the president. Indeed, constitutional scholars have advanced powerful refutation of the unitary executive theory, and Justice Scalia did not even acknowledge their arguments.[70]

Second, the Court did not engage in a functional analysis of whether delegating this power to the states significantly undermines presidential power. Rather, the Court seemed to apply a bright-line rule (a rule that offers an unambiguous guideline): Congress never can give executive responsibility to the states. In fact, from a functional perspective, the executive branch is far better off delegating background checks to state and local governments. After all, the burden on federal law enforcement is enormously reduced.

Finally, it is important to remember that President Ronald Reagan favored the Brady Bill and argued for its constitutionality in the Supreme Court. The encroachment on presidential power in this case seems suspect. If the concern is with Congress unduly taking tasks away from the president, then the appropriate approach would be to inquire in each case whether such erosion occurred. A bright-line rule is misguided.

Printz is thus classic judicial formalism, both in its method of reasoning and in its refusal to consider the functional benefits of the law that it invalidated. Dean Evan Caminker notes this and explains:

Justice Scalia's opinion for the Court is decidedly formalistic in two distinct senses. First, the Court embraces "doctrinal formalism," by which I mean the Court takes a formalist approach to constructing a judicially enforceable doctrine. The Court announced a categorical anti-commandeering rule, one not subject to any case-by-case balancing of interests or measurement of burden. . . . Justice Scalia's opinion also embraces "interpretive formalism," by which I mean the Court takes a formalist approach to interpreting the meaning of the constitution.[71]

City of Boerne v. Flores

City of Boerne v. Flores, another major federalism-based decision of the 1990s, was every bit as formalistic as the others. As explained earlier, *City of Boerne v. Flores* declared unconstitutional the Religious Freedom Restoration Act, as it exceeded the scope of Congress's power under Section 5 of the Fourteenth Amendment. The act required that courts use strict scrutiny in considering challenges to laws as infringing free exercise of religion. Once more, the Court's opinion can be summarized as a syllogism:

> *Major premise:* Under Section 5 of the Fourteenth Amendment, Congress only may provide remedies for rights recognized by the courts; Congress may not expand the scope of rights or create new rights.
> *Minor premise:* The Religious Freedom Restoration Act expands the scope of rights.
> *Conclusion:* The Religious Freedom Restoration Act is unconstitutional.

The major premise, narrowly interpreting Congress's Section 5 power, cannot be defended on textual grounds or even with regard to the framers' intent; rather, the Court made a policy choice that was very much based on a desire to limit the scope of Congress's power to allow state and local governments more latitude as regulators. Yet, the Court never defended this as a policy choice at all.

Section 5 states: "The Congress shall have power to enforce, by appropriate legislation, the provisions of this article." Justice Kennedy defended the major premise of the syllogism by declaring: "Congress's power under §5, however, extends only to 'enforc[ing]' the provisions of the Fourteenth Amendment. . . . The design of the Fourteenth Amendment and the text of §5 are inconsistent with the suggestion that Congress has the power to decree the substance of the Fourteenth Amendment's restrictions on the states. *Legislation which alters the meaning of the Free Exercise Clause cannot be said to be enforcing the Clause. Congress does not enforce a constitutional right by changing what the right is.*"[72]

The key issue in *Flores*, and in defining Congress's power, thus is what "enforce" means in Section 5 of the Fourteenth Amendment. As is usually the case with difficult constitutional issues, the answer to this question cannot be found in the text or in the framers' intent. The word *enforce* is sufficiently ambiguous to allow either view as a plausible interpretation of Section 5. The Supreme Court in *Flores* claimed that the word necessarily means that Congress only can remedy and that Congress cannot determine the substantive meaning of rights.

Justice Kennedy begged the key question of what *enforce* means. One dictionary defines it as: "Urge, press home (argument, demand); impose (action, conduct upon person); compel observance of."[73] Another dictionary defines *enforce* as: "1. to give force to: strengthen; 2. to urge with energy; 3. constrain, compel; 4. to effect or gain by force; 5. to carry out effectively."[74] From the perspective of these definitions, Congress very much is "enforcing" the Fourteenth Amendment when it broadens the scope of liberty under the due-process clause and when it expands equal protection. In this sense, Congressional expansion of rights is enforced by strengthening the Fourteenth Amendment.

Dictionaries, of course, do not determine the meaning of the words in the Constitution. My point simply is that there is nothing certain about the meaning of the word *enforce* which supports Justice Kennedy's claim that it precludes Congress from using it to expand the scope of constitutional rights. Justice Kennedy argued as if the term *enforce* had a precise meaning that supported his position as the correct way to understand Congress's Section 5 power. No such precise meaning exists.

Phrased slightly differently, the word *enforce* might be defined in many alternative ways, two of which are "to implement" and "to remedy." Justice Kennedy chooses the latter. But the former seems equally plausible in the context of Section 5. Congress, by that provision, is given the authority to implement, as best it can, the protections of the Fourteenth Amendment, such as due process and equal protection. Congress can do this by expanding the scope of these rights if it decides that it is the best way to ensure, or to implement, these protections.

I am not making the strong claim that my definition is correct and Justice Kennedy's is wrong. Rather, my point is that the literal language of the Fourteenth Amendment does not answer the question of whether Congress may use its Section 5 power to expand the scope of constitutional rights or provide support for the major premise of Justice Kennedy's syllogism. This is hardly surprising; rarely does the literal language of the Constitution resolve difficult contemporary constitutional issues.

Nor does the framers' intent behind the Fourteenth Amendment answer the issue. Even assuming that framers' intent should be controlling in constitutional interpretation, a premise that I reject,[75] there is no indication that the issue was ever considered when the Fourteenth Amendment was drafted and ratified. Justice Kennedy's opinion in *Flores* argues that the legislative history of Section 5 resolves the issue. Justice Kennedy declared: "The Fourteenth Amendment's history confirms the remedial, rather than substantive, nature of the enforcement clause."[76]

Justice Kennedy said that the rejection of the Bingham Amendment shows that Congress meant Section 5 power solely to be remedial.[77] Specifically, Representative John Bingham had introduced a draft amendment summarized as follows: "The Congress shall have power to make all laws which shall be necessary and proper to secure to the citizens of each State all privileges and immunities of citizens in the several States, and to all persons in the several States equal protection in the rights of life, liberty, and property."[78] Justice Kennedy maintained that there was strong opposition to this provision and that the revised provision, Section 5, was not opposed in the same manner.

There is no doubt that the revised Section 5 has less sweeping sounding language than the Bingham proposal. Yet, there is not a word in the debates quoted by Justice Kennedy about whether Congress's power should be only to remedy what the Court determines to be a constitutional violation, or whether it includes congressional authority to expand rights. All that Justice Kennedy showed was that language with a narrower phrasing was enacted. The substantive difference in the phrasing is completely assumed by the justice.

In fact, the quotations used by Justice Kennedy did not support his position that Section 5 was intended to be only remedial in scope. Justice Kennedy quoted Representative Bingham, saying that the new draft would give Congress "the power . . . to protect by national law the privileges and immunities of all the citizens of the Republic . . . whenever the same shall be abridged or denied by the unconstitutional acts of any State."[79] Justice Kennedy next quoted Representative Thaddeus Stevens, that the new draft amendment "allows Congress to correct the unjust legislation of the States."[80] Finally, Justice Kennedy quoted Senator Jacob Howard as saying that Section 5 "enables Congress, in case the States shall enact laws in conflict with the principles of the amendment, to correct that legislation by a formal congressional enactment."[81]

None of these quotations support the view that Congress's power is solely to remedy violations of rights found by the Court, and not to expand rights safeguarded by the Fourteenth Amendment. Surely, the Religious Freedom Restoration Act can be seen, in Representative Bingham's words, as "protecting" rights or as "correcting unjust state practices," in Representative Stevens's language. Laws expanding the scope of rights are very much in accord with Senator Howard's goal of advancing the principles of the amendment. A careful reading of the very legislative history that Justice Kennedy invoked shows that it could be used equally persuasively to support either view.

Again, I am not making the strong claim that the legislative history of Section 5 means that my interpretation is correct, and Justice

Kennedy's was incorrect. Once more, the point is more limited: nothing in the framers' intent answers the question as to which approach to Section 5 is preferable, and nothing in this intent justifies the major premise that Justice Kennedy reasoned from. The framers simply did not consider whether Congress was limited to remedying violations of judicially recognized rights or whether Congress could use its power to recognize new rights.

In addition to text and framers' intent, the Court claimed that precedent supports its view that Congress's power is solely remedial. Justice Kennedy said that "[t]he Court has defined this power as 'remedial.'"[82] Yet, a close look at the precedents show that they better support the opposing view: Congress may use its Section 5 power to expand rights.

Katzenbach v. Morgan is the leading case interpreting Section 5, and it held that Congress, under Section 5 of the Fourteenth Amendment, may independently interpret the Constitution and even overturn the Supreme Court.[83] *Katzenbach* focused on the constitutionality of Section 4(e) of the Voting Rights Act of 1965, which provided that no person who has completed sixth grade in a Puerto Rican school, where instruction was in Spanish, shall be denied the right to vote over the issue of English literacy. Earlier, *Lassiter v. Northampton Election Board* upheld the constitutionality of an English-language literacy requirement for voting.[84]

Congress, in the Voting Rights Act, sought to partially overturn *Lassiter* by providing that failing a literacy test could not bar a person from voting if the person was educated through the sixth grade in Puerto Rico. The Supreme Court in *Katzenbach v. Morgan* upheld this provision as "a proper exercise of the powers granted to Congress by §5 of the Fourteenth Amendment."[85]

The Court offered two reasons to support this conclusion. One was that Congress could have concluded that granting Puerto Ricans the right to vote would empower them and help eliminate the discrimination they experienced.[86] In essence, this is an argument that the law was constitutional because it was a remedy for discrimination.

Second, the Court held that Congress could find that the literacy test denied equal protection, even though this was contrary to the Court's earlier holding in *Lassiter*. This aspect of the ruling is much more significant because it accords Congress the authority to define the meaning of the Fourteenth Amendment. Despite Justice Kennedy's attempt to minimize this aspect of the decision, the *Katzenbach* case clearly articulates the view that Congress, under its Section 5 power, could expand the protection against discrimination by prohibiting the literacy tests.

A specific issue before the Supreme Court was whether Congress was limited to remedying what the Court deemed in violation of the Constitution, or whether Congress could independently interpret the Constitution. The state of New York argued the former position, that Congress could not use its Section 5 power to independently determine the meaning of the Fourteenth Amendment, but rather it could only provide remedies for practices that the Court had ruled unconstitutional.[87]

The Court rejected this approach and spoke broadly of Congress's power under Section 5 and expressly rejected the view that the legislative power is confined "to the insignificant role of abrogating only those state laws that the judicial branch was prepared to adjudge unconstitutional."[88] The Court explained that "[b]y including §5 the draftsmen sought to grant to Congress, by a specific provision applicable to the Fourteenth Amendment, the same broad powers expressed in the Necessary and Proper Clause."[89]

In fact, Justice John Marshall Harlan, in dissent, took exactly the same view in *Katzenbach* as did Justice Kennedy in *Flores*. He contended that "enforcing" meant remedying and that Congress cannot use its section five powers to determine the substantive meaning of the Fourteenth Amendment.[90] Justice Harlan wrote:

The question here is not whether the statute is appropriate remedial legislation to cure an established violation of a constitutional command, but whether there has in fact been an infringement of that constitutional command, that is, whether a particular state practice, or, as here, a statute is so arbitrary or irrational as to offend the command of the Equal Protection Clause of the Fourteenth Amendment. That question is one for the judicial branch ultimately to determine.[91]

But Justice Harlan was the dissent; his position was explicitly rejected by Justice William Brennan's majority opinion.

Justice Kennedy deals with *Katzenbach* by saying: "There is language in our opinion in *Katzenbach v. Morgan* which could be interpreted as acknowledging a power in Congress to enact legislation that expands the rights contained in §1 of the Fourteenth Amendment. This is not a necessary interpretation, however, or even the best one."[92] Nevertheless, Justice Brennan's majority opinion in *Katzenbach* made it clear that Congress under Section 5 may expand, just not dilute, rights. In a footnote, Justice Brennan stated: "Contrary to the suggestion of the dissent, §5 does not grant Congress power to exercise discretion in the other direction and to enact 'statutes so as in effect to dilute equal protection and due process decisions of this Court.' We emphasize that Congress' power under §5 is limited to adopting measures to enforce the guarantees of the Amendment; §5 grants Congress no power to restrict, abrogate, or dilute these guarantees."[93] Justice Brennan was completely clear that he rejected Justice Harlan's position that Congress's power was purely remedial.

Moreover, other cases support Congress's authority under the post–Civil War, or Reconstruction, amendments to independently interpret the Constitution.[94] In *City of Rome v. United States*, the Court clearly ruled that Congress has the authority under Section 2 to interpret the meaning of the Fifteenth Amendment,[95] which prohibits racial discrimination with respect to voting. *Rome* involved a challenge to changes that the city of Rome adopted after the Voting Rights Act was enacted in 1965. Specifically, the city had annexed a substantial number of outlying areas and thus altered the racial composition of its electorate. It also had adopted an at-large system for selecting city commissioners. The federal district court found no evidence that these changes were motivated by a discriminatory purpose. Also, on the same day *Rome* was decided, the Court held, in *City of Mobile v. Bolden*, that at-large election systems are constitutional unless there is proof of a discriminatory purpose.[96] Therefore, the city of Rome's actions did not appear to be in violation of the Fourteenth or Fifteenth Amendments.

Nonetheless, the Supreme Court ruled against the city based on the Voting Rights Act. Although *City of Mobile v. Bolden* held that proof of a discriminatory intent was a prerequisite to finding a constitutional violation, the Court in *City of Rome* concluded that Congress could "prohibit changes that have a discriminatory impact."[97] *Rome* thus authorized Congress independently to interpret the meaning of the Fifteenth Amendment and even to adopt a view contrary to that of the Supreme Court. The Court had said that discriminatory impact was insufficient to show a violation of the Fourteenth Amendment, but the Court upheld a statute allowing discriminatory impact to suffice to establish liability.

Showing that precedents support allowing Congress to expand rights only demonstrates that Justice Kennedy was disingenuous in claiming that his position was backed by prior case law. However, that does not resolve the issue of what is the best way to interpret the scope of Congress's Section 5 power. The response to the invocation of precedents simply could be that they should be overruled.

As with the other cases, this review of *City of Boerne v. Flores* is meant to show that the Court's reasoning is formalistic, in that it is deductive and follows from inadequately defended premises. The decision also is formalistic in the sense that the Court gave no consideration to the benefits to the law that it was striking down. The invalidation of the Religious Freedom Restoration Act (RFRA) means that people in the United States will have far less protection for their religious practices. Laws of general applicability—whether prison regulations or zoning ordinances or historical landmark laws—that seriously burden religion might have been successfully challenged under RFRA but not any longer. Put most simply, *Flores* means that many claims of free exercise of religion that would have prevailed, now certainly will lose. People in the United States have less protection of their rights after *Flores* than they did before it. Yet, this was not discussed or even acknowledged in Justice Kennedy's opinion for the Court.

Thus, the federalism decisions of the 1990s, like the separation of powers rulings of the 1980s, have been formalistic in the classic sense of that term. The Supreme Court has emphasized deductive reasoning from asserted premises and has refused to give weight to functional considerations, whether based on public policy needs—such as cleaning up nuclear waste or keeping guns away from schools—or constitutional values, such as ensuring state compliance with federal law or enhancing the free exercise of religion.

THE FORMALISM OF THE FEDERALISM DECISIONS
OF THE EARLY TWENTY-FIRST CENTURY

One last example of formalism is important. The final decisions of the Rehnquist Court upheld federal laws concerning the scope of Congress's powers under Section 5 of the Fourteenth Amendment and the power of Congress to authorize suits against state governments. *Nevada Department of Human Resources v. Hibbs*[98] held that state governments may be sued for violating the family leave provisions of the Family and Medical Leave Act (FMLA).[99] In recent years, the Court had ruled that Congress may authorize suits against state governments only when it acts pursuant to Section 5 of the Fourteenth Amendment and not under any other congressional power. The Court thus concluded that federal laws prohibiting patent infringement,[100] age discrimination in employment,[101] and disability discrimination in employment could not be used to sue state governments because they were not within the scope of Congress's authority under Section 5.[102]

But *Hibbs* found that the federal law requiring employers to give employees unpaid time off for family leave could be used to sue state governments. Chief Justice Rehnquist, writing in a 6–3 decision, said that Congress was concerned about preventing and remedying gender discrimination in employment and that Congress has more authority to act under Section 5 when it is dealing with specific types of discrimination, such as those based on race or gender, which receive heightened scrutiny under equal protection.

The Court followed this a year later with *Tennessee v. Lane*.[103] The issue was whether state governments could be sued for violating Title II of the Americans with Disabilities Act, which prohibits discrimination against people with disabilities in state and local programs, services, and activities. The case involved a criminal defendant who had to crawl on his hands and knees to access a second floor courtroom that was not accessible to people with disabilities.

Tennessee v. Lane, in a 5–4 decision, held that state governments may be sued for discriminating against people with disabilities with regard to the fundamental right of access to the courts. Justice Stevens, writing the opinion in the case, emphasized that there is a well-established fundamental right of access to the courts and that Congress may enforce it by authorizing suits against state governments. The decision thus fits with the ruling from a year earlier, in *Nevada Department of Human Resources v. Hibbs*. Together the cases establish that Congress has much more power to act under Section 5 of the Fourteenth Amendment when it is dealing with a type of discrimination that receives heightened scrutiny or involves a fundamental right.

In fact, the cases establish a basic framework for analysis as to whether a state can be sued under a statute authorizing suits against state governments. If the statute concerns a type of discrimination that receives heightened scrutiny or involves a fundamental right, then the state can be sued even without any findings by Congress of unconstitutional state behavior. For example, there were no findings by Congress, in adopting the family leave provisions of the Family and Medical Leave Act, of unconstitutional gender discrimination by state governments. The concern was how the lack of family leave had a discriminatory impact on women and, of course, it is well established that disparate effects are not sufficient for an equal protection violation.

On the other hand, if the claims involve neither a type of discrimination that receives heightened scrutiny nor a fundamental right, then Congress may authorize suits against state governments only by finding a pervasive pattern of unconstitutional behavior. In *University of Alabama v. Garrett*, the Court found that state governments could not be sued under Title I of the Americans with Disabilities Act (ADA), even though there was a voluminous congressional record of discrimination against people with disabilities. The former director of nursing at the University of Alabama at Birmingham Hospital sued after she was let go for taking time off for breast cancer treatment. Chief Justice Rehnquist declared: "The legislative record of the ADA, however, simply fails to show that Congress did in fact identify a pattern of irrational state discrimination in employment against the disabled."[104] Justice Breyer attached a thirty-nine-page appendix to his dissenting opinion in which he listed the numerous references in the legislative history to government discrimination against the disabled.[105] Chief Justice Rehnquist's majority opinion found these insufficient, saying some were just anecdotes. He explained that most involved local governments, not state governments, and local governments are not protected by state sovereign immunity. Chief Justice Rehnquist further stated that some of the evidence concerned government discrimination against the disabled in providing services, which is Title II, not Title I, of the ADA. He observed that "[in] 1990, the States alone employed more than 4.5 million people. It is telling, we think, that given these large numbers, Congress assembled only such minimal evidence of unconstitutional state discrimination in employment against the disabled."[106]

Again, the Court's approach is highly formalistic and can be depicted as a traditional syllogism. To use *Hibbs* as the illustration:

> *Major premise:* Congress has broad power to authorize suits against states when dealing with types of discrimination that receive heightened scrutiny or involve fundamental rights, but otherwise must prove pervasive unconstitutional state behavior.
> *Minor premise:* The family leave provision of the Family and Medical Leave Act involves gender discrimination, which receives heightened scrutiny.
> *Conclusion:* States can be sued for violating the family leave provision of the Family and Medical Leave Act.

As with the formalism of the other cases described above, the major premise of this syllogism has not been justified by the Court, and would seem difficult to do so. Why should Congress's power under Section 5 depend on the Court's applied level of scrutiny for a particular right? Moreover, this has a perverse effect. The Court in *Hibbs* and *Lane* draws a distinction among types of discrimination, allowing Congress latitude to enact laws preventing and remedying some forms of discrimination but not others, by state governments. Under current equal protection law, constitutional challenges have relatively little chance of success in suits objecting to forms of discrimination, such as those based on age and disability, which receive only rational-basis review. Under rational-basis review, the government prevails so long as its action is reasonable, related to a legitimate government purpose. Thus, it is especially important that Congress have the authority to deal with these types of discrimination by statute. Yet, the effect of *Hibbs* and *Lane*, and its predecessor decisions over the prior decade is exactly the opposite: Congress is denied the authority to act where it is most needed because the Constitution will provide the least protection.

The crucial question is why Congress's power under Section 5 depends on the level of scrutiny applied by the Court in terms of equal protection. The only answer given can be seen in Chief Justice Rehnquist's majority opinion: "Because the standard for demonstrating the constitutionality of a gender-based classification is more difficult to meet than our rational basis test . . . it was easier for Congress to show a pattern of state constitutional violations."[107] There are several problems with this.

First, *Hibbs* never found that the denial of family leave constituted a constitutional violation. Since the failure to provide family leave was gender-neutral, and since it is highly doubtful that it was motivated by a discriminatory purpose, the FMLA cannot be seen as remedying constitutional violations. Second, other statutes dealing with the types of discrimination that receive only rational-basis review may very well be about remedying constitutional violations. Under this view, the Age Discrimination in Employment Act and Title I of the Americans with Disabilities Act, neither of which the Supreme Court had found to be within the scope of Section 5 of the Fourteenth Amendment, could be seen as remedying constitutional violations as well. The fact that rational-basis review is used under equal protection does not mean that there are no constitutional violations; arbitrary discrimination based on age or disability violates equal protection. In fact, Congress expressed concern with unconstitutional state discrimination in adopting the Americans with Disabilities Act.

Nor is there any other apparent reason why the level of scrutiny for a type of discrimination should define the scope of Congress's power to act under Section 5. In fact, as explained above, the Court's approach seems to have it exactly backward. In areas where constitutional protection is least likely to exist, statutory protection is most important. Under the Court's rational-basis jurisprudence, it is very difficult to successfully challenge discrimination that does not receive heightened scrutiny.

Especially in these areas, such as age and disability discrimination, Congress needs to have the authority to prevent and remedy wrongful government actions. The effect of *Hibbs* is that some types of discrimination matter and others do not; both constitutional and statutory protection is limited to the former.

Again, the key point is that even in rejecting federalism challenges and siding with federal power in *Hibbs* and *Lane*, the Court was highly formalistic. It reasoned deductively from unjustified and highly questionable premises. Indeed, the formalism of these decisions, and their tension with the earlier federalism decisions of the Rehnquist Court, may make these later decisions ripe for overruling. *Hibbs* was a 6–3 decision, with both Chief Justice Rehnquist and Justice O'Connor in the majority. *Lane* was a 5–4 decision, with Justice O'Connor in the majority. With two new conservative justices, these recent rulings may not survive long.

PUTTING FUNCTIONALISM BACK INTO FEDERAL GOVERNANCE

Earlier in this century, the legal realists exposed the fatal flaws in formalistic analysis.[108] Today, their criticisms of formalism are just as cogent and applicable to the Supreme Court's modern use of formalism in the area of federalism. Benjamin Cardozo says that "the demon of formalism tempts the intellect with the lure of scientific order," and further declared that when "judges are called upon to say how far existing rules are to be extended or restricted, they must let the welfare of society fix the path, its direction and its distance."[109] The formalism of the 1990s likewise appears to offer "scientific order" in the form of the certainty of deductive reasoning and ignores considerations of the "welfare of society."[110]

In part, the flaw of formalism in the area of federalism is the assumption of highly debatable premises. If formalism ever is possible and desirable, it must be in an area where premises for deductive reasoning can be established. With regard to federalism, however, the premises cannot be based on the text, the framers' intent, or the Court's prior decisions. Any premises must be founded on a normative theory about the appropriate relationship between federal and state governments. This has been completely absent from the Court's decisions.

The text of the Constitution says virtually nothing about the allocation of power between the federal and state governments. Moreover, the Constitution provides almost no guidance as to federalism. Several constitutional provisions focus on federalism. Most importantly, Articles I, II, and III of the Constitution create a national government with broad powers, and there is no dispute that the central difference between the Constitution and its predecessor, the Articles of Confederation, was in the establishment of the federal government. Article VI of the Constitution is crucial in understanding federalism because it provides that the Constitution, and laws and treaties made pursuant to it, are the supreme law of the land.

No provision of the Constitution speaks directly to the allocation of power between the national and state governments. Sometimes, both in political rhetoric and in court decisions, the Tenth Amendment is invoked as protecting state governments from federal encroachments. The text of the Tenth Amendment, however, simply does not say this. The Tenth Amendment states: "The powers not delegated to the United States by the Constitution, nor prohibited by it to the States, are reserved to the States respectively, or to the people."

Put another way, the Tenth Amendment states that Congress may act only if power is granted to it by the Constitution. States, in contrast, may act unless the Constitution prohibits the conduct. Phrased slightly differently, the Tenth Amendment is an important reminder that states possess the police power—the ability to do anything not forbidden by the Constitution; Congress does not have this kind of authority—Congress may act only when empowered by the Constitution. The text of the Tenth Amendment simply does not say that legislation within Congress's Article I authority is invalid if it interferes with state prerogatives. It certainly says nothing about not commandeering state governments. Nothing in the language of the Tenth Amendment provides a basis for declaring federal laws unconstitutional if they are adopted within the scope of powers given Congress by the Constitution.

Likewise, the text of other key constitutional provisions used by the

Court to protect federalism offers little guidance in decision making. The commerce clause in Article I empowers Congress to regulate commerce among the states, but leaves open what is "commerce" and what constitutes "among the states." The text of the Eleventh Amendment provides only that a state cannot be sued "by citizens of another state, or by citizens or subjects of any foreign state." Nothing in its text mentions barring suits against a state by its own citizens.

Nor is the framers' intent behind any of these provisions sufficiently clear as to provide premises for deductive reasoning. The framers were largely silent about the issue of federalism, and their views are of limited relevance anyway in dealing with a government so vastly different from what they envisioned. The absence of guidance from the framers in interpreting the Tenth Amendment is powerfully illustrated by the Court's decision in *Printz*, which, relying on the absence of laws in the first Congresses, compelled state government action as its sole evidence of framers' intent.[111] As to the Eleventh Amendment, there is strong historical evidence that the framers meant solely to preclude suits against state governments where jurisdiction was founded on diversity of citizenship and that they did not mean to bar federal questions from being heard in the federal courts.[112]

Nor do the Supreme Court's decisions concerning federalism provide clear guidance as to the appropriate content of federalism analysis. Over the course of American history, the Supreme Court has shifted back and forth between two different interpretations of the Tenth Amendment. One is that the Tenth Amendment is a reminder that Congress may act only if it has express or implied authority. By this view, no law within Congress's power is to be invalidated for interfering with states' rights. From the earliest days of the nation until the late nineteenth century, this approach prevailed. For example, in *Gibbons v. Ogden*, Chief Justice John Marshall explained that when Congress has the authority to act, such as under the commerce power, it may legislate as if there are no state governments.[113] This position was rejected for the first third of the century, until it again was taken up from 1937 to 1992, with the brief exception of *National League of Cities v. Usery* in 1976,[114] which was overruled in 1985.[115]

The other view is that the Tenth Amendment reserves a zone of activities to the states and that Congress may not intrude into this zone, even when it is exercising power under Article I of the Constitution. Beginning in the late nineteenth century and continuing until 1937, the Supreme Court aggressively used federalism and the Tenth Amendment to limit the scope of Congress's authority and to declare many federal laws unconstitutional. As discussed in Chapter 1, under this approach, the Court declared unconstitutional a federal law prohibiting the shipment in interstate commerce of goods made by child labor,[116] and a federal law requiring employers to pay a minimum wage.[117] This view was rejected by the Court from 1937 until 1992, with the exception of *National League of Cities* in 1976.

That is to say, two hundred years of Supreme Court precedents simply does not yield clearly established premises that can be assumed in the area of federalism. The Court's decisions can be invoked to support either position, although it should be recognized that for the vast majority of American history, the Court has rejected using federalism as a limit on legislative power.

There is simply no defined meaning to federalism to be found in any constitutional source, text, framers' intent, or Court decision. The premises in *New York v. United States, United States v. Lopez, Seminole Tribe of Florida v. Florida, City of Boerne v. Flores,* and *Printz v. United States* were assertions with little, if any, support. In *New York v. United States,* the Court offered no explanation as to why Congress cannot compel states to implement federal regulatory programs, except for the assertion that such conscription violates state sovereignty and a claim about government accountability that never was justified as a constitutionally based principle.

United States v. Lopez offered no explanation as to why Congress could regulate in three, and only three, circumstances. In *Seminole Tribe,* the Court relied on the highly dubious premise that the Eleventh Amendment is a constitutional bar on subject matter jurisdiction even for suits against a state by its own citizens—a premise that is inconsistent with the very text of the amendment.

Printz, as explained above, justified neither why Congress cannot compel state actions nor why there must be a unitary executive. As Professor Caminker observes in criticizing the formalism of the *Printz* decision: "[T]here is a comparative dearth of textual, historical, structural, and conceptual guideposts with respect to the congressional regulation of state government actions."[118]

In *City of Boerne v. Flores*, as discussed earlier, the Court's premises could not be justified by text, history, or precedent. There was a need for policy arguments to support the premises that were simply absent from Justice Kennedy's majority opinion.

This is not to say that the Court's premises are indefensible. Rather, any support from them must come from a normative theory about the appropriate content of federalism analysis. In other words, the premises must be justified by policy arguments and a functional approach to what is the best way to define the constitutional relationship between the federal and state governments.

Even more importantly, analysis must be functional because ultimately the issue of federalism posits which allocation of power provides the best governance with the least chances of abuse.[119] Federalism is about how power should be allocated between federal and state governments, and this must be based on the functional analysis of what provides for best governance in each context. Federalism, like all aspects of the structure of government, is designed to achieve basic goals; it is meant to provide a framework for governance that is most likely to be effective, while minimizing the likelihood of abuses of power. In other words, federalism is not an end in itself but a means to ends. Therefore, analysis must be functional as to what content of federalism is best for achieving the ultimate goals.

Furthermore, federalism itself is based on certain values that are thought to be served by dividing government power vertically between the nation and the states. The Court, for example, often justifies federalism based on states being more responsive to the voters and on decentralization of power facilitating desirable experimentation.[120] A functional analysis of federalism is necessary in order to consider how to best achieve these underlying goals. That, of course, requires in-depth exploration both as to the goals themselves and as to how best to achieve them.

However, most Supreme Court decisions protecting federalism say relatively little about the underlying values that are being served. When the Court does speak of the values of federalism, it usually does little more than present conclusions that federalism is desirable because it decreases the likelihood of federal tyranny, enhances democratic rule by providing government that is closer to the people, and allows states to be laboratories for new ideas.[121] Yet, as I argue in Chapter 3, these values have little relationship to the Supreme Court's decisions in the area of federalism.

In *New York v. United States*, for instance, there is no apparent relationship between the ruling and the values of federalism. It seems farfetched to see federal requirements for safe state disposal of nuclear waste as putting the country more at risk to federal tyranny. Surely, people in the state of New York want to see safe disposal of the nuclear waste in their midst. If New York was responsive to the people's wishes and assured safe disposal, the federal law is redundant as to what would occur, anyway, and thus minimally intrusive upon state autonomy. But if New York is unresponsive to its citizens—perhaps because of a desire to avoid cleanup costs or because of pressure from particular industries—federal regulation increases responsiveness. Little seems to be gained from experimenting with not cleaning up the waste. Under the federal law, states had the ability to experiment with techniques and mechanisms for the cleanup. The one thing that states could not do was experiment by providing inadequate cleanup. The federal law hardly seems an intrusion upon desirable and reasonable state experimentation.

Ultimately, the absence of a functional analysis can lead to Supreme Court decisions that are counterproductive in terms of the desired goals. For instance, in *New York v. United States*, the Court's express purpose is protecting state governments. Yet, the ruling in the case actually could have exactly the opposite of that effect. *New York v. United States* found that Congress could set out detailed standards for how nuclear waste is to be handled and could require that states comply with them. *New York* stipulated that what Congress could not do, however, is force states to devise means for dealing with the problem. Put another way, it is impermissible for Congress to let the states decide for themselves how to handle the waste, but it is permissible for Congress to force the states to do so in a particular manner. Yet, the latter would allow the states more discretion and choices and thus would be more protective of state sovereignty than the approach that the Court was willing to permit.[122]

It would seem that the Court's formalism with regard to federalism obscures consideration of competing values. Inherent to federalism is the tension between the competing interests of the federal and state governments. A formalistic approach to federalism places limits on federal power without any consideration of the competing federal interests— often constitutionally based interests. Dean Caminker writes that the formalistic "line of reasoning fails completely to take account of another essential postulate of the constitutional structure—federal supremacy. All sovereigns are not equal. . . . The difficult question is how to integrate the principles of dual sovereignty and federal supremacy properly."[123] This accommodation of dual sovereignty and federal supremacy requires balancing of competing values and a functional analysis.

For example, immunizing state governments from federal control and federal court review is one value, but a crucial competing constitutional value is ensuring the supremacy of federal law. The Constitution's most explicit, and most significant, provision concerning federalism is the supremacy clause in Article VI, which declares that the Constitution, and the laws and treaties made pursuant to it, is the supreme law of the land. Yet, consideration of this constitutional value is absent in the recent federalism decisions. This is most apparent in *Seminole Tribe of Florida v. Florida.*

In *Seminole Tribe*, the Court does not question that Congress has the authority to require that states negotiate with Indian tribes in good faith to allow gambling on Indian reservations.[124] The question, then, is how Congress can ensure the supremacy of federal law and secure state compliance with this mandate. The Court declared unconstitutional the primary enforcement mechanism, the ability to sue states in federal court for alleged noncompliance. The Court also ruled that state officers could not be sued in federal court to enforce federal laws that have comprehensive enforcement mechanisms.

Traditionally, suits against state officers have been a key way of enforcing the Eleventh Amendment and ensuring state compliance with federal law. Ever since *Ex parte Young*, it has been the law that state officers may be sued in federal court, even though the state government was immune from suit.[125] Suits against state officers have been indispensable in holding state governments accountable and in maintaining the supremacy of federal law. Indeed, Professor Charles Alan Wright observes that "the doctrine of *Ex parte Young* seems indispensable to the establishment of constitutional government and the rule of law."[126] *Seminole Tribe*, though, carves an unprecedented exception to *Ex parte Young*: state officers cannot be sued in federal court to enforce federal laws that have comprehensive enforcement mechanisms.

The key question after *Seminole Tribe* is how can the federal Indian Gaming Act, or other similar laws, be enforced? There is no doubt that Congress had the constitutional authority to enact the law pursuant to its Article I power to regulate commerce with Indian tribes. If Congress can legislate, surely it must also have the power to ensure the enforcement of its statutes. Yet, after *Seminole Tribe*, enforcement of this law seems an impossibility. The Supreme Court expressly held that neither the state government nor the state officers can be sued to enforce the statute. Chief Justice Rehnquist's opinion for the Court said that suits against state officials were barred because of the comprehensive enforcement mechanisms in the law. But the only real enforcement mechanism was the ability to sue state governments to accomplish compliance; the very provision declared unconstitutional in the first part of the opinion.

Nor is this federal statute unique. If suits against both the state and the state officer are precluded, there will be no way for the federal court to ensure state compliance with federal law. The constitutional value of federal supremacy is sacrificed to the value of state immunity.

Ultimately, the greatest failing of formalism is that it treats the structure of government as an end in itself, rather than as a means to the end of effective governance. Analysis must be functional. Which situations are best dealt with by the federal government and which by the states? There is no substitute for facing these questions directly in Congress, in the courts, or in scholarly analysis. Chapter 3 focuses on how to develop a functional approach to federalism by examining the values of federalism.

CHAPTER 3

The Values of Federalism

IN TEACHING CONSTITUTIONAL LAW, I have been continually struck by the absence of careful exploration of the values of federalism in the cases. From time to time, the Court alludes to the underlying benefits of federalism in terms of four basic values: limiting tyranny by the federal government; enhancing democracy by providing governance that is closer to the people; providing laboratories for experimentation; protecting and advancing liberty. But these values are seldom more than just slogans. Rarely, if ever, is there any explanation as to how these particular values are compromised by particular federal laws.

Initially in this chapter, I consider these values and especially the Court's treatment of them. Then I return to the paradox of post-1937 federalism described in Chapter 1 and suggest that neither aspect of the paradox has any relationship to the underlying values of federalism. More significantly, I contend that even the Supreme Court's decisions that have been most protective of states' institutional interests have little relation to these often-stated underlying values of federalism.

A functional approach to federalism requires the careful identification and analysis of the underlying values of federalism. Federalism—like all government arrangements—has been chosen for instrumental reasons. What values are served by dividing power between the federal and state governments?

I argue that federalism analysis by the courts and Congress must include consideration of these and other values, and that decision making must be based on an explicit weighing of such considerations. But the Supreme Court's federalism decisions over the past ten years have had no relationship to these underlying values. I conclude the chapter by focusing on an important example—the recent decisions expanding sovereign immunity—and contend that they powerfully illustrate the Court's failure to consider or advance the values of federalism.

Chapter 4 then considers the implications of this functional analysis and especially how federalism can be reinvented primarily in terms of empowerment, not limits. The remainder of this book considers how the functional approach of federalism as empowerment should be used in defining the powers of Congress, the role of the federal courts, and the scope of preemption of state and local actions.

THE TRADITIONALLY STATED VALUES OF FEDERALISM

Many Supreme Court decisions protecting federalism say relatively little about the underlying values that are being served. Occasionally, the Court mentions the benefits of protecting states, but never does the Court explain how its decision is advancing these goals. When the Court does speak of the values of federalism, usually the four benefits of protecting state governments, alluded to above, are identified: reducing the likelihood of federal tyranny; enhancing democratic rule by providing government that is closer to the people; allowing states to be laboratories for new ideas; and protecting and advancing individual liberty. Each of these justifications for limiting federal power and judicial protection of state governments warrants examination, particularly as to its relationship to the Court's recent federalism decisions.

Reducing the Likelihood of Federal Tyranny

The first justification for protecting states from federal intrusions is that the division of power vertically, between federal and state governments, lessens the chance of federal tyranny. Professor Andrzej Rapaczynski notes that "[p]erhaps the most frequently mentioned function of the federal system is the one it shares to a large extent with separation of powers, namely the protection of the citizen against governmental opposition—the 'tyranny' that the Framers were so concerned about." [1] The framers of the Constitution relied primarily on the structure of government as a protection against tyrannical governance. The Constitution itself, apart from the amendments, has relatively few protections of individual rights. Instead, the framers viewed the separation of powers horizontally, among the branches of the federal government, and vertically, between the federal and state governments, as the best safeguard against autocratic rule.

How do state governments prevent federal tyranny? Perhaps the framers thought that the possibility of federal abuses could be best limited by restricting the authority of the federal government. The framers envisioned that governance would be most concentrated at the state and local levels and that federal actions would be relatively rare and limited. Alexander Hamilton explained that "[the] necessity of local administration for local purposes would be a complete barrier against the oppressive use of such power." [2] If the powers of the federal government are limited, most governing, of necessity, must be done at the state and local levels.

Yet, the notion of radically limited federal power seems anachronistic in the face of a modern national market economy and decades of extensive federal regulations. Not surprisingly, the Supreme Court's approval of increased federal power occurred at a time of great economic distress and a world war. These were events that clearly called for action by the federal government. The Rehnquist Court's federalism decisions of the 1990s, by contrast, occurred during a time of economic prosperity and peace. There has been less focus on federalism in the rhetoric of the Bush Administration than during the Reagan presidency. This, in part, is likely due to the events of September 11 and the perceived need for federal actions of many sorts to deal with the terrorist threat.

Additionally, there has been a major shift over time as to how best to control abusive government. Currently, it is thought that if a federal action intrudes upon individual liberties, the federal judiciary will invalidate it as unconstitutional. Judicial review is seen as an important check against tyrannical government actions.

Professor Rapaczynski offers a more sophisticated and contemporary explanation as to why state governments limit the likelihood of federal tyranny. He writes:

[T]he most influential protection that states offer against tyranny is the protection against the special interest of government itself. For the fact that the federal government may be less likely than the states, in what we may call "normal times," to oppress small minorities whose mode of life offends a homogeneous majority does not mean that it is never likely to oppress them as well as to deprive the citizenry as a whole of their legitimate voice in running national affairs. Should the federal government ever be captured by an authoritarian movement or assert itself as a special cohesive interest, the resulting oppression would almost certainly be much more severe and durable than any state would be capable.[3]

Professor Rapaczynski is undoubtedly correct that a tyrannical federal action stemming from the capture of the federal government would be extremely undesirable. But the relationship of this observation to the content of federalism is not clear. Is it an argument that the fewer the powers accorded to the federal government the better it is because federal power might be used for ill? Ultimately, this is an argument against having *any* federal power, because all authority could be abused. Once it is decided that there should be a federal government and federal power, it is necessary to decide which federal powers offer enough prospect for benefits to outweigh their potential for tyrannical use. Put another way, the problem with the "less is better" approach is that the powers of the federal government also can be used to advance freedom and thus provide the antithesis of tyrannical rule.

Alternatively, Rapaczynski might be arguing that particular federal powers are undesirable because if there is capture of the federal government, these could be used in especially abusive ways. For example, it might be better to have most policing done at the local level and avoid a national police force. This would help protect civil liberties in the event of a capture by autocratic rulers at the national level. This is an important concern and it requires careful consideration of what particular federal powers so risk abuse as to outweigh their likely benefits. But it is not, as is assumed, an argument against the very existence of federal power. Indeed, to the extent that federal authority is used to advance rights and equality, such as through the Religious Freedom Restoration Act or the Violence Against Women Act or the Age Discrimination in Employment Act, it is perverse to justify restricting federal power on the grounds that it inherently risks tyranny.

Have the Rehnquist Court's recent federalism decisions in any way lessened the likelihood of federal tyranny; do they really advance this value?[4] It is impossible for me to understand why a federal law that forces states to clean up nuclear waste—the issue in *New York v. United States*—increases in the slightest the chances of a tyrannical government. Nor do federal laws prohibiting guns near schools or requiring state and local background checks for firearms seem related in the slightest to lessening tyranny, unless, of course, one believes that such laws violate the Second Amendment's right to bear arms. I do not have this view, but if I did, then the objection would be on that basis and not for fear of tyranny. I could go through each and every one of the federalism decisions and raise the same question, because none has the slightest relationship to preventing tyranny.

Enhancing Democratic Rule

A second frequently invoked value of federalism is that states are closer to the people and thus more likely to be responsive to public needs and concerns. Professor David Shapiro clearly summarizes this argument when he writes: "[O]ne of the stronger arguments for a decentralized political structure is that, to the extent that the electorate is small, and elected representatives are thus more immediately accountable to individuals and their concerns, government is brought closer to the people and democratic ideals are more fully realized."[5] This argument has intuitive appeal. It suggests that the smaller the area governed, the more responsive the government will be to the interests of the voters.

However, it must be recognized that this value of federalism could be inconsistent with the first value discussed above. To the extent that voters at the state and local levels prefer what might be regarded as tyrannical decisions—or more likely, rule that abuses a particular minority group—greater responsiveness increases the dangers of government tyranny. That is, the substantive reduction of tyranny will not always be best achieved by the process approach of maximizing electoral responsiveness; indeed, the reverse might well be the result.

In fact, there is a greater danger of special interests capturing government at smaller and more local levels. James Madison wrote of the danger of "factions" in *Federalist 10*, and modern political science literature offers support for his fears.[6] In *J. A. Croson v. City of Richmond*, the Supreme Court emphasized the dangers of special interest capture at the local level in invalidating a city's affirmative action to benefit minority businesses.[7] The Court distinguished an earlier case that had upheld a similar federal program on the grounds that capture by special interests was much less likely at the federal level than at the local level.[8]

Arguments about responsiveness likely must rest on one of two assumptions. One premise might be that voters more closely monitor the conduct of representatives the more local the level of government. Yet, this is an empirical proposition that is at odds with reality. Presidential and senatorial elections usually attract more voter interest and more knowledgeable electoral decisions than do elections for purely local offices. Alternatively, the premise might be that the smaller the governing unit the greater the likelihood of voter homogeneity and the ability of government to easily ascertain the will of the voters. But it is not clear what size of government unit is necessary for such homogeneity. For example, is a state the size of California, or for that matter a city the size of Los Angeles, sufficiently more homogeneous in its interests as to increase the likelihood of responsive government? Professor Shapiro writes: "[T]he goal of realizing democratic values to the maximum extent feasible may not be significantly enhanced by reducing the relevant polity from one of some 280,000,000 (the United States) to one of, say, 30,000,000 (the State of California)."[9] He explains that "[i]n either case, the size of the electorate and its heterogeneity tend to dwarf participation by the individual and to frustrate the recognition of small group preferences."[10]

The point is that assertions about the responsiveness of government are descriptively shaky and normatively not necessarily desirable. There is little historical evidence that one level of government is inherently more responsive than any other.

Interestingly, if the real issue is responsiveness, the concern should be with protecting *local* governments much more than state governments. But as Professors Rubin and Feeley point out: "[F]ederalism only protects the autonomy of states, not the autonomy or variability of local governments."[11] For example, sovereign immunity protects state governments from suits but cannot be invoked by cities, counties, or other local governments.[12]

Again, nor do the Supreme Court's recent federalism decisions seem to have anything to do with this value. What is striking, and often overlooked, is that the federalism rulings of the Rehnquist Court have, almost without exception, invalidated very popular federal laws that clearly were responsive to the public's desires. Several of these statutes, such as the Religious Freedom Restoration Act, the Americans with Disabilities Act, and the Violence Against Women Act, were passed overwhelmingly and sometimes almost unanimously.

Allowing States to Experiment

A third argument that is frequently made for protecting federalism is that states can serve as laboratories for experimentation. Justice Louis Brandeis apparently first articulated this idea when he declared: "To say experimentation in things social and economic is a grave responsibility. Denial of the right experiment might be fraught with serious consequences to the Nation. It is one of the happy incidents of the federal system that a single courageous State may, if its citizens choose, serve as a laboratory and try novel social and economic experiments without risk to the rest of the country." [13]

More recent federalism opinions, too, have invoked this notion. Justice Lewis Franklin Powell, dissenting in *Garcia*, lamented that "the Court does not explain how leaving the States, virtually at the mercy of the federal government, without recourse to judicial review will enhance their opportunities to experiment and serve as laboratories." [14] Likewise, Justice Sandra Day O'Connor, dissenting in *Federal Energy Regulatory Commission v. Mississippi*, stated that the "Court's decision undermines the most valuable aspects of our federalism. Courts and commentators frequently have recognized that the 50 states serve as laboratories for the development of new social, economic, and political ideas." [15]

However, any federal legislation preempting state or local laws limits experimentation. For that matter, the application of constitutional rights to the states limits their experimenting with providing less safeguards of individual liberties. The key questions are, When is it worth experimenting? and When is experimentation to be rejected because of a need to impose a national mandate? The value of states as laboratories provides no answer to this issue.

There also is a related process question: Who is in the best position to decide when further experimentation is warranted or when there is enough knowledge to justify federal action? A strong argument can be made that the need for using states as laboratories is a policy argument to be made to Congress against federal legislation and not a judicial argument that should be used to invalidate particular federal laws on the grounds that they unduly limit experimentation. Additionally, Congress and even federal agencies, can design experiments and try different approaches in various parts of the country.

Professors Rubin and Feeley take this argument even further. They argue that political realities mean that relatively few experiments will be done at the state and local levels. They write:

To experiment with different approaches for achieving a single, agreed-upon goal, one sub-unit must be assigned an option that initially seems less desirable, either because that option requires changes in existing practices, or because it offers lower, although still-significant chances of success. . . . As a result, individual states will have no incentive to invest in experiments that involve any substantive or political risk, but will prefer to wait for other states to generate them; this will, of course, produce relatively few experiments.[16]

On the other hand, Rubin and Feeley contend that Congress has far more incentive to structure and monitor experiments. They thus conclude "that most significant 'experimental' programs in recent years have in fact been organized and financed by the national government." [17]

Again, it must be asked whether the Supreme Court's recent federalism decisions have had the slightest to do with promoting positive experimentation. Does anyone really believe that states should be able to experiment with not cleaning up the nuclear waste in their midst, or with allowing children to bring guns near schools, or with tabling an adequate remedy for women who are victims of gender-motivated violence? The Court often mentions the value of experimentation, but for obvious reasons, never even hints that these are areas where experimentation is a good thing.

Protecting Liberty

The fourth, and final, justification often invoked for preserving federalism is, I believe, the most important: that federalism protects liberty. Perhaps this is just another way of presenting the first justification, that federalism avoids tyranny. But I think that the justices invoking this value have something else in mind: they see that freedom is increased when a particular conception of the proper structure of American government is enforced. For example, Chief Justice William Rehnquist wrote: "This constitutionally mandated division of authority was adopted by the Framers to ensure protection of our fundamental liberties." [18] Similarly, Justice Antonin Scalia declared: "The separation of the two spheres is one of the Constitution's protections of liberty." [19] Justice O'Connor wrote: "Just as the separation and independence of the coordinate branches of the Federal Government serves to prevent the accumulation of excessive power in any one branch, a healthy balance of power between the States and the Federal Government will reduce the risk of tyranny and abuse from either front." [20] It is striking that so many of the Supreme Court's recent federalism decisions repeat the same language as a premise for judicial invalidation of federal laws. [21]

Unfortunately, none of the cases explains how federalism enhances liberty. The idea expressed is the simple one that limiting federal power means restricting the ability of the federal government to enact laws inimical to individual freedom. The problem with this claim is that the federal government could use its authority to advance liberty or to restrict it. The Court's assumption is that the latter, federal actions limiting liberty, are more likely than the former, federal laws significantly enhancing individual rights. The Court never has justified this premise.

Actually, proving the majority's claim with regard to individual freedom is quite complicated. In all likelihood, over time, limiting the federal government's power in the name of federalism probably will be used to strike down some laws that advance liberty and some that restrict it. The majority needs to offer some reason to believe that, on balance, federal actions will be more harmful than beneficial to liberty. Nothing of this sort is found in any of the Supreme Court's federalism decisions, or for that matter in any of the scholarly literature that champions federalism.

One way of looking at this is to consider whether the Supreme Court's decisions protecting federalism have advanced liberty. Over the course of American history, and particularly during the Rehnquist Court, have the Supreme Court's federalism decisions been "rights progressive," advancing rights, or "rights regressive," limiting individual liberty?[22] Examining the decisions, it is startling how often they are rights regressive and how rarely the federalism rulings have ever expanded the scope of rights.

Perhaps the Court's most rights regressive actions have been the decisions limiting the scope of Congress's power under Section 5 of the Fourteenth Amendment. Section 5 broadly empowers Congress to enact laws to enforce the Fourteenth Amendment. In the past five years, the Court has greatly narrowed this authority in two respects: first, it has held that Congress cannot expand the scope of rights but rather can provide only remedies for rights recognized by the judiciary; and second, it has held that Congress, under Section 5 may not regulate private conduct.

As to the former, in a series of decisions beginning with *City of Boerne v. Flores*,[23] the Court has held that Congress, under Section 5, cannot expand the scope of rights. Rather, Congress can enact laws only to prevent or remedy violations of rights recognized by the courts and these laws must be "proportionate" and "congruent" to the violations. Individually and collectively, these decisions are tremendously rights regressive. They dramatically limit the ability of Congress to expand the scope and protections of individual liberties.

As described in Chapter 1, again, in *City of Boerne v. Flores*, for example, the Court struck down a federal statute, the Religious Freedom Restoration Act, that expanded the safeguards accorded to the free exercise of religion.[24] The act was adopted in 1993 to overturn a then-recent Supreme Court decision that offered a narrow interpretation of the First Amendment's free exercise clause. In *Employment Division of the Department of Human Resources of Oregon v. Smith*, in 1990, the

Supreme Court significantly lessened the protections of the free exercise clause.[25] The Supreme Court, in *Smith*, changed the law and held that the free exercise clause cannot be used to challenge neutral laws of general applicability.

In response to this decision, in 1993, Congress overwhelmingly adopted the Religious Freedom Restoration Act (RFRA), which was signed into law by President Bill Clinton. The RFRA expressly indicated its goal to be that of overturning *Smith* and restoring the test that was administered before *Smith*. The act required courts considering free exercise challenges, including to neutral laws of general applicability, to uphold the government's actions only if they were necessary to achieve a compelling purpose. Specifically, the RFRA prohibited "[g]overnment" from "substantially burden[ing]" a person's exercise of religion even if the burden results from a rule of general applicability unless the government can demonstrate the burden "(1) is in furtherance of a compelling governmental interest; and (2) is the least restrictive means of furthering that compelling governmental interest." [26]

City of Boerne v. Flores involved a church in Texas that was prevented from constructing a new facility because its building was classified a historic landmark. The church sued under the Religious Freedom Restoration Act, and the city challenged the constitutionality of the law. Justice Anthony Kennedy wrote that the act is unconstitutional. The Court held that Congress, under Section 5 of the Fourteenth Amendment, may not create new rights or expand the scope of rights; rather Congress is limited to laws that prevent or remedy violations of rights recognized by the Supreme Court and these must be narrowly tailored—"proportionate" and "congruent"—to constitutional violation.

Justice Kennedy defended this conclusion by invoking the need to preserve the Court as the authoritative interpreter of the Constitution. He quoted *Marbury v. Madison*, from the early nineteenth century, and wrote: "If Congress could define its own powers by altering the Fourteenth Amendment's meaning, no longer would the Constitution be 'superior paramount law unchangeable by ordinary means.' It would be 'on a level with ordinary legislative acts, and like other acts, . . . alterable when the legislature shall please to alter it.' " [27] Justice Kennedy concluded this part of the majority opinion by declaring: "Shifting legislative majorities could change the Constitution and effectively circumvent the difficult and detailed amendment process contained in Article V." [28]

Justice Kennedy's majority opinion then declared the RFRA unconstitutional on the grounds that it impermissibly expanded the scope of rights and that it was not proportionate or congruent as a preventative or remedial measure. He wrote:

RFRA is not so confined. Sweeping coverage ensures its intrusion at every level of government, displacing laws and prohibiting official actions of almost every description and regardless of subject matter. . . . Any law is subject to challenge at any time by any individual who alleges a substantial burden on his or her free exercise of religion. The reach and scope of RFRA distinguish it from other measures passed under Congress' enforcement power, even in the area of voting rights. The stringent test RFRA demands of state laws reflects a lack of proportionality or congruence between the means adopted and the legitimate end to be achieved. [29]

The RFRA prohibits much that would not violate the Constitution and thus was deemed to exceed the scope of Congress's Section 5 power.

There seems little doubt that this decision is rights regressive. The striking down of *Flores* means that people in the United States will have far less protection for their religious practices. Laws of general applicability—whether prison regulations or zoning ordinances or historical landmark laws—that seriously burden religion might have been successfully challenged under the RFRA, but not any longer. Put most simply, the striking down of *Flores* means that many claims of free exercise of religion that would have prevailed, now certainly will lose. People in the United States have less protection of their rights after *Flores* than they did before it.

The decisions following *City of Boerne v. Flores* have likewise been rights regressive. Three times so far—in *Florida Prepaid Postsecondary Education Expense Board v. College Savings Bank*,[30] *Kimel v. Florida Board of Regents*,[31] and *University of Alabama v. Garrett*[32]—the Court has considered whether laws are valid exercises of Congress's Section 5 power and a permissible basis for suits against state governments. In all three cases, the Court applied *City of Boerne v. Flores* and found the law invalid as an exercise of Congress's Section 5 power and precluded the suit against the state government.

In *Florida Prepaid Postsecondary Education Expense Board v. College Savings Bank*, the Supreme Court ruled that Congress, under Section 5, could not authorize suits against states for patent infringement. *Kimel v. Florida Board of Regents* decided that Congress lacked authority to enact the Age Discrimination in Employment Act under section five. The Court came to the same conclusion in *University of Alabama v. Garrett*, about Title I of the Americans with Disabilities Act, which prohibits employment discrimination based on, and requires reasonable accommodations for, disabilities.

Again, there seems no question that these decisions are rights regressive. *Florida Prepaid* means that patent (and copyright) owners have less protection of their rights because they cannot sue state governments that engage in infringement. *Kimel* and *Garrett* limited the ability of Congress to prohibit employment discrimination based on age and disability. The result of these two cases is that state government employees have much less protection from discrimination.

There has been one other aspect of the Court's Section 5 decisions that has not been mentioned in earlier chapters: the Court has ruled that Congress cannot use this provision to regulate private conduct. In the Civil Rights Cases, in 1883, the Supreme Court greatly limited Congress's ability to use its power under the Reconstruction amendments to regulate private conduct.

In *United States v. Guest*, five Justices, although not in a single opinion, concluded that Congress may outlaw private discrimination pursuant to Section 5 of the Fourteenth Amendment.[33] *Guest* involved the federal law that makes it a crime for two or more persons to go "in disguise on the highway, or on the premises of another, with intent to prevent or hinder his free exercise or enjoyment of any right or privilege."[34] The Court held that interference with the use of facilities in interstate commerce violated the law, whether or not motivated by a racial animus.

The majority opinion did not broach the question of whether Congress could regulate private conduct under Section 5. However, six of the justices—three in a concurring opinion and three in a dissenting opinion—expressed the view that Congress could prohibit private discrimination under its Section 5 power. Justice Tom Clark, in a concurring opinion joined by Justices Hugo Black and Abe Fortas, said that "the specific language of section 5 empowers the Congress to enact laws punishing all conspiracies—with or without state action—that interfere with Fourteenth Amendment rights." [35] Likewise, Justice William Brennan in an opinion that concurred in part and dissented in part, and that was joined by Chief Justice Earl Warren and Justice William Douglas, concluded that Congress may prohibit private discrimination pursuant to Section 5. [36]

But in *United States v. Morrison*,[37] the Supreme Court expressly reaffirmed the Civil Rights Cases and disavowed, in *United States v. Guest*, the opinions to the contrary. *Morrison* involved a constitutional challenge to the civil damages provision of the Violence Against Women Act, which of course authorized victims of gender-motivated violence to sue under federal law. As mentioned in Chapter 1, the case was brought by Christy Brzonkala who allegedly was raped by football players while a freshman at Virginia Polytechnic Institute. The players ultimately avoided punishment by the University, and Brzonkala filed suit against her assailants and the university under the Violence Against Women Act. The case presented the question as to whether the civil damages provision of the federal Violence Against Women Act [38] is constitutional. The provision authorizes victims of gender-motivated violence to sue for money damages. Congress enacted the Violence Against Women Act based on detailed findings of the inadequacy of state laws in protecting women who are victims of domestic violence and sexual assaults. For example, Congress found that gender-motivated violence costs the American economy billions of dollars a year and is a substantial constraint on freedom of travel by women throughout the country. The Violence Against Women Act obviously increased the rights of women to sue and to gain some redress for gender-motivated violence.

The United States government intervened to defend the law, and it and the plaintiff argued that the civil damages provision was constitutional both as an exercise of Congress's commerce clause power and of its authority under Section 5. The Court, in a 5–4 decision, held that the law exceeds the scope of the commerce clause because Congress cannot regulate noneconomic activity based on a cumulative impact on interstate commerce.[39] By the same 5–4 margin, the Court held that the law is unconstitutional as an exercise of Congress's Section 5 power. Chief Justice Rehnquist, writing the opinion, said that Congress under this authority may regulate only state and local governments, not private conduct. Chief Justice Rehnquist relied on "the time-honored principle that the Fourteenth Amendment, by its very terms, prohibits only state action." [40] He said that the opinions in *United States v. Guest*, indicating congressional power to regulate private conduct, were only dicta.[41] Thus, the civil damages provision of the Violence Against Women Act was deemed to exceed the scope of Congress's power because it "is not aimed at proscribing discrimination by officials which the Fourteenth Amendment might not itself proscribe; it is directed not at any State or state actor, but at individuals who have committed criminal acts motivated by gender bias." [42]

Again, limiting the scope of Congress's Section 5 power in the name of federalism is very rights regressive. Congress is denied the ability to expand rights and protections against private infringers of liberty. More generally, the Court's narrowing of Congress's ability to protect rights is inherently rights regressive. Perhaps there is some other justification for what the Court has done, but the limitation on Congress's power clearly lessens the protection of rights.

Whatever its other merits, there seems no possible argument that *Morrison* is rights progressive. Congress enacted a law to expand the rights of victims of gender-motivated violence based on the findings of a serious social problem and the inadequacy of remedies in the state courts. The Supreme Court's invalidation of the statute thus restricts the rights of women throughout the country. Conceivably, it could be argued that *Morrison* protects the rights of those accused of sexual violence by preventing them from being sued in federal court. Then the question would have to be, Which is more rights progressive: expanding the ability of victims of gender-motivated violence to sue, or protecting those accused of such acts from being sued? Merely stating the question makes the answer obvious.

A final aspect of the Court's federalism decisions has been a substantial expansion of state sovereign immunity. The Court held, in *Seminole Tribe of Florida v. Florida*, that Congress may authorize suits against state governments pursuant only to Section 5 of the Fourteenth Amendment and not under any other congressional power.[43] It was based on this decision that the Court handed down the rulings described above, in *Florida Prepaid, Kimel,* and *Garrett,* that state governments could not be sued for patent infringement, for violating the Age Discrimination in Employment Act, or for infringing Title I of the Americans with Disabilities Act. Also, in *Alden v. Maine,* the Court held that state governments cannot be sued in state court, even on federal claims, without their consent.[44]

Expanding sovereign immunity is clearly rights regressive. Sovereign immunity protects the government as an entity and denies relief to those that are injured. Rights are undermined whenever there is a violation and no remedy for it.

None of this discussion is to imply that the traditional justifications for protecting federalism are wrong. The goals themselves—preventing tyranny, enhancing government responsiveness, promoting experimentation, and advancing liberty—are all desirable. But each is much more complicated than the traditional judicial treatment makes it seem. Each proposition is primarily a descriptive statement—states will limit the likelihood for federal tyranny; states are responsive to the people; states will serve as beneficial laboratories for experimentation. Yet, the descriptive accuracy of each statement is largely asserted and not proven. Moreover, the normative implications of each descriptive proposition is very uncertain. Will limiting the powers of the federal government to prevent tyranny, on balance, preclude more beneficial federal actions or more undesirable ones? When is responsiveness to the people a virtue? As to efficiency, sometimes it is more efficient to have action at the national level and sometimes at the local. With respect to participation, sometimes national action better engages involvement and other times localism does so. When is experimentation desirable and worth encouraging? None of these questions have been explored in any depth by the Supreme Court.

Original Meaning?

There is one other justification for the Supreme Court's federalism decisions that must be considered: that they are mandated by the text of the Constitution and its original meaning. For an originalist, the argument would be that the decisions are correct because they follow the written provisions of the Constitution and its original understanding. From this perspective, the values of federalism help inform and explain the original meaning, but ultimately the decisions are correct because of their fidelity to the text and its original meaning.

For the past several decades, discussions about constitutional interpretation have been dominated by a debate between originalist and non-originalist modes of interpretation. Originalism is the view that "judges deciding constitutional issues should confine themselves to enforcing norms that are stated or clearly implicit in the written Constitution."[45] In contrast, non-originalism is the "contrary view that courts should go beyond that set of references and enforce norms that cannot be discovered within the four corners of the document."[46] Originalists believe that the Court should find a right to exist in the Constitution only if it is expressly stated in the text or was clearly intended by its framers. If the Constitution is silent, originalists say, it is for the legislature, unconstrained by the courts, to decide the law. Non-originalists think that it is permissible for the Court to interpret the Constitution to protect rights that are not expressly stated or clearly intended. Sovereign immunity cannot be found in the Constitution under either of these theories of constitutional interpretation.

One response to the originalist defense of the federalism decisions, of course, is to disagree with originalism as a method of constitutional interpretation. Powerful critiques of originalism have been advanced over the past thirty years.[47] For broad, open-textured constitutional provisions—whether it is "cruel and unusual punishment" or "due process of law" or "commerce among the states"—there is not an answer to be found in the text or the original meaning.[48] Also, as Jeff Powell persuasively argued, the framers did not intend that their original understanding would be binding; thus, a justice truly committed to following original intent would be obligated under it to abandon the enterprise.[49]

It makes no sense to have the country governed in the twenty-first century by the conceptions of the late eighteenth century, or even 1868, when the Fourteenth Amendment was ratified. My favorite example of this always has been that under originalism it would be unconstitutional to elect a woman as president or vice president because Article II refers to these offices with the pronoun, "he," and the framers undoubtedly intended that these office holders would be male. Likewise, the conceptions of Congress's commerce power from the late eighteenth century seem to have little relevance in deciding the scope of congressional authority for the modern twenty-first century economy.

Obviously, a full examination of the originalism debate is beyond the scope of this book. Those who reject originalism are not going to use it in defining the scope of federal power. But for those who embrace originalism, I realize that this brief critique will be unconvincing. For these individuals, the key point is that the Supreme Court's federalism decisions of the past fifteen years cannot possibly be defended based on originalism.

To start with the easiest examples, as explained in Chapter 2, the text of the Tenth and Eleventh Amendments do not support the Court's recent interpretations of them. The Tenth Amendment says simply that all powers not granted to the United States nor prohibited to the states are reserved to the states and the people. There is nothing in the text of that provision or any discussion at the ratifying conventions that would support the interpretation that the amendment reserves a zone of activities to the states or prohibits Congress from commandeering state governments. The Eleventh Amendment says only that the judicial power of the United States does not extend to suits against a state by citizens of another state or a foreign country.[50] There is strong reason to believe, based on the text and historical evidence, that this was meant merely to prevent suits against state governments based solely on diversity of citizenship and was not intended to enshrine a broad principle of state sovereign immunity.[51]

As explained in the earlier chapters, there is strong evidence that the original understanding of Section 5 of the Fourteenth Amendment was to equip Congress with broad authority to enforce its provisions. The Court's restrictive interpretation, in cases like *City of Boerne v. Flores*, is very much at odds with the expansive remedial power intended by the Congress and states that ratified the Fourteenth Amendment.

In other words, the Supreme Court's recent federalism decisions cannot claim a basis in originalism, even assuming the desirability of that interpretive approach, any more than they can be explained by the underlying values of federalism.

THE RELATIONSHIP BETWEEN SUPREME COURT DECISIONS AND THE VALUES OF FEDERALISM

What is striking is that the Supreme Court's decisions since 1937 have had no relationship to the underlying values of federalism. Chapter 1 described the paradox of post-1937, pre-1990s federalism: aggressive use of federalism to limit the power of the federal courts and rejection of federalism as a limit on the power of Congress. But neither side of this paradox can be explained by the underlying values of federalism. For example, if the goal is preventing tyranny, it makes little sense to disempower the federal courts while leaving Congress unchecked. Limiting the power of the federal courts assumes that they are more likely to be "tyrannical" than state courts. Not even the most ardent defenders of "Our Federalism" have ever suggested that as a rationale for limiting federal court power.[52]

Likewise, if the goal is letting states be laboratories for experimentation, the choice would be to limit federal legislative power, which displaces states' choice. But that was not what occurred in the judicial decisions from 1937 through the 1990s. Nor is restricting federal judicial power defended in terms of experimentation. The claim for those who want to limit federal courts is that state courts are on parity with federal courts in their ability and willingness to enforce federal rights.[53] No one suggests that state courts should be able to experiment with less than full compliance with the Constitution.

Finally, neither can the post-1937 paradox be defended in terms of advancing liberty. Some federal laws, such as the 1964 Civil Rights Act advanced liberty, others, such as the tremendous expansion of federal criminal laws,[54] limited liberty. Restricting federal judicial power is about advancing liberty only if one believes state courts will do a *better* job in advancing individual rights. Again, I have seen no one advance that proposition as a justification for the decisions advancing judicial federalism in the post-1937 era.

Just as the post-1937 paradox cannot be explained in terms of the underlying values of federalism, neither can the post-1990s decisions. As mentioned above, there is a profound disconnect between the values, professed by the Court, to underlie federalism and the decisions of the past ten years. The Court's failure is not simply a matter of exposition in not adequately explaining how its rulings advance the underlying goals of federalism. The central point is that the Rehnquist Court's federalism decisions have nothing to do with the values that it invokes as the justifications for limiting federal power and protecting state sovereignty.

WHAT ARE THE VALUES OF FEDERALISM?

The goal must be to get past the slogans and develop a theory of federalism that serves the underlying goals for having a government structure that includes both the federal and state governments. Thus, in constructing a theory of federalism, the starting question must be, What are the values of federalism?

Two objectives should be regarded as paramount: providing an effective government and advancing liberty. Indeed, I would suggest that these are the primary objectives of the United States Constitution. The framers of the Constitution wanted a structure to meet society's needs in both the short and the long term. They replaced the Articles of Confederation because it was failing to meet social needs. The absence of a federal commerce power, the lack of federal authority to tax and spend, the lack of a chief executive, and the lack of a federal judiciary all caused problems that the new Constitution was meant to address.[55] Even a cursory glance at *The Federalist Papers* or the debates at the Constitutional Convention confirms that the framers deeply hoped to create a structure for effective government. The reality is that sometimes effective governance requires the resources and expertise of the national government, whereas sometimes this can be done locally. Stephen Griffin, a professor at Tulane Law School, has recently written a compelling article titled, *Stop Federalism Before It Kills Again: Reflections on Hurricane Katrina*. In it he argues that the tragedy in New Orleans powerfully shows the need for actions that only the federal government can take.[56]

At the same time, of course, the framers were concerned about freedom and avoiding tyranny. They thought that they could safeguard liberty through the structure of government, dividing power horizontally among the branches and vertically between the federal government and the states. The states in considering whether to ratify the Constitution felt that there were not sufficient assurances of liberty and insisted that a Bill of Rights be added.

Thus, any junior high school civics student surely could identify the underlying goals for the Constitution, including its federalist structure, as providing effective government and advancing liberty. Yet, it is surprising how the Court never has linked its federalism rulings to these basic objectives.

It also is possible to identify several more specific values that are served by having both a federal and state governments. Some of these objectives include dealing with spillovers and externalities; providing for efficiency; empowering communities; enhancing accountability; and meeting diverse needs. What is interesting is that sometimes these values point toward national action, sometimes toward leaving matters to the states, and perhaps most often they point in conflicting directions.

Spillovers and Externalities

There often is an important reason for national action in dealing with spillovers and externalities. Environmental regulation provides many examples of this. If a northerly state at the top of a river allows dumping of pollutants without controls, it may experience none of the adverse consequences when the water takes the effluents south to downriver states. The northerly state, which allows the pollution, may gain great economic benefits from not having pollution control; it may attract more businesses, and its businesses may have a competitive advantage for not having to pay for pollution-control devices. The downriver states, though, are powerless to protect themselves from the consequences of the pollution. The same story could be told about a state that permits air pollution, knowing that the winds will carry the harmful particulates across state lines and away from the originating state.

There are also more subtle ways, that ultimately can have profound consequences, in which a state's environmental actions seriously affect other states. For instance, the decision of one state to allow the destruction of an endangered species indigenous to that state has the effect of depriving the entire country of the species. If it is a species that could be used for positive social ends, the entire country is the loser.

National action often may be desirable to prevent spillovers and externalities. For example, a key justification for having a federal law to prohibit child labor was that states realistically could not do this on their own. Businesses in a state that allowed child labor would have a significant competitive advantage over businesses in states that prohibited it because wages and production costs would be so much lower. Ultimately, states allowing child labor would put so much economic pressure on other states that they would have no choice but to give in and repeal their prohibitions of child labor. This was exactly the argument made to the Supreme Court for allowing the federal ban on child labor and it was expressly rejected by the Court as irrelevant.[57] The Court's key failing was in not seeing that the national market was as much a threat, if not more of one, to state autonomy than any federal regulation.

In other words, one important value often to be considered is whether national action is needed to deal with externalities and spillover problems. There are many areas in which such national consequences require national action.

Efficiency

Sometimes it is more efficient to deal with matters locally, sometimes nationally. For example, economies of scale are such that often national regulation is better than local regulation. An easy example of this is the regulation of pharmaceutical products. It makes no sense to have each state engage in the expensive and time-consuming process of reviewing applications for new drugs to make sure that they are safe and effective.

It is far more efficient to have one agency, such as the Food and Drug Administration, do this for the entire country.

But there are other times when it is more efficient to have matters handled at the local level.[58] For example, fire protection for communities always has been handled in a decentralized manner. Why? Creating a national bureaucracy for fire departments, with a central administration, is not advantageous. It would add cost to the system, and with little apparent benefit. Dealing with fire protection at the local level lets each area choose the equipment and staffing best suited to its needs. In the event of fire, it obviously is better to call the local fire department than a national system.

In terms of local versus national action, one approach isn't necessarily inherently more efficient than the other. Each, at times, might be the most cost-effective. Undoubtedly there will be many times when it is uncertain and unknowable as to whether the most efficient approach is to deal with a problem through the national government or through state and local governments.

Empowering Communities

A strong argument for local control is the autonomy that comes with permitting communities to make their own choices. This allows people to have a greater say in the nature of the community in which they live. This is intrinsically desirable and reflected in the traditional claim that states are closer to the people. This can be seen in many Supreme Court cases that are not traditionally regarded as being about federalism. For example, in defining obscenity, the Supreme Court has placed an emphasis on using community standards to determine what appeals to the prurient interest and what is patently offensive.[59] In the area of zoning, the Court has given great deference to local governments, which in large part is about allowing communities to have a greater say in determining their environment.[60]

Additionally, community empowerment can be defended as intrinsically desirable if one believes that people's lives are benefited and enriched from being part of their community. The more communities are empowered to make choices, the more people will see a reason for identifying with and being part of one.

But the relationship between community empowerment and federalism is not obvious. Federalism, as implemented by the Supreme Court throughout American history, has been about protecting *state* governments. Even the smallest states do not function as communities in any meaningful sense. In fact, it is hard to think of a city like Los Angeles as a community in itself; it is a collection of many very distinct and different communities.

Even more important, there is the inescapable question of when it is better to leave matters for communities to decide and when it is better to have national choices made. For example, in the area of civil rights, the choice was rightly made—by the Supreme Court in the desegregation cases and by Congress in adopting the Civil Rights Act of 1964—that these were not matters to be left to communities. Clearly, the opposition to both desegregation and the 1964 Civil Rights Act was on states' rights grounds. But the national commitment to equality was rightly found more critical than federalism and community control.

Enhancing Accountability

Obviously, a central commitment of democratic government is holding the governors accountable. This is reflected in countless aspects of the Constitution, including its mandate for regular elections for government officials, its having representatives and senators chosen locally, and its protection of freedom of speech. The Supreme Court has spoken of the ability to criticize government and its officers as "the central meaning of the First Amendment" precisely because it facilitates accountability.[61]

Yet, the relationship between federalism and accountability is unclear. On the one hand, having decisions made at a local level might increase accountability. People can monitor how their local officials are doing on a specific issue and vote them out of office if there is dissatisfaction. Exercising control over local actions seems easier than doing it for national actions. Far fewer people need to be mobilized at much less cost when the focus is local. Additionally, the Supreme Court has invoked accountability in the context of protecting states' rights under federalism. As described earlier,[62] *New York v. United States* held that it violates the Tenth Amendment for Congress to compel state and local governments to enact laws or adopt regulations.[63] Justice O'Connor's opinion stressed that it would undermine accountability for states to act pursuant to a federal mandate because voters will not know which level of government to hold responsible for the actions.[64]

But accountability sometimes is easier at the national than the local level. National elections receive far more media attention and have much greater levels of voter participation than do local elections. People much more commonly know national political figures than local ones. Also, if the comparison is between state governments and the federal government, it is not clear that there is a real difference in terms of political accountability given the size of state governments and the number of constituents represented. In other words, although accountability is an important value to be served, it cannot be assumed that it always favors local as opposed to national concerns.

Meeting Diverse Needs

Another key value of decentralized decision making is that it allows government to better meet diverse needs. Each area of the country has some ways in which it is different from others, and decentralized decision making can better serve this. Sometimes it is a matter of climate or of dominant businesses or even of culture, but there are significant differences between the needs in Manhattan as compared to, say, rural Mississippi. Policing is an example of this. The reason why most policing in the United States is done at the local level is because of the very different needs presented by different communities.

But the countervailing interest to meeting diverse needs is uniformity. The question often is whether it is better to have geographic diversity or national uniformity. A classic older example of this is railroad regulation. Rather than leave regulation of railroad rates and safety to each state, Congress decided that national uniformity was necessary and created the Interstate Commerce Commission.[65]

Another, very different, example is the incorporation of the Bill of Rights. The document's application to state and local governments is about uniformity over diversity of choice. If the Bill of Rights did not apply to the states, then each area could choose for itself how to proceed. Justice Clarence Thomas, for instance, has recently argued in several opinions that the establishment clause of the First Amendment should not be applied to the states. If the clause were applied, a state or local government could declare an official state religion or require school prayer or advance religion in any way it wanted.[66] This certainly would have the advantage of providing diversity. But the application of the establishment clause to state and local governments reflects the choice that uniformity matters here. The entire country should have to follow the same principles with regard to separation of church and state, and for all of the Bill of Rights.

I list these additional values of federalism, albeit briefly, to suggest that a full consideration as to how to structure government must include many aspects beyond the few that the Supreme Court consistently has identified. Also, it is striking that the Supreme Court's recent federalism decisions really advance none of these. Is there any social benefit in allowing children to have guns near schools, the issue in *United States v. Lopez*? Perhaps there is some sense, in this case, in meeting diverse needs, because in some communities guns are more necessary. But overall, isn't it clearly better to keep guns away from schools? Is there any social benefit in having nuclear waste kept in an unsafe manner (*New York v. United States*), or in allowing firearms to be purchased without background checks (*Printz v. United States*)? I am willing to concede, though skeptically, that there are arguments that these laws are socially undesirable; but that should be the focus of the discussion, and yet it wasn't in the Supreme Court decisions or even in much of the commentary about the rulings.

The recent federalism decisions of the Supreme Court neither provide for more effective government nor advance liberty. They seem very much to be about protecting the form of federalism and states' control, but not about serving any of the underlying values of federalism.

DEALING WITH COMPETING CONSIDERATIONS:
THE EXAMPLE OF SOVEREIGN IMMUNITY

I definitely do not mean to suggest that national is always better than local. Quite the contrary, I think that often there are competing considerations; some values point toward national control, and some toward more local decision making. In part, the question then is who should make this choice. Should it be for the courts to decide what is national and what is local, or should it be left to the political process? In part, too, it's a matter of how the choice should be made. I contend that decisions about the structure of government have to be based on a functional consideration of competing issues and not on any kind of formalism.

To illustrate and to make this less abstract, consider a critical example in recent developments concerning federalism: sovereign immunity. Should state governments be immune from suit in federal courts, state courts, and federal agencies? This very much seems to be about balancing competing considerations: the states' desire for accountability, which is gained by allowing suits, versus states' desire for autonomy, meaning freedom from judicial scrutiny and damage judgments, which is advanced by providing immunity. Yet, the Supreme Court never has based its decisions on careful consideration of these competing issues and, in fact, rarely does more than allude to them (if that) in its decisions.

Careful analysis of these competing considerations points in the opposite direction of the Supreme Court's decisions. The remainder of this chapter looks in depth at the issue of sovereign immunity and the Court's rulings concerning it over the past ten years. Sovereign immunity powerfully illustrates the central points of this chapter: the Supreme Court's decisions have not advanced the underlying values of federalism; nor has the Court focused on the competing functional considerations. Doing so leads to the conclusion that the protection of sovereign immunity has been misguided. I begin with background on judicial protection of sovereign immunity and then continue with the justifications for sovereign immunity. I conclude by looking at its costs and conclude, based on these functional considerations, that sovereign immunity deserves no place in a country that believes in the rule of law and government accountability.

The principle of sovereign immunity is derived from English law, which assumed that "the King can do no wrong."[67] Since the time of Edward I, the Crown of England, unless specifically offering its consent, has been immune from suit.[68] Throughout American history, United States courts have applied this principle, although they often have admitted that its justification in this country is unclear.[69]

A doctrine derived from the premise, "the King can do no wrong," deserves no place in American law. The United States was founded on the rejection of monarchy and of royal prerogatives.[70] American government is based on the fundamental recognition that the government and government officials can do wrong, and when they do, they must be held accountable. Sovereign immunity undermines that basic notion.

The doctrine is inconsistent with the United States Constitution. Nowhere does the document mention or even imply that governments have complete immunity from suits. Sovereign immunity is a doctrine based on a *common law* principle borrowed from English common law. However, Article VI of the Constitution states that the Constitution and laws made pursuant to them are the supreme law and, as such, it should be prevail over claims of sovereign immunity. Yet, sovereign immunity, a common law doctrine, trumps even the United States Constitution and bars suits against government entities for relief when they violate the Constitution and federal laws.

Sovereign immunity is inconsistent with a central maxim of American government: that no one, not even the government, is above the law. The effect of sovereign immunity is to place the government above the law and to ensure that some individuals who have suffered egregious harm will be unable to receive redress for their injuries.[71] The judicial role of enforcing and upholding the Constitution is rendered illusory when the government has complete immunity from suits. Moreover, sovereign immunity undermines the basic principle, announced in *Marbury v. Madison*, that "[t]he very essence of civil liberty certainly consists in the right of every individual to claim the protection of the laws, whenever he receives an injury."[72]

All of this seems so clear and obvious. Yet sovereign immunity is not fading from American jurisprudence; quite the contrary, the Supreme

Court is dramatically expanding its scope. *Alden v. Maine* held that sovereign immunity broadly protects state governments from being sued in state court without their consent, even to enforce federal laws.[73] In *Seminole Tribe of Florida v. Florida*, the Court greatly limited the ability of Congress to authorize suits against state governments and to override sovereign immunity.[74] The Court applied this in the past couple of years to bar suits against states for patent infringement[75] and for age discrimination.[76] Thus, it is crucial to consider whether sovereign immunity advances the values of federalism.

Is Sovereign Immunity Required by the Constitution?

If sovereign immunity were required by the Constitution, there would be no place for a functional analysis, except in defining its scope to the extent that the Constitution is unclear. But if the Constitution does not expressly provide for sovereign immunity, then it is necessary to consider whether it advances the underlying values of federalism.

The Supreme Court has found that sovereign immunity, particularly for state governments, is unquestionably a constitutional requirement. *Alden v. Maine* declared: "We hold that the powers delegated to Congress under Article I of the United States Constitution do not include the power to subject nonconsenting States to private suits for damages in state courts." [77] In *Seminole Tribe of Florida v. Florida*, the Court was explicit that the Eleventh Amendment is a constitutional limit on federal subject matter jurisdiction and that Congress, by statute, can override it only pursuant to Section 5 of the Fourteenth Amendment.[78] Put another way, the Court has found state sovereign immunity to be part of the Constitution and thus prevented Congress, by statute, from overriding it. In essence, the Court holds that sovereign immunity is a right of state governments and operates just like individual rights: it limits the legislative power and trumps all other claims.

What's more, the sovereign immunity of the United States government is firmly established. Long ago, Chief Justice John Marshall declared that "[t]he universally received opinion is, that no suit can be commenced or prosecuted against the United States." [79] Many times the Supreme Court has reiterated this principle, holding that "the United States cannot be lawfully sued without its consent in any case."[80]

I make two distinct arguments. First, I contend that sovereign immunity is not a constitutional doctrine. Second, I argue that sovereign immunity should be regarded as an unconstitutional doctrine; it conflicts with many aspects of the United States Constitution. It is important to separate these two steps in the analysis. The former explains why the doctrine should not be found in the United States Constitution. By itself, this does not justify abolishing the doctrine, though if this conclusion is accepted, it would mean that Congress, by statute, could authorize suits against governments. The latter argument, however, goes further by maintaining that the doctrine should be deemed unconstitutional and therefore must be eliminated.

First, is there, indeed, a constitutional basis for sovereign immunity? As alluded to above, sovereign immunity cannot be justified under an originalist approach. All of the recent cases—*Seminole Tribe*, *Alden*, *Florida Prepaid*, and *Kimel*—that expand the scope of sovereign immunity have been decided by 5–4 margins. In each case, the majority was comprised of the five most conservative justices on the Court: Chief Justice Rehnquist and Justices O'Connor, Scalia, Kennedy, and Thomas. These are the justices who most frequently profess an originalist philosophy.[81] Yet, sovereign immunity cannot be justified under a faithful adherence to an originalist approach to constitutional interpretation.

Originalists maintain that rights should be found in the Constitution only if stated in the text or clearly intended by its framers. Sovereign immunity, as applied by the Rehnquist Court, is a right of state governments to be free from suit without their consent. Yet, it is a right that cannot be found in the text or the framers' intent.

The text of the Constitution is silent about sovereign immunity. Not one clause of the first seven articles remotely even hints at the idea that the government has immunity from suit. No constitutional amendment has bestowed sovereign immunity on the federal government.

A claim might be made that the Eleventh Amendment provides sovereign immunity to state governments. Yet, if this is a textual argument, a careful reading of the text does not support the claim. The Eleventh Amendment states, "The Judicial power of the United States shall not be construed to extend to any suit in law or equity, commenced or prosecuted against one of the United States by Citizens of another State, or by Citizens or Subjects of any foreign state." Initially, it should be noted that the Eleventh Amendment applies only in federal court; it is a restriction solely on "the judicial power of the United States." Indeed, in *Alden v. Maine*, the Court recognized this and based its holding entirely on the broad principle of state sovereign immunity and not in any way on the text of the Eleventh Amendment. Justice Kennedy, writing for the majority, stated: "[S]overeign immunity derives not from the Eleventh Amendment but from the structure of the original Constitution itself." [82]

Moreover, the text of the Eleventh Amendment restricts suits against states to those based on diversity of citizenship; it says that the federal judicial power does not permit suits against states by a citizen of another state or of a foreign country. Nothing within it bars a suit against a state by its own citizens. This was the holding of *Hans v. Louisiana* more than a century ago, but it certainly isn't based on a textual argument regarding the Eleventh Amendment. [83]

In *Alden v. Maine*, Justice Kennedy made a textual argument for sovereign immunity by stating that the existence of states is mandated by the Constitution. He wrote: "The founding document 'specifically recognizes the States as sovereign entities.' . . . Various textual provisions of the Constitution assume the States' continued existence and active participation in the fundamental processes of governance." [84] Yet, the fact that the Constitution preserves states as entities says absolutely nothing about whether states should have immunity in state court or sovereign immunity more generally. The Constitution, of course, recognizes the existence of state governments, but it does not give any indication of the scope of state power or the existence of state immunity.

Sovereign immunity cannot by justified textually, neither can it be justified from an originalist perspective based on framers' intent. It is important to remember: originalists believe that if the Constitution is silent as to whether a right is protected, protection is granted only when the framers' intent is clear. [85] When the intent is unclear, the right is not constitutionally protected. At the very least, the framers' intent is completely ambiguous as to sovereign immunity.

There was no discussion of sovereign immunity at the Constitutional Convention in Philadelphia in 1787. The issue did arise, however, in the state ratifying conventions. The dispute was over whether Article III authorized suits against non-consenting states in federal court. Two of the clauses of Article III, Section 2, specifically deal with suits against state governments. These provisions permit suits "between a State and Citizens of another state" and "between a State . . . and foreign . . . Citizens." The dispute was over whether the above-quoted language of Article III was meant to override the sovereign immunity that kept states from being sued in state courts. As Justice Souter recently observed, "The 1787 draft in fact said nothing on the subject and it was this very silence that occasioned some, though apparently not widespread, dispute among the framers and others over whether ratification of the Constitution would preclude a state sued in federal court from asserting sovereign immunity as it could have done on any nonfederal matter litigated in its own courts."[86] There is no record of any debate about this issue or these clauses at the Constitutional Convention.

However, at the state ratification conventions, the question of suits against state governments in federal court was raised and received a great deal of attention. States had incurred substantial debts, especially during the Revolutionary War, and there was a great fear of suits being brought against the states in federal court to collect on these debts. More generally, the concern was expressed that although sovereign immunity was a defense to state law claims in state court, immunity would be unavailable if the same matter were raised against a state in a diversity suit in federal court.

Thus, at the state ratification conventions, there was a debate over whether states could be sued in federal court without their consent.[87] One group argued that the text of Article III clearly made states subject to suit in federal court. In Virginia, George Mason, author of the Virginia Declaration of Rights, opposed ratification of the Constitution. He particularly disliked the provisions that made the states liable in federal court:

Claims respecting those lands, every liquidated account, or other claim against this state, will be tried before the federal court. Is not this disgraceful? Is this state to be brought to the bar of justice like a delinquent individual? Is the sovereignty of the state to be arraigned like a culprit, or private offender?[88]

Mason believed that Article III's explicit provision for suits against the states would have the effect of abrogating the states' sovereign immunity defense.[89]

Likewise, Patrick Henry opposed the Constitution at the Virginia convention, in part based on his belief that Article III unmistakably permitted litigation against states in federal court. He labeled as "incomprehensible" the claim that Article III allowed states to be plaintiffs, but not defendants.[90] Henry said, "There is nothing to warrant such an assertion. . . . What says the paper? That it shall have cognizance of controversies between a state and citizens of another state, without discriminating between plaintiff and defendant."[91]

Further, this view that Article III overrides state sovereignty and permits suits against non-consenting states in federal court was held not just in Virginia or only by opponents of ratification. In Pennsylvania, North Carolina, and New York there were major objections to this part of the Constitution.[92] Many of the Constitution's supporters also agreed that Article III permitted states to be sued in federal court. In fact, they argued that this lack of immunity was desirable to ensure that states could not escape their liabilities or avoid litigation that was necessary to hold states properly accountable. Edmund Randolph, a member of the Committee of Detail at the Constitutional Convention, argued: "I ask the Convention of the free people of Virginia if there can be honesty in rejecting the government because justice is to be done by it? . . . Are we to say that we shall discard this government because it would make us all honest?"[93] In Pennsylvania, Timothy Pickering argued that it was important for federal courts to be able to give relief against states to citizens of other states or nations who had been wronged and might be unable to receive fair treatment in a state's own courts.[94]

In sharp contrast, many other supporters of the Constitution argued that Article III did not override state sovereignty and that, notwithstanding its provisions, states could be sued in federal court only if they consented to be a party to the litigation. Alexander Hamilton wrote in *The Federalist Papers*:

It is inherent in the nature of sovereignty not to be amenable to the suit of an individual *without its consent*. This is the general sense and the general practice of mankind; and the exemption, as one of the attributes of sovereignty, is now enjoyed by the government of every State in the Union. Unless, therefore, there is a surrender of this immunity . . . it will remain with the States.[95]

Similarly, James Madison argued that states have sovereign immunity, and Article III serves to allow states to come to federal court only as plaintiffs, permitting them to be sued as defendants provided consent is given.[96] Madison said that "jurisdiction in controversies between a state and citizens of another state is much objected to, and perhaps without reason. It is not in the power of individuals to call any state into court."[97]

This recounting of the ratification debates reveals that there was no consensus, even among the Constitution's supporters, about whether state sovereign immunity survived Article III. Justice Souter, after a detailed recounting of this history, observed: "[T]he framers and their contemporaries did not agree about the place of common-law state sovereign immunity even as to federal jurisdiction resting on the citizen-state diversity clause."[98] In reviewing the Eleventh Amendment's history, the Supreme Court has rightly observed that "[a]t most, then, the historical materials show that . . . the intentions of the Framers and Ratifiers were ambiguous."[99] Justice Souter explained: "There is almost no evidence that the generation of the Framers thought sovereign immunity was fundamental in the sense of being unalterable. Whether one looks at the period before the framing, to the ratification controversies, or to the early republican era, the evidence is the same. Some Framers thought sovereign immunity was an obsolete royal prerogative inapplicable in a republic; some thought sovereign immunity was a common-law power defeasible, like other common-law rights, by statute; and perhaps a few thought, in keeping with a natural law view distinct from the common-law conception, that immunity was inherent in a sovereign because the body that made a law could not logically be bound by it. Natural law thinking on the part of a doubtful few will not, however, support the Court's position." [100]

Clearly, sovereign immunity cannot be based on the contemporary practices at the time.[101] The reality is that there was not uniformity among the states. As Justice Souter explained, in dissent, in *Alden v. Maine*, "The American Colonies did not enjoy sovereign immunity, that being a privilege understood in English law to be reserved for the Crown alone; 'antecedent to the Declaration of Independence, none of the colonies were, or pretended to be, sovereign states.' Several colonial charters, including those of Massachusetts, Connecticut, Rhode Island, and Georgia, expressly specified that the corporate body established thereunder could sue and be sued." [102]

An argument might be made in response that the ratification of the Eleventh Amendment indicates the framers' desire to protect sovereign immunity. Yet, as scholars such as John Gibbons and William Fletcher have persuasively argued, the purpose of the Eleventh Amendment was limited to precluding diversity suits against the states.[103] The Eleventh Amendment was to overrule *Chisholm v. Georgia*, and *Chisholm* involved only this latter part of Article III.[104] Therefore, it makes sense to view the Eleventh Amendment as restricting only diversity suits against state governments.

As a result, Justice Kennedy, in *Alden v. Maine*, was reduced to defending sovereign immunity as implicit in the framers' silence. Justice Kennedy invoked this silence as key evidence of the framers' intent. He wrote:

We believe, however, that the founders' silence is best explained by the simple fact that no one, not even the Constitution's most ardent opponents, suggested the document might strip the States of the immunity. In light of the overriding concern regarding the States' war-time debts, together with the well known creativity, foresight, and vivid imagination of the Constitution's opponents, the silence is most instructive. It suggests the sovereign's right to assert immunity from suit in its own courts was a principle so well established that no one conceived it would be altered by the new Constitution.[105]

The problem with this argument is that silence is inherently ambiguous. Perhaps Justice Kennedy was correct that the framers were silent because they thought it obvious that states could not be sued in state court. Alternatively, maybe they were silent because they thought it clear that states could be sued in state court. Most likely, though, the framers were silent because the issue did not come up, and they never thought about it. Silence is inherently uncertain and a highly questionable basis for judging intent. I am deeply skeptical that originalists such as Justices Scalia and Kennedy would accept the argument that the framers' silence about, say, the right to privacy is indicative that they thought it so obvious and clear that it was unnecessary to enumerate.

My point is simply that sovereign immunity cannot be found in the Constitution from an originalist perspective. From a non-originalist viewpoint, the issue is whether sovereign immunity is a value that should be seen as embodied in the Constitution. I provide an implicit answer in the next section of this chapter by arguing that sovereign immunity should be seen as inconsistent with the Constitution. Finally, I consider the policy justifications of sovereign immunity and conclude by demonstrating how these justifications fail to warrant the continued existence of the doctrine.

Does Sovereign Immunity Violate Fundamental Constitutional Principles?

In this section, I argue that sovereign immunity is inconsistent with three fundamental constitutional principles: the supremacy of the Constitution and federal laws; the accountability of government; and due process of law. Each of these constitutional doctrines should be regarded as sufficient to justify declaring sovereign immunity unconstitutional.

The Supremacy of the Constitution and Federal Laws

Article VI of the Constitution states: "This Constitution, and the Laws of the United States which shall be made in Pursuance thereof; and all treaties made, or which shall be made under the Authority of the United States, shall be the Supreme Law of the Land; and the Judges in every State shall be bound thereby, anything in the Constitution or Laws of any State to the Contrary Notwithstanding." This is one of the most significant provisions in the entire Constitution, for it ensures that the document is not merely aspirational but that it shall trump all other law. Indeed, in *Marbury v. Madison*, Chief Justice John Marshall relied, in part, on the supremacy clause to explain the authority for judicial review.[106] Without judicial review, there is no way to ensure that the Constitution and federal laws are supreme.

In *McCulloch v. Maryland*, Chief Justice John Marshall further elaborated on the importance of the supremacy clause: "This great principle is, that the constitution and the laws made in pursuance thereof are supreme; that they control the constitution and laws of the respective states, and cannot be controlled by them." [107] Chief Justice Marshall went on to say:

If any one proposition could command the universal assent of mankind, we might expect it would be this—that the government of the Union, though limited in its powers, is supreme within its sphere of action. This would seem to result, necessarily, from its nature. It is the government of all; its powers are delegated by all; it represents all, and acts for all. . . . The nation, on those subjects on which it can act, must necessarily bind its component parts. But this question is not left to mere reason: the people have, in express terms, decided it, by saying, "this constitution, and the laws of the United States, which shall be made in pursuance thereof, shall be the supreme law of the land," and by requiring that the members of the state legislatures, and the officers of the executive and judicial departments of the states, shall take the oath of fidelity to it. The government of the United States, then, though limited in its powers, is supreme; and its laws, when made in pursuance of the constitution, form the supreme law of the land, "anything in the constitution or laws of any state to the contrary notwithstanding." [108]

The doctrine of sovereign immunity is inconsistent with the supremacy clause. Most simply, this is because it allows a non-constitutional common law doctrine to have primacy over the Constitution and the federal laws made pursuant to it. A plaintiff asserting a federal constitutional or statutory claim against the federal or a state government loses because of the defendant's invocation of sovereign immunity.

In other words, the common law doctrine is supreme over the Constitution and federal law.

Moreover, sovereign immunity frustrates the supremacy of federal law by preventing the enforcement of the Constitution and federal statutes. How can the supremacy of federal law be assured and vindicated if states can violate the Constitution or federal laws and not be held accountable? The probation officers in *Alden* have a federal right to overtime pay. But there is no way of forcing the states to meet their federal obligation. College Savings Bank has a federal patent right that was allegedly infringed by the state of Florida, but there is no way to hold Florida liable for patent infringement. In *Kimel*, the Court did not declare unconstitutional the application of the Age Discrimination Act to state governments. Instead, it said that states cannot be sued for violating it. In other words, the states are left free to disregard federal law.

In an oral argument in *Alden*, Solicitor General Seth Waxman quoted to the Court from the supremacy clause of Article VI. He contended that suits against states are essential to assure the supremacy of federal law. Justice Kennedy's response to this argument is astounding. It is quoted earlier and it bears repeating. I think that it is the single most crucial and revealing statement about the conservative view of the relationship between the federal and state governments:

The constitutional privilege of a State to assert its sovereign immunity in its own courts does not confer upon the State a concomitant right to disregard the Constitution or valid federal law. The States and their officers are bound by obligations imposed by the Constitution and by federal statutes that comport with the constitutional design. We are unwilling to assume the States will refuse to honor the Constitution or obey the binding laws of the United States. The good faith of the States thus provides an important assurance that "[t]his Constitution, and the Laws of the United States which shall be made in Pursuance thereof . . . shall be the supreme Law of the Land." (U.S.C., Article VI)[109]

What, then, is the assurance that state governments will comply with federal law?: trust in the good faith of state governments. It is inconceivable that thirty or forty years ago, at the height of the civil rights movement, the Supreme Court might have issued such a statement, that state governments simply could be trusted to voluntarily comply with federal law. James Madison said that if people were angels there would be no need for a Constitution, but there would be no need for a government, either.[110] The reality is that from time to time state governments, intentionally or unintentionally, will violate federal law. To rely on trust in the good faith of state governments is no assurance whatsoever of the supremacy of federal law.

The Supreme Court should declare that claims of sovereign immunity by federal and state governments are inconsistent with the supremacy clause of the Constitution. The Court should hold that sovereign immunity cannot be used as a defense to a federal constitutional or statutory claim.

Government Accountability

As explained above, I believe that the principle of government accountability is inherent in the structure of the Constitution and embodied in many specific constitutional provisions. Long ago, in *Marbury v. Madison*, Chief Justice John Marshall explained that the central purpose of the Constitution is to limit the actions of government and government officers.[111] This is all about ensuring that the government is accountable for its actions. In *Marbury*, the Court emphasized the need for accountability and redress in its declaration that "[t]he very essence of civil liberty certainly consists in the right of every individual to claim the protection of the laws, whenever he receives an injury." [112] Chief Justice Marshall declared that "[t]he government of the United States has been emphatically termed a government of laws, and not of men." [113]

Sovereign immunity is inconsistent with all of these basic principles. It allows the government to violate the Constitution and laws of the United States without being held accountable. It obviously means that constitutional and statutory rights can be violated, and individuals are left with no remedies. The probation officers in *Alden*, the company with the patent in *Florida Prepaid*, and the state employees in *Kimel* all have federal rights, but because of sovereign immunity, they have no remedies. Sovereign immunity makes the laws of the United States subordinate to the will of the men and women making government decisions.

The principle that the government must be accountable can be found in many parts of the Constitution. Professor Akhil Amar has argued that it is embodied in the first words of the Constitution—"We the People"—which serves to make the people sovereign.[114]

Moreover, the Constitution rejects, implicitly and explicitly, royal prerogatives of all sorts. Scholars have shown that sovereign immunity in the United States is very much based on English law and particularly the idea that "the King can do no wrong."[115] Yet, if there is any universally agreed upon proposition about the American Constitution, it is its rejection of a monarchy and royal prerogatives. Article II's simple declaration that the "executive Power shall be vested in a President of the United States," who serves for a limited four-year term, is an emphatic rejection of royalty in the United States. Article I, Section 9, prohibits any title of nobility being granted by the United States. This is all about ensuring an accountable government.

A constitutional principle of accountability can be found in other constitutional provisions as well. Professor James Pfander has persuasively argued that the right to petition clause, found in the First Amendment, is inconsistent with the notion of sovereign immunity.[116] Professor Pfander demonstrates that "the Petition Clause guarantees the right of individuals to pursue judicial remedies for government misconduct."[117] In a lengthy and carefully researched article, he shows that "[t]he Petition Clause affirms the right of the individual to seek redress from government wrongdoing in court, a right historically calculated to overcome any threshold government immunity from suit."[118]

My point is that a constitutional principle of government accountability can be found in many parts of the Constitution. Sovereign immunity is inconsistent with this basic precept because it prevents accountability, even when the government egregiously violates the Constitution and federal laws.

Due Process of Law

Even if sovereign immunity is found in the structure of the Constitution, and I argue above that there is no basis for such a conclusion, two constitutional amendments should be seen as modifying and eliminating sovereign immunity: the Fifth and Fourteenth Amendments' assurance that no person will be deprived of life, liberty, or property without due process of law. The due process clause certainly can be used to strengthen the above argument as to the Constitution's assurance of government accountability. But even more specifically, it should be understood as imposing a constitutional mandate that those who suffer a loss of life, liberty, or property at the hands of the government are entitled to redress.

On many occasions, the Supreme Court has recognized that the absence of any court, state or federal, raises a serious due process issue.[119] In a long line of cases, the Court has said that because due process requires a judicial forum, it would interpret federal laws that appeared to preclude all jurisdiction as not doing so.[120] The Court has emphasized in these cases the importance of a judicial forum to provide redress when there is a deprivation of life, liberty, or property.[121]

However, the Court's recent sovereign immunity decisions mean that there will be many instances in which individuals will be injured without having any judicial forum available. The probation officers in Maine have a federal property right to overtime pay,[122] but there is no way for them to get due process. College Savings Bank has a federal property right in its patent, but it cannot get any due process; both federal and state judicial forums are closed to it. The state employees in *Kimel* have a liberty and property interest, created by federal law, in being free from age discrimination, but they are denied due process by the absence of any forum.

Thus, I contend that sovereign immunity is inconsistent with the supremacy of the Constitution and federal statutes, the basic principle of government accountability, and the central requirements of due process of law. On all of these grounds, the Supreme Court should banish the doctrine from American law.

The Values of Federalism and Sovereign Immunity

But what values are served by sovereign immunity? Is there any functional justification for it?

Conceptions of tort law (law that addresses wrongful acts rather than breaches of contract) have changed dramatically from the time that the United States Constitution was written and ratified. Today, liability is justified primarily based on two rationales: the need to provide compensation to injured individuals and the desire to deter future wrongdoing. In fact, the Supreme Court has recognized the importance of these rationales in the context of suits against the government. In *Owen v. City of Independence*, which dictated that local governments are not protected from liability by good-faith immunity, the Supreme Court held that local governments are liable even when their constitutional violations are a result of actions taken in good faith.[123] The Court stressed that allowing cities good-faith immunity would frustrate the underlying purposes of Section 1983 in terms of deterrence and risk spreading.[124]

Sovereign immunity frustrates compensation and deterrence. Individuals injured by government wrongdoing are left without a remedy. Stanley received no compensation for the human experimentation inflicted on him; neither were the probation officers in *Alden* nor the company in *College Savings Bank* nor the state employees in *Kimel* compensated for their injuries. Moreover, sovereign immunity frustrates deterrence because the violating government knows it can sidestep federal law without risking liability.

Rationales for Sovereign Immunity

What, then, are the justifications for sovereign immunity, and do they warrant its continued existence? Five primary rationales are discussed below: the importance of protecting government treasuries; separation of powers; the absence of authority for suits against the government; the existence of adequate alternative remedies; and tradition. I argue, in turn, that none of these are persuasive or justify the continued existence of sovereign immunity.

Protecting Government Treasuries

Sovereign immunity unquestionably has the virtue of protecting government treasuries from the costs of damage suits.[125] Indeed, that is its main effect. Doctrines exist to facilitate suits for injunctive relief against the government through the ability to sue individual government officers for prospective remedies.[126] But sovereign immunity protects government treasuries from damage judgments.

In *Alden v. Maine*, Justice Kennedy expressly spoke of this justification for sovereign immunity: "Not only must a State defend or default but also it must face the prospect of being thrust, by federal fiat and against its will, into the disfavored status of a debtor, subject to the power of private citizens to levy on its treasury or perhaps even government buildings or property which the State administers on the public's behalf." [127] This concern underlies all of the Court's sovereign immunity decisions. Allowing the government to be sued means that it can be held liable and the ultimate cost is to the taxpayer.

But this argument rests on an unsupported, and I believe unsupportable, assumption: that protecting the government treasury is more important than the benefits of liability in terms of ensuring compensation and deterrence. Sovereign immunity assumes that providing the government immunity, so as to safeguard government treasuries, is more important than ensuring government accountability. Yet, in none of the sovereign immunity cases has the Supreme Court ever justified this value choice.

Moreover, I believe that it is the wrong value priority under the Constitution. As argued in the prior section, basic constitutional principles such as ensuring the supremacy of federal law, holding the government accountable, and providing due process, all make sovereign immunity unacceptable. Although abolishing sovereign immunity would impose financial burdens on the government, it is better to spread the costs of injuries from illegal government actions among the entire citizenry than to make the wronged individual bear the entire loss.

Separation of Powers

A separate, though interrelated argument for sovereign immunity, is based on separation of powers. The claim is that the operation of government would be hindered if it were liable for every injury it inflicted.[128] The argument is that sovereign immunity is necessary to protect the government from undue interference by the judiciary.[129] Sovereign immunity preserves the unhampered exercise of discretion and limits the amount of time the government must spend responding to lawsuits. The Supreme Court declared that the "[g]overnment, as representative of the community as a whole, cannot be stopped in its tracks by any plaintiff who presents a disputed question of property or contract right."[130]

Again, this argument rests on assumptions that are unsupported and seemingly unsupportable. There is no evidence offered that suits against the government would prevent effective governance. In fact, the evidence is to the contrary. The Supreme Court has held that local governments are not protected by sovereign immunity[131] and that they can be sued under Section 1983.[132] Yet, there is no evidence that such liability has unduly disrupted the actions of government.

Moreover, it is unclear why suits for money damages would be more disruptive of government than suits for injunctive relief against government officers, which already are allowed. The likely answer is that suits for monetary compensation might cost money that could be used for other government activities. This, though, collapses the separation of powers argument into the prior claim concerning the need to protect the government fiscally.

Separation of powers never has been understood as insulating the activities of other branches of government from judicial review. Quite the contrary, ever since *Marbury v. Madison*, it has been accepted that separation of powers is judicially enforceable. As Chief Justice John Marshall emphasized, enforcing the limits of the Constitution necessitates judicial review and government accountability.

Also, the effect of sovereign immunity is to cause lawsuits to be filed against the individual government officers. The Supreme Court long has held that sovereign immunity prevents suits against the government entity, but not against the officers.[133] Hence, individuals seeking redress from the federal government must sue its officers for money damages to be paid from their own pockets.[134] Many believe that this is undesirable and that it would be preferable to have the government entity sued rather than its officers.[135] For example, it is argued that the exercise of discretion is more likely to be chilled if officers are personally liable than if the government entity is held responsible.

Absence of Authority for Suits against the Government

A third justification for sovereign immunity is that there is no authority in the Constitution or federal laws for suits against the government. Justice Oliver Wendell Holmes made the argument that liability cannot exist unless the law provides for it.[136] Justice Holmes said that claiming a right to sue the government is "like shaking one's fist at the sky, when the sky furnishes the energy that enables one to raise the fist." [137] From this viewpoint, rights do not exist independent of positive law. The right to sue must be grounded in a statute in order for it to exist.

However, this argument would mean that any statute can override sovereign immunity. Justice Holmes's argument is simply that there must be authority for suits. It means that Congress can override sovereign immunity and authorize suits if it is acting pursuant to any congressional power. This was the approach taken by the Court in *Pennsylvania v. Union Gas*[138] but rejected in *Seminole Tribe of Florida v. Florida*.

Moreover, the positive argument for sovereign immunity ignores the Constitution as a basis for suits. The authority for litigation against the government is the Constitution itself and its assurance of the supremacy of federal law, government accountability, and due process.

Existence of Adequate Alternatives

Implicit in many defenses of sovereign immunity is the claim that government liability is unwarranted because there are adequate alternatives. Most notably, individual government officers can be sued, particularly for injunctive relief, and this makes suits against government entities unnecessary.

Although such suits are critical in ensuring the supremacy of federal law, they are inadequate and do not replace litigation leveled against government entities. Injunctive relief obviously can prevent future violations, but it does nothing to provide redress for past infringements; something I argue above is a constitutional mandate. The probation officers in *Alden* can sue for an injunction to ensure that they are paid overtime in the future, but that does nothing to provide them a remedy for the prior violations of their rights under the federal Fair Labor Standards Act. College Savings Bank might get an injunction against state officers to protect their patents from future infringements by the state of Florida, but that gives the bank no remedy for past wrongful actions. For all of the states' violations of federal law that occurred prior to the injunction, and for many reasons these violations could be extensive and impose great harm, the supremacy of federal law is undermined.

Suits against government officers for money damages are not a substitute for litigation against government entities. Sometimes, the Court has ruled that there is no cause of action. Even when a cause of action exists, whether under Section 1983, some officers, such as judges, prosecutors, and legislators, have absolute immunity from suits for money damages.[139] Consider, for example, a claim that state court judges are systematically violating criminal defendants rights, such as by racism in setting bail or by paying criminal defense attorneys too little to protect defendants Sixth Amendment rights.[140] Who can be sued in such an instance? The state government cannot be named as a defendant in federal or state law. State judges cannot be sued for damages or for injunctive relief because of a federal law that expressly bars such suits.[141] It seems that no suit could be brought, even though there is an allegation of a serious violation of a basic constitutional right.

Government officials who do not have absolute immunity at least have qualified immunity, which often makes recovery for violations of federal law impossible. The Supreme Court has ruled that government officials can be held liable only if they violate a clearly established right that a reasonable officer should know.[142] The result is that often injured individuals have no recourse except to sue the government entity. Without such litigation, the supremacy of federal law often cannot be protected. Again, *McCulloch v. Maryland* is instructive: "It is of the very essence of supremacy, to remove all obstacles to its action within its own sphere. . . . This effect need not be stated in terms. It is so involved in the declaration of supremacy, so necessarily implied in it, that the expression of it could not make it more certain." [143]

Tradition

The strongest argument for sovereign immunity is tradition: it has existed, in some form, through most of American history and is based on English law. But this begs the central question: Is this a tradition that should continue? As Justice Harry Blackmun remarked in another context: "Like Justice Holmes, I believe that '[i]t is revolting to have no better reason for a rule of law than that so it was laid down in the time of Henry IV.' "[144] Sovereign immunity conflicts with other, more important, traditions in American law: enforcing the Constitution and federal laws, ensuring government accountability, and providing due process of law.

I do not think that it is possible to deny that there is a tradition of protecting sovereign immunity. The nature and extent of the tradition might be open to question; for example, as Justice Souter has demonstrated, there was no such clear tradition in the early American states.[145] Also, there was no tradition prior to 1999 and *Alden v. Maine* that accorded states sovereign immunity in their own courts. But these reservations aside, sovereign immunity long has been a part of American law.

This descriptive statement, though, says nothing about the normative desirability of continuing sovereign immunity. Slavery, enforced racial segregation, and the subjugation of women were also deeply embedded traditions. Like these traditions, sovereign immunity is a repugnant concept, at odds with the most basic precepts of the American Constitution, and it should be repudiated.

Criticisms of sovereign immunity are not new. President Abraham Lincoln declared: "It is . . . as much the duty of Government to render prompt justice against itself in favor of citizens as it is to administer the same between private individuals."[146] Unfortunately, the current Supreme Court is unpersuaded by such criticisms and is expanding, not narrowing, the reach of sovereign immunity.

Most troubling, the Court's decisions have failed to consider or serve the underlying values of federalism. I focus on sovereign immunity in detail to show the enormous gap between the values that federalism is supposed to serve and the doctrines that have been developed.

Federalism must be reinvented so that it advances the reasons why American government is structured with federal, state, and local governments. I begin to describe this approach, seeing federalism as empowerment, in the next chapter.

CHAPTER 4

Conceiving Federalism as Empowerment, Not Limits

THROUGHOUT AMERICAN HISTORY, the Supreme Court has shifted between two different views of federalism. One, which might be termed a "nationalist" perspective, seeks to broadly define the powers of the national government and gives little, if any, weight to protecting the prerogatives of state governments. The other view, which might be termed a "federalist" perspective, seeks to narrowly define the authority of the national government to preserve governance for the states.[1]

The history that is described in the first chapters of this book can be understood in terms of a Supreme Court that has shifted back and forth between these two very different views of federalism. During the first one hundred years of American history, not one federal law was struck down as exceeding the scope of Congress's power under the commerce clause or as violating the Tenth Amendment. The very broad definition of federal power articulated in *Gibbons v. Ogden*[2] was followed without exception during this era.

As is well known, and described earlier, from the late nineteenth century until 1937, the Court shifted to a federalist perspective. During this time, the Court narrowly defined the scope of Congress's commerce power and said that even laws within this authority or within the scope of the taxing and spending power could not infringe the zone of activities protected by the Tenth Amendment.[3]

A third era existed from 1937 until 1992. The Court completely shifted to a nationalist perspective, thereby enhancing federal legislative power and rejecting the Tenth Amendment as a limit on Congress's authority. During this period, not one federal law was invalidated as exceeding the scope of Congress's commerce clause or its spending power. Only once was a law struck down as violating the Tenth Amendment,[4] and that case was overruled less than a decade later.[5] However, as discussed in

Chapter 1, the Court regularly used federalism to narrow the jurisdiction of federal courts in this post-1937 era.

Finally, in recent years, which I see as beginning with *New York v. United States* in 1992,[6] the Court has shifted back to a federalist perspective. The Court has narrowed the scope of Congress's power under the commerce clause and Section 5 of the Fourteenth Amendment.[7] Also, it has revived the Tenth Amendment as a limit on federal power and has tremendously expanded state sovereign immunity.

In the last two chapters, I have focused on criticizing the shift to this federalist perspective. I have argued that the Supreme Court decisions during this time have been highly formalistic and that they don't achieve the underlying goals of government. In this chapter, I want to move from criticizing the federalism cases of the past fifteen years and propose an alternative vision: federalism should be reconceived to empower government at all levels. As I explain, what I am arguing for is different from the nationalist approach, especially as it was followed during the period from 1937 to the 1990s. For example, my vision of federalism as empowerment would include a broad definition of congressional authority, but it also would expansively define federal court jurisdiction, and at the same time, restrict the scope of preemption to empower state and local governments.

This chapter begins by describing what federalism as empowerment would mean and then explains why this best serves the underlying values of federalism. The chapter concludes by responding to objections to this vision of federalism. Chapter 5 then describes in detail how the role of the federal courts is defined under this approach, and Chapter 6 looks at how preemption doctrines should be defined with federalism reconceived as empowerment. Because each of these topics has its own complexities, each is discussed in more detail in subsequent chapters and is only briefly mentioned here.

WHAT WOULD FEDERALISM AS EMPOWERMENT MEAN?

The central thesis of federalism as empowerment is the genius of having multiple levels of government; that is, an array of alternative actors equipped to deal with society's problems and needs. If one level of government fails, another is there to take over the responsibility. For example, if state governments can't or don't require the clean up of radioactive waste, the federal government can act to ensure its safe disposal.[8] If states fail to provide adequate remedies to deter gender-motivated violence and to compensate victims, the federal government can create a cause of action in federal court.[9] If the federal government decides not to require insurance companies to disclose their Holocaust-era policies, state governments can implement this rule within their boundaries.[10]

To be clear, this does not mean that government at any level has unlimited power and that there is no judicial role. Quite the contrary, the courts should aggressively enforce the Constitution's protections of individual liberties and civil rights. This is the primary protection against tyranny, whereas federalism-based limits on government power offer no safeguard, and as argued in the previous chapter, have actually been rights regressive.

Also, I should be clear that I am not saying that the political process adequately enforces the structural limits on federal power and adequately safeguards the interests of state governments. This is the position taken by Herbert Wechsler in his famous article on the political safeguards of federalism,[11] and which I criticized in Chapter 1. Also, appraising whether the political process adequately protects the interests of states as states requires a normative vision of what is "adequate." I am making a much different claim: that the structural limits federalism imposes on government power are minimal. The real limits on government power, apart from the political process, come from the provisions of the Constitution providing for liberty and equality.

The Tenets of Federalism as Empowerment

What, then, are the tenets of federalism as empowerment? In this section, I summarize the tenets in a seven-point list. At this stage, I simply want to describe what I mean by federalism as empowerment. The subsequent sections of this chapter, and Chapters 5 and 6, defend this vision.

Tenet No. 1: Commerce Clause Power

Congress under the commerce clause may regulate any activity that it reasonably believes has an effect on commerce with foreign nations, Indians tribes, and among the states. The effect may be found from the cumulative impact of activities across the country.

Here, I am arguing for the approach to the commerce clause that was followed from 1937 to 1995. To be clear, I would reject the test for the commerce power that the Court developed in *United States v. Lopez*. This test, which I've described in previous chapters, limits Congress to regulating in three circumstances: the channels of interstate commerce, the instrumentalities of and persons or things in interstate commerce, and the activities that have a substantial effect on commerce.[12] Likewise, I would reject any distinction between economic and noneconomic activity in defining commerce power, such as the Court drew in *United States v. Morrison*.[13]

Or put another way, I am arguing for exactly the position urged by the four dissenting justices in cases such as *Lopez* and *Morrison*. Their view, and the law that was followed for almost sixty years, allowed Congress to regulate under the commerce clause, so long as there was a reasonable basis for believing that the activity, looked at cumulatively across the country, had an effect on commerce. I urge a return to this approach. As argued in the previous chapters, the abandonment of this approach has been highly formalistic and has not served the underlying goals of providing effective government that expands liberty. As I lay out below, the Court's approach from 1937 to 1995 better achieves the underlying goals for federalism.

Tenet No. 2: Spending and Taxing Power

Congress under its taxing and spending power should continue to have the power to tax and spend for the general welfare. In other words, Congress can adopt any tax to raise revenue or any spending program to expend it that Congress believes will serve the interests of the country. This is the approach taken by the Court in *United States v. Butler* in 1936 and followed ever since.[14] Interestingly, while the Court has shifted to a federalist approach in defining Congress's power under the commerce clause and the post–Civil War, or Reconstruction, amendments, it has not limited the taxing or spending power.[15] Nor should it.

Moreover, as inducements for action, Congress should be able to attach strings to grants at the state and local levels. In *South Dakota v. Dole*, the Supreme Court upheld a federal law that conditioned a percentage of federal highway money to state governments on their setting a twenty-one-year-old drinking age.[16] Chief Justice Rehnquist, an ardent advocate for states' rights, wrote the opinion for the Court, and said that Congress may attach strings to grants so long as the conditions are clearly stated and so long as they relate to the purpose of the program. This approach should be continued.[17]

Tenet No. 3: Post–Civil War Power

Congress's power under the post–Civil War amendments should be broadly defined in terms of which entities Congress may regulate and what laws Congress may enact. This point deserves more discussion than some of the others, as it has gotten little coverage in previous chapters.

These powers, of course, refer to Congress's power under Section 2 of the Thirteenth Amendment, Section 5 of the Fourteenth Amendment, and Section 2 of the Fifteenth Amendment. The Thirteenth Amendment prohibits slavery and involuntary servitude. Section 1 of the Fourteenth Amendment most importantly prohibits states from denying any person equal protection under the law, or life, liberty, or property without due process of law. The Fifteenth Amendment forbids denying the right to vote on the basis of race or previous conditions of servitude. Each amendment has a provision, or section, as outlined above that declares: "Congress shall have power to enforce this article by appropriate legislation."

These powers should be defined broadly to equip Congress with the authority to advance the goals of these amendments. First, Congress should be able to regulate both government *and* private actors. In the Civil Rights Cases, in 1883, the Supreme Court greatly limited Congress's ability to use its power under the Reconstruction amendments to regulate private conduct.[18] The Civil Rights Act of 1875 provided that all persons were "entitled to the full and equal enjoyment of the accommodations, advantages, facilities and privileges of inns, public conveyances, on land or water, theatres, and other places of public amusement; subject only to the conditions and limitations established by law, and applicable to citizens of every race and color, regardless of any previous condition of servitude." In other words, the law broadly prohibited private racial discrimination by hotels, restaurants, transportation, and other public accommodations.

By an 8–1 decision, the Court held that the act was unconstitutional, adopting a restrictive view as to the power of Congress to use these provisions to regulate private behavior. As to the Thirteenth Amendment, the Court recognized that it applies to private conduct; it prohibits people from being or owning slaves. The Court, however, said that Congress's authority was limited to ensuring an end to slavery; Congress could not use this power to eliminate discrimination. The Court explained that "it would be running the slavery argument into the ground to make it apply to every act of discrimination which a person may see fit to make as to the guests he will entertain, or as to the people he will take into his coach or cab or car, or admit to his concert or theatre, or deal with in other matters of intercourse or business." [19] Indeed, the Court stated that Congress could abolish "all badges and incidents of slavery," but it could not use its power under the Thirteenth Amendment to "adjust what may be called the social rights of men and races in the community." [20]

Amazingly for a decision in 1883, less than two decades after the end of the Civil War, the Court suggested that slavery was a thing of the past and that there was little need for civil rights legislation to protect blacks. Justice Joseph P. Bradley, writing for the Court, stated: "When a man has emerged from slavery, and by the aid of beneficent legislation has shaken off the inseparable concomitants of that state, there must be some stage in the progress of his elevation when he takes the rank of a mere citizen and ceases to be the special favorite of the laws, and when his rights as a citizen, or a man, are to be protected in the ordinary modes by which other men's rights are protected." [21]

The Court also held that Congress lacked authority to enact the law under the Fourteenth Amendment. In fact, the Court broadly declared that the Fourteenth Amendment applies only to government action and that therefore it cannot be used by Congress to regulate private behavior. The Court stated that "the fourteenth amendment is prohibitory . . . upon the states. [Individual] invasion of individual rights is not the subject matter of the amendment." [22] The Court made it clear that Congress's authority was only over state and local governments and their officials, not over private conduct: "It does not authorize Congress to create a code of municipal law for the regulation of private rights; but to provide modes of redress against the operation of State laws, and the actions of State officers." [23]

For almost eighty years, the Court continued to adhere to the holding of the Civil Rights Cases, that Congress, pursuant to the Thirteenth Amendment, could not regulate private conduct. For example, in *Hodges v. United States*, in 1906, the Court declared unconstitutional a federal law that made it a crime for private individuals to intimidate blacks to keep them from performing their contracts of employment.[24] The Court explained that the Thirteenth Amendment was intended only to prohibit slavery, and the Court again stated its view that blacks should not be protected by special legislation. The Court said that the Reconstruction amendments "declined to constitute them wards of the Nation . . . doubtless believing that thereby in the long run their best interests would be subserved, they taking their chances with other citizens in the states where they should make their homes." [25]

However, in the past quarter century, the Court has overruled these earlier decisions and has accorded Congress broad power under the Thirteenth Amendment to prohibit private racial discrimination. The seminal case is *Jones v. Alfred H. Mayer Co.*, which held that Congress could prohibit private discrimination in selling and leasing property.[26] The case involved a private real estate developer who refused to sell housing or land to blacks. A black couple sued under 42 U.S.C. (United States Constitution), Section 1982, which provides that all citizens have "the same right, in every State and Territory, as is enjoyed by white citizens thereof to inherit, purchase, lease, sell, hold and convey real and personal property."

The Court held that Section 1982 applies to prohibit private discrimination and that Congress had the authority under the Thirteenth

Amendment to adopt the law.[27] Indeed, the Court said that Congress has broad legislative power under the Thirteenth Amendment: "Congress has the power under the Thirteenth Amendment rationally to determine what are the badges and incidents of slavery, and the authority to translate that determination into effective legislation."[28]

Subsequently, the Court has upheld the constitutionality of other federal statutes regulating private behavior that were adopted under Section 2 of the Thirteenth Amendment.[29] In *Runyon v. McCrary*, the Court held that 42 U.S.C., Section 1981, applies to prohibit discrimination in private contracting and that this is within the scope of Congress's power under Section 2 of the Thirteenth Amendment.[30] Section 1981 provides that "[a]ll persons within the jurisdiction of the United States shall have the same right in every State and Territory to make and enforce contracts, to sue, be parties, give evidence, and to the full and equal benefit of all laws and proceedings for the security of persons and property as is enjoyed by white citizens." *Runyon* raised the question of whether Section 1981 prohibits private schools from excluding qualified black children solely because of their race.

The Supreme Court saw no basis for distinguishing *Jones v. Alfred H. Mayer Co.* and concluded "that Section 1981, like Section 1982, reaches private conduct."[31] The Court unanimously reaffirmed this conclusion in 1989, in *Patterson v. McLean Credit Union*.[32]

The Court also has held that Congress had authority under the Thirteenth Amendment to enact 42 U.S.C., Section 1985(3), which creates a civil cause of action for conspiracies to violate civil rights.[33] In *Griffin v. Breckenridge*, the Court allowed a private suit by black victims of a racially motivated assault.[34] The incident occurred in Mississippi in 1966, when two whites stopped five black people in a car and severely beat them. The Court found that there was a cause of action under Section 1985(3) because there was "nothing inherent in [the provision] that requires the action working the deprivation to come from the State."[35]

In *Jones, Runyon, Patterson*, and *Griffin*, the Court gave Congress broad power under Section 2 of the Thirteenth Amendment to prohibit private racial discrimination. Yet, it should be noted that in other cases, the Court has spoken in a more qualified manner about this power. *Nor-*

wood v. Harrison held that a Mississippi program to give free textbooks to private schools violated the Constitution.[36] In discussing Congress's authority under Section 2 of the Thirteenth Amendment, the Court said that "some private discrimination is subject to special remedial legislation in certain circumstances."[37] Despite these qualifiers, *Jones*, *Runyon*, and *Patterson* give Congress the ability to prohibit private racial discrimination as part of its authority to eliminate the badges and incidents of slavery.

This is enormously important federal authority. So far, the Court has not suggested that it will back away from this definition of federal power. It is critical that the Supreme Court continues to uphold this broad definition of congressional power to prohibit private racial discrimination pursuant to Section 2 of the Thirteenth Amendment.

Unlike the Thirteenth Amendment, which Congress can use to prevent private discrimination, it is now clear that Section 5 of the Fourteenth Amendment cannot be used to regulate private activity. I would reject this narrow approach and allow Congress to regulate private behavior to advance due process and equal protection, the focus of Section 1 of the Fourteenth Amendment.

As described earlier, in *United States v. Guest*, in 1966, five justices, although not in a single opinion, took this approach and concluded that Congress may outlaw private discrimination pursuant to Section 5 of the Fourteenth Amendment.[38] But in *United States v. Morrison*,[39] in 2000, the Supreme Court expressly reaffirmed the Civil Rights Cases and disavowed the opinions to the contrary in *United States v. Guest*. As described earlier, *Morrison* involved a constitutional challenge to the civil damages provision of the Violence Against Women Act, which authorized victims of gender-motivated violence to sue under federal law. The federal government defended the law as constitutional under both Congress's commerce clause authority and under Section five of the Fourteenth Amendment. The Court rejected both arguments, and as to the latter, Chief Justice Rehnquist wrote that under this power, only state and local governments, not Congress, may regulate private conduct.

Morrison thus reinstates an unfortunate limit on Congress's power under Section 5 of the Fourteenth Amendment. I believe that the decision is an unduly narrow interpretation of a constitutional provision that was intended to have broad scope. The Violence Against Women Act was adopted because of documented inadequacies in state courts and state laws. The text of Section 5 does not limit Congress's enforcement authority to regulating government entities. In terms of the underlying goals of federalism—providing effective government and enhancing liberty—a broader reading of Section 5 to allow regulation of private behavior would accomplish both of these. *Morrison*, itself, is illustrative in that providing federal remedies for victims of sexual violence in the face of congressionally documented inadequacies in state courts both enhances the effectiveness of government and advances equality.

A second major issue concerning Congress's power under the Reconstruction amendments is the scope of authority under these provisions. Is Congress limited to providing remedies for only those violations of constitutional rights recognized by the Supreme Court; or may Congress use its power under these amendments to adopt an independent interpretation of the Constitution, even overruling Supreme Court decisions?

There are two possible answers to these questions concerning the scope of Congress's authority under Section 5 of the Fourteenth Amendment. One view, which might be labeled the "nationalist" perspective, is that Congress can use its Section 5 authority to expand the scope of rights. *Katzenbach v. Morgan*, in 1966,[40] appeared to adopt this approach. An alternative view, which might be called a "federalist" perspective, is that Congress under Section 5 cannot create new rights or expand the scope of existing rights; Congress can act only to prevent or remedy violations of rights, and such laws must be narrowly tailored. In *City of Boerne v. Flores*, in 1997, discussed in Chapter 2, the Court unequivocally adopted this second perspective and has reaffirmed it in several decisions over the past ten years. Earlier, I criticized the narrow reading of Congress's Section 5 power in these recent decisions. Under federalism as empowerment, Congress's Section 5 authority would be broadly defined to include the ability to expand the scope of rights or even to create new rights, so long as there was not a dilution of rights. Again, this is not a radical change. This is exactly the position urged by Justice William Brennan, in his opinion, in *Katzenbach v. Morgan*.[41]

Again, it is consistent with the text of Section 5, which gives Congress the power to adopt laws "to enforce" the amendment. This was intended to create expansive authority to remedy state violations of rights. What's more, it would empower Congress to deal effectively with serious problems in a manner that advances liberty and equality.

Tenet No. 4: The Tenth Amendment

The Tenth Amendment should be understood as allowing Congress to act only where there is constitutional authority, while states may do anything except that which is prohibited by the Constitution. This is the approach that the Court followed throughout the nineteenth century, and from 1937 to 1992, with one exception that was overruled. It should be followed again.

The Tenth Amendment says: "The powers not delegated to the United States by the Constitution, nor prohibited by it to the States, are reserved to the States respectively, or to the people." The key question about the Tenth Amendment is whether it is a judicially enforceable limit on Congress's powers; can federal laws be declared unconstitutional as violating this constitutional provision? Over the course of American history, the Court has been inconsistent in answering this question and has shifted between two different approaches.

The nationalist perspective is that the Tenth Amendment is not a separate constraint on Congress, but rather it is simply a reminder that Congress can legislate only if it has authority under the Constitution. Under this approach, a federal law could never be found unconstitutional in terms of violating the Tenth Amendment, but it could be invalidated for exceeding the scope of Congress's power under Article I of the Constitution or for violating another constitutional provision. This is what the Court meant in *United States v. Darby*, in 1941, when it declared that the "Amendment states but a truism that all is retained which has not been surrendered." [42]

The alternative federalist perspective is that the Tenth Amendment protects state sovereignty from federal intrusion. Under this approach, the Tenth Amendment is a key protection of states' rights and federalism. The Tenth Amendment reserves a zone of activity to the states for their exclusive control, and federal laws intruding into this zone should be declared unconstitutional by the courts. In the first third of this century, until 1937, the Court adopted this view and found that the Tenth Amendment reserved to the states control over production, and federal laws attempting to regulate production were deemed unconstitutional.[43] Since 1992, in cases such as *New York v. United States*[44] and *Printz v. United States*,[45] the Supreme Court has returned to this latter view and held that federal laws that compel states to adopt laws or to administer federal mandates violate the Tenth Amendment.

Federalism as empowerment would take the language of the Tenth Amendment literally. It does not speak of a zone of activities for the states. It just says that Congress can exercise only the powers granted, while states can do all that is not prohibited.

Tenet No. 5: Sovereign Immunity

Sovereign immunity should not be a bar to suits. The Eleventh Amendment should be interpreted to preclude suits only if the sole basis for jurisdiction is diversity of citizenship between the parties. That is, cases based on federal question jurisdiction—suits for violations of the Constitution and laws of the United States—should not be deemed barred by the Eleventh Amendment. Nor should sovereign immunity be a bar to suits against state governments in state courts or in federal administrative agencies.

As explained in the previous chapter, a major limit on federal judicial power—and now on the authority of state courts as well—is the doctrine of sovereign immunity. Sovereign immunity in the federal courts is based on the Supreme Court's interpretation of the Eleventh Amendment. The Eleventh Amendment states, "The Judicial power of the United States shall not be construed to extend to any suit in law or equity, commenced or prosecuted against one of the United States by Citizens of another State, or by Citizens or Subjects of any foreign state." As interpreted, the Eleventh Amendment prohibits suits in federal courts against state governments in law, equity, or admiralty, by a state's own citizens, by citizens of another state, or by citizens of foreign countries. Additionally, the Supreme Court recently held that sovereign immunity bars suits against state governments in state court without their consent.[46] The Court thus has ruled that there is a broad principle of sovereign immunity that applies in both federal and state courts; the Eleventh Amendment is a reflection and embodiment of part of that principle. As Justice Anthony Kennedy, writing the opinion in *Alden v. Maine*, declared: "[S]overeign immunity derives not from the Eleventh Amendment but from the structure of the original Constitution itself." [47]

But this is the federalist perspective of sovereign immunity. Although five justices have supported it in recent years, four have taken a very different, nationalist, view. This approach sees the Eleventh Amendment as restricting only the diversity jurisdiction of federal courts.[48] Article III of the Constitution permits subject matter jurisdiction, either based on the content of the litigation—for example, federal question jurisdiction—or based on the identity of the parties—for example, diversity jurisdiction. Article III, Section 2, identifies nine categories of cases and controversies that might be heard in federal court. One of these is "Cases, in Law and Equity, arising under this Constitution, the Laws of the United States, and Treaties made, or which shall be made, under their Authority." This is the provision that authorizes federal question jurisdiction. A different, later, passage of Article III, Section 2, allows for "Controversies . . . between a State and Citizens of another state." This is an authorization for suits against a state based on diversity of citizenship.

The language of the Eleventh Amendment clearly is directed at modifying this latter provision. In fact, the amendment simply states: "The Judicial Power of the United States shall not be construed to extend to any suit . . . against one of the United States by Citizens of another state." Therefore, according to this view, the Eleventh Amendment does not bar suits against states based on other parts of Article III. Most notably, the amendment does not preclude suits based on federal question jurisdiction. Thus, all claims of state violations of the United States Constitution or federal laws could be heard in federal courts.[49]

Those who take this latter view completely reject the idea of sovereign immunity as a constitutional principle. As explained at the end of Chapter 3, sovereign immunity is nowhere mentioned in the Constitution and is inconsistent with the enforcement of the Constitution. Thus, federalism as empowerment would reject the idea that state governments cannot be sued to enforce the Constitution and laws of the United States.

Tenet No. 6: The Power of Choice for Litigants

Principles defining federal court jurisdiction should be modified so as to maximize the ability of litigants to choose whether to have their claims heard in federal or state court. As explained in the next chapter, for the past few decades, the Supreme Court has rejected federal court jurisdiction based on the assumption, often made explicit in opinions, that state courts are on parity with federal courts in their ability and willingness to enforce federal rights. I argue in Chapter 5 that there is no way to assess the relative competence of federal and state courts; even if competence could be defined, inevitably it will vary based on geography, time, and issue. The appropriate way to empower both federal and state courts is to allow litigants with constitutional claims the maximum opportunity to litigate in the forum of their choice. How this would be implemented is discussed extensively in the next chapter.

Tenet No. 7: The Power of Narrowly Defined Preemption

Preemption doctrines should be narrowly defined so that state and local laws are deemed preempted only if a federal statute expressly preempts state and local laws, or if there is a direct conflict between federal law and state and local laws. One way to empower state and local governments is to narrow the preemptive effect of federal laws. Interestingly, this has not occurred in the past two decades, despite a Court committed to states' rights. This is discussed in detail in Chapter 6, and this revised approach to preemption is defended.

WHY FEDERALISM AS EMPOWERMENT IS DESIRABLE

In Chapter 3, I argued that, above all, the structure of government exists to achieve two objectives: provide an effective government and advance liberty. The crucial question is, Which approach to federalism will maximize the likelihood of attaining these goals? Is effective government better achieved by limiting federal and state government powers in the name of federalism, or by federalism as empowerment as it is defined above? Is liberty better ensured by limiting federal and state government powers in the name of federalism, or by federalism as empowerment?

The answer is clear. As for effective government, using federalism to limit federal and state power inevitably prevents government from successfully acting to deal with social problems. This has been true throughout American history. Whenever the Supreme Court has used federalism as a restriction on government power, critical societal issues are often ignored. For example, during the first third of the twentieth century, the Supreme Court's use of federalism and dual sovereignty prevented government from achieving important objectives. When Congress sought to prohibit child labor, undoubtedly a desirable goal with which few could disagree, the Supreme Court declared the law unconstitutional, saying it violated the Tenth Amendment.[50] As I mentioned earlier in the book, Congress was concerned that market pressures would prevent state governments from being able to act effectively. States that prohibited child labor would find that their manufacturers were at a competitive disadvantage relative to those in states that allowed child labor. The result was inevitable pressure to the least common denominator: child labor was permitted across the country. Congress, knowing of the restrictive interpretation of the commerce power followed by the Supreme Court at the time, prohibited the shipment in interstate commerce of goods made by child labor. The Supreme Court's invalidation of this statute meant that child labor continued for decades until ultimately the Court shifted course.

The other Supreme Court decisions of the time that employed federalism as a limit likewise reflect how effective government was thwarted. For instance, the Court used a narrow definition of commerce to overturn federal laws regulating monopolies in agricultural production,[51] invalidate the regulation of wages and hours in the coal industry,[52] reverse a pension system for railroad workers,[53] and upset agricultural price supports.[54] These examples are striking because all are instances in which few would deny that they were desirable government objectives. Simply put, effective government was thwarted by using federalism as a limit on Congress's powers. Had the Court seen federalism in terms of empowering government, all of these laws would have been upheld, and the country would have been better for it.

The same is true of federalism in the modern era. Again, it is striking that the Supreme Court's use of federalism as limits has invalidated laws that are enormously desirable. The Rehnquist Court, as I've pointed out before, used federalism to overturn federal statutes prohibiting guns near schools,[55] allowing victims of gender-motivated violence to sue,[56] protecting intrastate waters from pollution and degradation,[57] enforcing the cleanup of radioactive waste,[58] and requiring background checks for firearm permits.[59] Can it really be argued that government was more effective because these laws were struck down? Few, I think, would push for guns near schools, or for the withholding of compensation to victims of violence, or for the degradation of wetlands, or for the release of radioactive waste, or for giving gun permits to dangerous individuals. It must be remembered that in each instance, Congress acted because it perceived at least some state and local governments as failing to do so.

Likewise, in the area of preemption, which I discuss in Chapter 6, the Supreme Court has thwarted effective government by striking down critical state and local laws. In recent years, the Court has preempted state laws limiting cigarette advertisements near schools,[60] requiring insurance companies to disclose their Holocaust-era policies,[61] and providing compensation to individuals hurt in automobiles lacking airbags.[62]

Under federalism as empowerment, all of these cases would have come out differently. Government would have been much more able to deal with the serious social problems that the legislatures were trying to tackle. It does not make sense to say that government would be more effective if its power is significantly limited. That is why federalism as empowerment is far more likely to produce good government than federalism as limits. In fact, I cannot think of any example of a Supreme Court decision invalidating a law on federalism grounds that made government more effective in addressing social issues.

The response, of course, can be that even though the use of federalism to limit government power might frustrate effective government, it is still desirable because it enhances individual liberties. From this perspective, enforcement of the limits on government authority in the name of federalism is a necessary evil in order to maximize freedom and equality.

But as explained in Chapter 3, that has not at all been the effect of the Supreme Court's enforcement of federalism as limits. Quite the contrary, the Supreme Court's federalism decisions, to use the terminology from the previous chapter, have been rights regressive. The Court has invalidated numerous laws that enhance liberty and has, through the expansion of sovereign immunity, thwarted deterrence of government wrongdoing and compensation to its victims. To choose a couple of examples discussed previously, the Court's invalidating the civil damages provision of the Violence Against Women Act,[63] and its striking down the Religious Freedom Restoration Act,[64] undermined rather than enhanced liberty. These were statutes advancing civil rights, and both were invalidated based on federalism as limits. Similarly, the expansion of sovereign immunity has meant that victims of age and disability discrimination by state governments have been left without damage remedies.[65]

Put more generally, using federalism to limit government authority prevents government from enacting laws to advance civil liberties and civil rights. Expanding state sovereign immunity inevitably means that victims of unconstitutional or illegal government action cannot secure a damages remedy from the state.

Additionally, as argued already, there is no basis for the often-stated assumption that enforcing federalism reduces the likelihood of tyrannical government action and enhances freedom. Besides, judicial review provides the best protection against government actions that violate rights. If the government acts tyrannically or infringes liberties, courts can and should invalidate the government's action. The indirect protection that comes from enforcing federalism as limits is unnecessary and counterproductive.

Providing for effective government and enhancing freedom are the primary goals for government, but there are other objectives as well. As explained previously, having both federal and state governments can be important in dealing with spillovers and externalities, providing for efficiency, empowering communities, enhancing accountability, and meeting diverse needs. However, there is no reason to believe that courts, in enforcing federalism as limits, would advance, rather than inhibit, the achievement of these objectives. Accomplishing these ends can require a different level of government action—federal, state, or local—depending on the need. Limiting Congress's commerce power or its authority under the post–Civil War amendments does not have any overall relationship to these objectives. Neither does a broad approach to preempting state laws.

In fact, it would seem that the political process, rather than the judiciary, is far better able to decide the structure of government that best maximizes these goals. For example, Congress can determine when externalities and spillover problems require federal environmental laws. Congress, rather than the courts, seems best able to pinpoint what structure of government is most efficient in managing administrative costs. To be clear, this is not saying that Congress would adequately protect states as states. I am not sure how even to define *adequate*, here. Rather, the point is that Congress is in the best position to decide when national action is needed to effectively address social problems, whether the issue is endangered species, or violence against women.

My defense of federalism as empowerment is thus a simple one: the objectives of government are best achieved if government at all levels is equipped to deal with society's problems, so long as the rights provided in the Constitution are upheld.

RESPONDING TO THE OBJECTIONS TO FEDERALISM
AS EMPOWERMENT

I know that many, even among those sympathetic to my goals, will be skeptical of federalism as empowerment as I've defined it above. Some may have the sense that I am arguing for something radical. It must be remembered that when it comes to federal authority, I am simply advocating a return to the law that was followed from 1937 until the 1990s. But when it comes to preemption law, I am urging for significant change, in order to lessen the instances in which state and local government action is forestalled. That, of course, would enhance state and local power, not diminish it. I am also arguing for far-reaching change in the doctrines of federal jurisdiction, which I defend in Chapter 5.

An Originalist Objection

I can anticipate a number of objections to federalism as empowerment. First, an originalist argument can be made: the framers of the Constitution did not intend a federal government of such broad powers. I confess that I am not an originalist and believe that the world of the twenty-first century is sufficiently different from the world of the late eighteenth century that the intention of the framers is not determinative of modern constitutional meaning.[66] Most importantly, every aspect of federalism as empowerment is consistent with the text of the Constitution. In fact, my approach is much more faithful to the text than the federalism as limits practiced by the Supreme Court. For example, it is impossible to find in the language of the Tenth Amendment the Supreme Court's principle that Congress cannot commandeer state governments and force them to enact laws or adopt regulations. And nowhere can it be found in the Eleventh Amendment the principle that state governments cannot be sued by their own citizens.

In fact, I believe that an originalist argument can be made *for* federalism as empowerment. After all, in *Gibbons v. Ogden*,[67] none other than Chief Justice John Marshall adopted a broad reading of Congress's commerce power and a rejection of the Tenth Amendment as a limit on federal authority. In *Chisholm v. Georgia*,[68] in 1793, four out of five justices on the Supreme Court rejected the idea that state governments retained sovereign immunity after the adoption of the Constitution. These cases are powerful evidence of the original understanding because the justices were part of the drafting and ratification of the Constitution.

In the end, though, originalism cannot provide the foundation for judicial enforcement of federalism as limits. It is impossible to know what the framers wanted in this regard, because they did not discuss judicial review, let alone how it should be used in the area of federalism. The argument for judicial enforcement of federalism as a limit on government authority must come from normative arguments, not from authoritative evidence as to framers' intent.

The strongest response from an originalist perspective would be that the framers intended to create a Congress of limited power and that my approach negates this. Article I of the Constitution restricts Congress to power "herein granted." Federalism as empowerment would mean that Congress could do virtually anything, so long as it did not violate the rights provided in the Constitution. This is an exceedingly worrisome statement from the originalist perspective, and it is the premise for Supreme Court decisions limiting the scope of Congress's powers. The claim is that if Congress is not to have limitless power, something rejected by the very language of Article I, then the Court must enforce restrictions on the scope of the commerce power.

Before replying directly to this argument, it is important to be clear that it only addresses some aspects of federalism as empowerment. For example, this argument, that no power of Congress should be structurally limitless, does not provide support for the Rehnquist Court's view of the Tenth Amendment or for its expansion of sovereign immunity. Nor does it provide a reason for restricting the scope of Congress's power under the post–Civil War amendments. Even the broad view of this authority confines it to certain types of laws.

But what of the argument that the broad definition of Congress's commerce power would mean that the legislature essentially would have police authority under this provision, which is inconsistent with the fundamental constitutional postulate prohibiting such authority? My response is that even under federalism as empowerment, courts would impose some constraint on Congress's commerce power: Congress could act only when it reasonably believed that an activity had an effect on commerce. Admittedly, this is not much of a limit, because few laws would fail this test. However, it is an outer boundary on federal power and answers those who object that my approach has no limits whatsoever. Also, of course, there are limits imposed on Congress by other constitutional provisions. Congress, for example, could not use its commerce clause power to require newspapers to have licenses. That would clearly violate the First Amendment. Though simple, the illustration is significant, because it belies the claim that my approach would mean *limitless* federal power.

Once it is recognized that there should be at least some limits, then the question becomes, where does one draw the line? How much of a constraint should be enforced to be true to the Constitution's vision of a Congress with limitless power? This, then, requires choosing as to whether federalism as empowerment or federalism as limits is a better way to define Congress's authority in achieving the goals of effective government and enhanced liberty.

Put another way, the premise that there must be some check on Congress's power does not provide an answer as to what the limits should be. Whether the limits on Congress's power should be great, so as to constrain federal authority, or whether the limits should be minimal, to empower the federal government, cannot be answered by the premise that there must be some limits. The answer to this must come from a choice as to which theory of federalism best achieves the goals for government, and I reiterate that federalism as empowerment is preferable.

Undesirable Government Actions

A second objection is that empowering government could lead to undesirable government actions. Power can be used for good or for ill. A more powerful Congress could use its authority to enact undesirable laws. As the past decades have shown, political pressures have compelled Congress to criminalize matters that previously had been handled at the state level; federalism as empowerment could exacerbate this tendency. And federalism as empowerment would lessen preemption, which could mean that more undesirable state and local laws might remain in force.

This is an important objection and one that is not easily answered. The question is whether allowing more government action would lead to more good or to more bad consequences. There seems no way to assess this. It is impossible to know, in terms of an overall assessment, what might be done in the future to determine which would be good and which bad government action. There's simply no way to figure out how to tally it all up.

Those who favor federalism as limits can argue from the premise that less government action is better. But this assumption is just as unjustified as the opposite assumption that government action, on balance, is better than government inaction. Precisely because government can be used for good or bad ends, it is impossible to make an overall assessment.

Ultimately, I think the only way to resolve this is by looking backward, not forward. Has society been better off when the Court has used federalism as limits, or when it has taken an approach much closer to federalism as empowerment? From this perspective, I think that the answer is clear. Over the course of American history, federalism as limits resulted in the invalidation of countless desirable laws, including statutes prohibiting child labor, requiring a minimum wage, mandating the clean up of radioactive waste, and forbidding guns near schools. Put more generally, as argued earlier, there are strong reasons to believe that federalism as empowerment would do a better job of providing for effective government and enhancing liberty.

But I acknowledge that empowering government can lead to undesirable government actions. Here, though, I'm confident that judicial review would protect individual freedom, and other types of misguided government actions ultimately would be checked by the political process. I recognize that there are instances in which the incentives of the political process may be perverse, and that bad laws may be enacted and survive that do not infringe other parts of the Constitution. In the end, under an empowered federalism that encourages government action, there is no reason to believe that the bad consequences of these laws would outweigh the good.

The Destruction of States as States

A third objection to federalism as empowerment is that it would render state governments meaningless. It is interesting that throughout American history, the Supreme Court has defended federalism as limits on the grounds that without it, there would be the destruction of states as states. For example, in striking down a federal law protecting coal miners in 1936, the Court declared: "Every journey to a forbidden end begins with the first step; and the danger of such a step by the federal government in the direction of taking over the powers of the states in that the end of the journey may find the states so despoiled of their powers, or—what amount to the same thing—so relieved of responsibilities . . . as to reduce them to little more than geographic subdivisions of the national domain."[69] Similarly, in striking down the federal law prohibiting child labor, the Supreme Court stated: "The far-reaching result of upholding the act cannot be more plainly indicated than by pointing out that if Congress can thus regulate matters entrusted to local authority by prohibition of the movement of commodities in interstate commerce, all freedom of commerce will be at an end, and the power of states over local matters may be eliminated, and thus our system of government practically destroyed."[70]

After 1937, though, the Supreme Court upheld a federal minimum wage and allowed a federal law prohibiting child labor, and our system of government was not destroyed. Even though the Court imposed no limits on the scope of Congress's commerce power for almost sixty years, states were not reduced to political subdivisions of the federal government.

Nor is this a risk. The reality is that most governance in the United States always has been, and always will be, done at the state and local levels. The sheer size of the country makes it inevitable that local governments will have the primary responsibility for providing police protection, education, and sanitation services. To be sure, the size and responsibilities of the federal government have increased dramatically over time. But this shows that such expansion does not end the primary governing responsibility of state and local governments.

If the real concern is empowering state and local governments, then preemption should be limited. Before moving to this aspect of federalism as empowerment, in Chapter 6, I address, in the next chapter, what federalism as empowerment would mean in defining the role of the federal courts.

CHAPTER 5

Federalism as Empowerment:
Redefining the Role of the Federal Courts

WHAT WOULD SHIFTING to empowerment as the core value of federalism mean in defining the role of the federal judiciary? In this chapter, I suggest that it would significantly change federal jurisdiction.

Throughout American history, and especially for the past thirty years, discussions about the scope of federal jurisdiction largely have focused on whether federal courts are more willing and able than state courts to protect constitutional rights. This issue has been labeled the question of "parity" between federal and state courts.[1] Those favoring expansive federal court availability to decide constitutional claims frequently argue that state courts are not to be trusted to adequately protect constitutional rights. They contend that, in constitutional litigation between the government and private citizens, federal courts are more likely than state courts to rule in favor of individual liberties and against the government.[2]

Some proponents of parity maintain that state courts are as likely to protect individual rights as are the federal courts.[3] Others who argue for parity contend that even when the federal and state courts reach different results, one set of outcomes is not necessarily preferable to the other.[4] They suggest that since both systems offer equally acceptable processes, jurisdiction should not be determined based on the assumption that one court system is superior.

The Earl Warren Court expanded federal court jurisdiction based on the expressly stated premise that federal courts often are necessary to ensure adequate protection of constitutional rights. By increasing the availability of federal habeas corpus for state prisoners,[5] expanding the scope of relief under 42 U.S.C., Section 1983,[6] limiting the circumstances in which federal courts must abstain,[7] and minimizing the preclusive effects of state court judgments in federal court,[8] courts should be accessible to protect constitutional rights.

In contrast, the Warren Burger and William Rehnquist Courts frequently narrowed federal court jurisdiction, declaring that state courts were equally trustworthy in deciding constitutional claims. The Burger and Rehnquist Courts' confidence in the state courts is reflected in its restrictions on habeas corpus relief,[9] limitations placed on Section 1983 suits,[10] expansion of the abstention doctrines,[11] and an increase in the preclusive effects of state court decisions on the federal courts.[12]

Academic discussions about the scope of federal jurisdiction frequently turn on whether state courts are thought to be as likely as federal courts to vindicate federal rights. While Professor Burt Neuborne, known for his seminal 1977 article, *The Myth of Parity*, and other critics of the Burger and Rehnquist Courts' jurisdictional decisions have assailed the assumption of parity as being an unjustifiable myth, others, such as Professor Paul Bator, defend the deference to state courts that is inherent in the Burger Court's approach.

The past two decades have brought major legislative actions based on assumptions of parity, or the lack of it. The 1996 Antiterrorism and Effective Death Penalty Act dramatically cut back on the availability of habeas corpus. This included the imposition of a strict statute of limitations, preventing successive habeas corpus petitions, and limiting the scope of review in federal court.[13] These changes, in part, were based on the premise that state courts are adequate to uphold the constitutional rights of criminal defendants. Interestingly, a few years ago, Congress enacted the Class Action Fairness Act to shift class action suits from state to federal court.[14] This, too, was based on a perception of the differences between federal and state courts and the judgment that many state courts were likely to be more receptive to class action plaintiffs; the shift to federal court was meant to decrease such suits and their success.

There is much irony to these new anti–habeas corpus and anti–class action statutes, both favored by conservatives. The former tries to keep federal courts away from reviewing state court decisions and is based on a claim that state courts are the same as federal courts in their willingness to uphold the Constitution. The latter seeks to shift cases from state to federal courts based on the belief that federal courts will be more favorable to business interests. In both instances, of course, the laws were adopted based on the goals Congress wanted to achieve: making it more difficult to overturn convictions and making it harder to bring class action suits against businesses.

The debate over parity continues with little sign of abatement or resolution. Each side musters quotations from the Supreme Court, declaring either state court parity or federal court superiority. Each side develops reasons for its position on the comparative quality of the courts. But neither side advances the debate past an intuitive judgment as to whether state courts are equal to federal courts in their willingness and ability to protect federal rights. I fear that the debate over parity is permanently stalemated because parity is an empirical question—whether one court system is as good as another—for which there never can be any meaningful empirical measure.

Because the issue of parity cannot be resolved, it is worth considering whether it is possible and desirable to defined a role for the federal courts without evaluating the comparative abilities of the federal and state courts in constitutional cases.

In this chapter, I argue that there is a way to avoid the parity debate by focusing on federalism as empowerment. The first part of the chapter shows that current decisions and debates about the scope of federal jurisdiction have focused on the question of parity between federal and state courts. The second section demonstrates that the debate about parity is unresolvable because parity is an empirical question for which there is no empirical answer. The third part argues that the alternatives which have attempted to define a role for the federal courts without regard to parity are unsatisfactory. The final section sketches a new definition of the role of the federal courts. Simply stated, I argue that viewing federalism as empowerment should mean that litigants with federal constitutional claims would generally be able to choose the forum, federal or state, in which to resolve their disputes. This principle should guide Congress in enacting statutes defining federal court jurisdiction and the Supreme Court in fashioning jurisdictional rules where congressional intent is uncertain.

Federal courts operate the way they do not because they are better than state courts, but rather because they are potentially different. The role of the federal courts is to provide an alternative forum for the vindication of constitutional rights. I will argue that such an approach is desirable because it maximizes the opportunity for upholding the Constitution, increases litigant autonomy, enhances federalism, and is consistent with the existing constitutional and statutory structure. After defending this principle of litigant choice, I consider the practical implications of such an approach and respond to some of the likely objections.

Several caveats about the limited scope of this chapter are necessary at the outset. First, this chapter focuses on the role of the lower federal courts, especially the federal district courts and courts of appeals; it does not address, except tangentially, the role of the United States Supreme Court or the place of specialized federal tribunals. In part, this is because the Supreme Court's role in assuring the uniformity and supremacy of federal law has not been the subject of substantial debate. Also, most of the discussion about parity has centered on jurisdictional doctrines determining whether parties can litigate their claims in federal district courts instead of state courts, or whether state court decisions on constitutional issues should have preclusive effect in federal court.

Second, this chapter examines the role of the federal courts only with respect to constitutional issues. I do not consider, for example, federal jurisdiction over either diversity cases or cases arising under federal statutes (except for those statutes that provide the vehicle for the vindication of constitutional rights, such as 42 U.S.C., Section 1983, and the federal habeas corpus statutes). In part, the scope of this discussion is limited because the parity debate in the cases and scholarly literature has centered on constitutional cases. Further, the policy rationales for federal jurisdiction might be sufficiently different in diversity and statutory cases as to warrant separate treatment.

THE ROLE OF PARITY IN DETERMINING THE SCOPE OF FEDERAL JURISDICTION

The issue of the relative competence and trustworthiness of state and federal courts is not new. In fact, a major controversy in the drafting of the Constitution was whether lower federal courts were necessary. Although all present at the Constitutional Convention accepted the need for a federal judiciary,[15] some believed that it was sufficient to create only a United States Supreme Court to review state court judgments. John Rutledge, who would eventually become chief justice, declared at the Convention that "the State Tribunals might and ought to be left in all cases to decide in the first instances, the right of appeal to the supreme national tribunal being sufficient to secure the national rights and uniformity of Judgments." [16]

Rutledge's views were strongly disputed by those who expressed distrust in the ability and willingness of state courts to uphold federal law. James Madison declared, "Confidence cannot be put in the State Tribunals as guardians of the national authority and interests." [17] Madison argued that state judges, who were likely to be biased against federal law, could not be trusted and that appeal to the Supreme Court was inadequate to protect federal interests.[18] Ultimately, the Convention compromised between these two positions and, pursuant to Article III, gave Congress discretion to create lower federal courts. Such courts were created by the Judiciary Act of 1789, and have existed ever since.

The ratification of the Constitution and the enactment of the first Judiciary Act did not end the debate over the relative competence of federal and state courts. In one of the first significant cases before the Supreme Court concerning the scope of federal question jurisdiction, *Osborn v. Bank of the United States*, Daniel Webster argued to the Court that the "[C]onstitution itself supposes that [state judicial systems] may not always be worthy of confidence, where the rights and interests of the national government are drawn into question." [19]

Because the scope of federal government activity before the Civil War was limited, there were relatively few situations in which the Court directly confronted the issue of whether to trust state courts. Furthermore, the absence of general federal question jurisdiction prior to 1875—which in itself reflected trust in the state courts to adequately decide federal issues—limited the circumstances in which the Supreme Court faced questions about the relative competence of the state and federal judiciaries. Before the Civil War, the primary argument that state courts were not to be trusted to protect federal rights concerned perceived state court hostility to the rights of slave owners.[20] Many believed that federal courts were more disposed to protecting the federal rights slave owners had to the possession and return of their slaves.

Doubts about the ability and willingness of state courts to protect federal rights surfaced with special force after the Civil War. There was widespread concern, particularly in Congress, that state courts in the South could not be trusted to protect the rights of the newly freed slaves. Simply put, "the Thirty-ninth Congress thoroughly distrusted the State courts and expected nothing from them but resistance and harassment."[21] One congressman after another declared, as did Representative William L. Stoughton, that "the State authorities and local courts are unable or unwilling to protect the constitutional rights of individuals or punish those who violated these rights."[22] Thus, Congress enacted statutes such as the Civil Rights Act of 1871 (which contained what is now known as 42 U.S.C., Section 1983) with the explicit purpose of "throwing open the doors of the United States courts to individuals claiming to have been deprived of constitutional rights at the hands of state and local governments."[23] Likewise, congressional creation of habeas corpus relief for state prisoners and the establishment of general federal question jurisdiction were accompanied by statements of distrust in the state courts.[24]

Yet, the experience of Reconstruction and the fervent expressions of federal court superiority in Congress did not end the dispute over the relative competence of federal and state courts. Even in the midst of Reconstruction, in 1875, the Supreme Court declared that "it is not lightly to be presumed that Congress acted upon a principle which implies a distrust of [the] integrity or . . . ability of the state courts."[25]

During the early part of the twentieth century, when the Supreme Court aggressively protected economic rights, federal courts were perceived as more disposed than state courts to enforce liberties such as freedom of contract and property rights.[26]

But the issue of parity has taken on special importance since the outset of the Warren Court in the early 1950s. In the past half century, the Supreme Court has relied frequently on explicit statements of federal court superiority as a basis for expanding federal jurisdiction, and conversely, the Court has relied on claims of state court parity as justification for restricting federal jurisdiction. Often parity has been at the core of the disagreement between the majority and the dissent.

Why did this issue become so important in the past fifty years? First, the application of the Bill of Rights to the states, through the incorporation process, greatly expanded the opportunity for state violations of constitutional liberties. Early in American history, the Supreme Court held that the Bill of Rights did not apply to state government actions.[27] But beginning late in the nineteenth century, slowly at first, and then at an accelerating pace after World War II, the Supreme Court held that the term "liberty" in the due process clause of the Fourteenth Amendment "incorporated" provisions of the Bill of Rights. Through this interpretive process, the Supreme Court began applying almost all of the Bill of Rights to the states, including most of the provisions dealing with criminal procedure.[28] As the opportunity for claims of state violations of constitutional rights thus increased, so did concern over whether state courts were adequate to the task of assuring sufficient protection.

A second reason this debate became so significant was the fact that the Supreme Court's expansion of individual liberties also created more opportunities for claims that states had violated constitutional rights. Especially during the Warren era, the Court interpreted the Constitution to include rights such as privacy and travel as well as procedural protections. Usually these rights were recognized by the United States Supreme Court in the process of declaring state statutes unconstitutional. Thus, there was concern over whether state courts would adequately enforce and protect the newly recognized liberties.

Third, and probably most critically, state resistance to civil rights, especially in the South, renewed distrust of the state courts. The post–World War II civil rights movement—from the invalidation of the Jim Crow laws that segregated every aspect of Southern life, to the school desegregation decisions and the civil rights marches and protests—highlighted that blacks in the South often were deprived of their constitutional rights and that they lacked adequate protection in state courts.

Together, these pressures raised the question as to whether state courts are equal to the federal judiciary in their willingness and ability to protect constitutional rights. At a time of increasing litigation, the Supreme Court was called on to define federal court jurisdiction and frequently did so with reference to conclusions about the relative competence and trustworthiness of federal and state courts. What is most striking about the Supreme Court's statements about parity is their inconsistency. There are as many declarations that state courts are equal to federal courts as there are statements that federal courts are superior to state courts in protecting federal rights.[29] The only pattern is that when the Court rules in favor of allowing federal jurisdiction it usually rejects the assumption of parity. But when it holds against permitting jurisdiction, the court declares that state courts are equal to federal courts in upholding the Constitution.

In general, the Warren Court expanded federal jurisdiction, relying on the premise that federal courts are necessary to vindicate constitutional rights.[30] The Burger and Rehnquist Courts, in contrast, rejected attempts to expand federal court jurisdiction, and often narrowed it, concluding that state courts could be trusted to adequately protect federal interests.[31] Yet, regardless of the position adopted by the particular Court, there was no unanimity or consistency with respect to rulings or declarations about parity. In almost every case there were dissents: when the Court ruled in favor of federal court jurisdiction, the dissents proclaimed that state court parity made federal jurisdiction unnecessary;[32] when the Court held against federal jurisdiction, the dissents challenged the majority's assumption of parity.[33] Furthermore, the Warren Court sometimes found parity,[34] and the Burger and Rehnquist Courts occasionally expanded federal court jurisdiction based on express statements that the federal judiciary is the primary guardian of constitutional rights.[35]

The result is that the Court's statements about parity have been totally inconsistent and irreconcilable. Nonetheless, the Court has repeatedly justified its holdings by invoking conclusions about the relative competence of federal and state courts.

A powerful example of this concerns the availability of habeas corpus relief for state prisoners. The Supreme Court has based its rulings

concerning the scope of habeas corpus upon judgments about the trustworthiness of state courts. Discussions concerning parity have been especially critical when the Court confronts the question of a defendant relitigating, via habeas corpus, issues that were already raised and litigated
in state court. The principle of collateral estoppel generally precludes a
party from relitigating a matter that previously was presented to a court
and decided by it. (Estoppel is a legal impediment to something proclaimed or denied because one's words or actions indicate otherwise.)
Brown v. Allen, decided in 1953, created an important exception to this
principle of finality for habeas petitions.[36] The Supreme Court, in an
opinion by Justice Felix Frankfurter, observed that "even the highest
state courts" have failed to give adequate protection to federal constitutional rights.[37] As such, the Court concluded that federal habeas corpus
review exists to remedy state court disregard or violations of a defendant's rights. *Brown v. Allen* thus held that state prisoners could present claims of denials of constitutional rights in federal court on habeas
corpus, even if they had fully litigated those arguments in state court. As
Professor Henry Hart notes a few years later, Brown established that "a
state prisoner ought to have an opportunity for a hearing on a federal
constitutional claim in a federal court."[38]

In marked contrast, the Burger Court in *Stone v. Powell* held that
Fourth Amendment search and seizure claims may not be relitigated
on habeas corpus if the state court provided an opportunity for full
and fair litigation of the issue.[39] In partially overruling *Brown v. Allen*, the Court concluded that state prisoners generally should not be
able to relitigate a contention that evidence obtained on the basis of an
unconstitutional search and seizure was improperly admitted at trial.
The Court emphasized that exclusionary rule claims do not relate to the
accuracy of the fact-finding process, rejecting the argument that state
judges would be less vigilant in protecting federal constitutional rights.
Justice Lewis Powell, writing for the majority in *Stone v. Powell,* said
that the Court is "unwilling to assume that there now exists a general
lack of appropriate sensitivity to constitutional rights in the trial and appellate courts of the several States."[40] Furthermore, the Court declared
that there is "no intrinsic reason why the fact that a man is a federal

judge should make him more competent, or conscientious, or learned with respect to constitutional claims than his neighbor in the state court-house." [41] Thus, *Brown* allowed relitigation of constitutional claims because of a belief that state courts were inadequately protecting rights; *Stone* found relitigation of Fourth Amendment claims in federal court unnecessary because state courts were fully able and willing to decide such issues.

Subsequently, the Rehnquist Court further limited habeas corpus for state prisoners, again based on the assumption that state court proceedings were adequate. [42] In 1996, Congress went even further in restricting habeas corpus in the Antiterrorism and Effective Death Penalty Act. The more state courts are perceived as equal to federal courts in their willingness to uphold constitutional claims, the less necessary habeas corpus becomes.

Parity has been central to the Supreme Court's consideration of many other issues concerning aspects of federal jurisdiction. Of course, by arguing that parity has been a key issue in decisions about federal jurisdiction, I do not mean to imply that it has been the only concern. The Warren, Burger, and Rehnquist Courts were influenced by other major considerations, such as the need for procedural protections for criminal defendants, the desirability of the exclusionary rule, and the benefits of the many tiers of review. But there is no doubt that the question of parity has been one very crucial consideration in the Supreme Court's decisions concerning federal court jurisdiction. If federal courts are viewed as superior in protecting federal rights, then expansive federal jurisdiction seems necessary. But to the extent that state courts are assumed to be equally able and willing to protect federal rights, then federal court jurisdiction is far less significant.

PARITY: A FUTILE DEBATE

Despite decades of arguments in both court opinions and scholarly literature, the debate remains unresolved as to whether state courts are equal to federal courts in their ability and willingness to protect federal rights. Each side postulates its position, marshals appropriate supporting quotations and citations, and criticizes decisions and articles that reflect its view. But that is as far as the dialogue goes. The debate over parity is the legal equivalent to the Miller Lite commercial of years' back, in which one side yells, "Tastes great!" and the other screams, "Less filling!!!" As the two sides of the parity debate indignantly shout, "Federal courts are better!" and "State courts are just as good!" the dialogue appears stalemated, fixed in a litany that appears as unresolvable and unchangeable as the scripts for the beer commercial.

The only change has been that now conservatives may be more inclined toward federal courts in some instances, as Republican appointees have increasingly become the majority in most circuits and districts. Thus, it was not surprising that it was a Republican Congress that passed the Class Action Fairness Act to shift large class action suits from state to federal court. This occurred because of a perception that some state courts were too pro-plaintiff. But even the debate over this act was very much centered on the relative merits of state as opposed to federal courts.

I contend that focusing on parity is futile, because ultimately the issue of parity is an empirical question for which no empirical measure is possible. Lacking a method to determine whether state courts are as good or whether federal courts are better, judges and scholars are left with their intuitions about the comparative virtues of the two systems.

To demonstrate this, first I'd like to explain why parity is an unanswerable empirical question. Then I want to discuss why no empirical attempts to answer the question—such as historical evidence or comparisons of institutional characteristics of state and federal courts—can end the deadlock. Saying that one thing is as good or better than another requires criteria for comparison and a standard for evaluation relative to the criteria. Comparing automobiles, for instance, initially requires criteria—for example, safety, reliability, cost, and so on—and then a basis for measuring the performance of those factors Likewise, claiming that one court system is as good or better than another requires a definition of *good* and a basis for evaluation relative to that standard. Yet, such a yardstick and data for comparing federal and state courts do not exist and are unlikely to be devised.

Defining Quality in the Parity Debate

The first problem with such a comparison is the difficulty in defining *quality*. By what criteria are federal and state courts to be compared? Because there rarely is consensus as to what constitutes a "correct" decision, measurement surely cannot take the form of counting the number of "right" results produced by each system. Nor is there likely to be meaningful comparison in terms of the technical competence of the state and federal judges. Devising a useful definition of judicial competence seems elusive; even if such a definition existed, the question would remain whether such differences really matter in determining outcomes.

Some who claim that federal courts should have a preeminent role in hearing constitutional claims do have a definition of quality. The core of their argument is that federal courts are more likely than state courts to rule in favor of individuals asserting constitutional claims. That is, by their definition of quality, the better court is the one that is more likely to rule against the government and in favor of an individual claiming a deprivation of a constitutional right or a denial of equality. Professor Burt Neuborne, for instance, explicitly adopts this definition of quality: "Comparative qualitative analysis, of course, presupposes the existence of a consensus as to what we mean by 'better.' My definition . . . views the better forum as the one more likely to assign a very high value to the protection of the individual, even the unreasonable or dangerous individual, against the collective, so that the definition of the individual right in question will receive its most expansive reading and its most energetic enforcement. Such a definition of 'better' is based on an assumption that it is socially desirable to route controversies involving asserted constitutional rights of individuals to those judicial forums most likely to resolve them in favor of the individual." [43]

Neuborne's definition of quality is not universally accepted, however. Those who champion the state courts might respond that constitutional cases often involve the balancing of government interests against individual liberties, and that it is wrong to presuppose that decisions in favor of the government are preferable. Professor Paul Bator makes exactly this argument. [44] Furthermore, Bator argues that the Constitution contains other values, espousing, for example, the importance of limitations on the Federal government's powers, and that state judges are likely to be more sensitive to these goals than are their federal counterparts. Thus, Bator challenges Neuborne's definition of quality and concludes that "the claim that cases should be channeled to the federal courts because of the special receptivity of federal judges to constitutional values may embody a narrow and partisan vision of what constitutional values are."[45] According to Bator, because neither set of results is demonstrably preferable, federal and state court systems should be treated as equals; both employ processes worthy of respect, even if they might yield different outcomes.

Although I believe a strong case can be made in favor of Professor Neuborne's definition and the position that the judicial system should maximize the opportunity for protecting individual rights, it is important to recognize that such a definition would be highly disputed. Ultimately, the argument over quality would dissolve into a dialogue about the underlying purposes of the Constitution and world views about the desirable content of constitutional decisions. Such discussions undoubtedly are enlightening but are unlikely to yield an accepted measure for comparing the quality of the courts.

Aggregate Measures

A second problem with empirically determining whether there is parity is that even if quality could be defined, and even if it could be measured, at best the result would be an aggregate comparison of all state courts with all federal courts. As the term *parity* is used, it refers to an overall comparison of the federal courts with the composite of all of the state judiciaries. The state courts differ greatly from one another, just as the federal courts are not homogeneous. There is an enormous variance among the different states and many federal districts in their disposition toward protecting individual rights.[46] Some state courts are more disposed toward upholding individual liberties than are some federal courts.[47] There are many examples of state courts that have recognized and protected constitutional rights that the federal courts have rejected.[48]

In fact, even if a particular state's court system is relatively similar to the corresponding federal method, there might be differences depending on the issue examined. A specific state court, for example, might be more likely than the federal court to side with an individual in one type of constitutional case, but the federal court in that state might be more protective of constitutional rights on other issues.

I question the usefulness of an aggregate evaluation of court systems as large and varied as those of the fifty states and ninety-one federal districts. Even if a net comparison could be done, it might hide true areas of concern. Imagine, for instance, that the aggregate data demonstrated that, overall, the state courts were as likely as federal courts to protect constitutional rights. Statistically, that would demonstrate parity as that term is commonly used. Yet, it is possible that such data might reflect that there are many state courts which are slightly better than the federal jurisdictions, but a few that are far worse in protecting individual liberties. In other words, according to this hypothetical data, in most instances the choice between federal and state courts generally would not matter, but in some states the availability of a federal forum would be essential for vindicating individual liberties. Overall data showing parity would mask a substantial need for federal jurisdiction in some areas.

Similarly, aggregate data might mask differences among the court systems as to particular issues. Conceivably, the data could show that state courts tend to side with individual rights' claims involving economic liberties, but federal courts tend to do better in protecting political liberties. A net comparison between state and federal courts and their overall likelihood to rule in favor of a constitutional right might hide important differences that could be crucial in deciding jurisdictional rules.

One could, of course, try to assess variance among the states, such as through complex statistical analysis. The measurement could be broken down into an assessment of performance on particular issues. This, however, would be a different inquiry from the current focus on parity, which is an overall comparison of the state with the federal system with regard to protecting individual liberties. Furthermore, if the goal is, as Neuborne argues, maximizing the protection of individual rights, it is undesirable to consign individuals to a less capable court system because in other areas of the country that level of court might be superior. Optimally, cases would be channeled to the particular court in each area that offered the best chance of protecting rights.

Empirical Comparisons

Finally, and most critically, even if quality were defined and even if aggregate measures were meaningful, an accurate empirical comparison of federal and state courts in constitutional cases does not exist and, methodologically, probably cannot be done. As Professor Martin Redish observes in 1980: "There are, to my knowledge, no statistical data to support the assertion that federal courts are, on the whole, better equipped to guard federal interests than their state counterparts. Indeed it would be difficult to devise a system of measurement which could be used to answer that question empirically."[49]

The most likely methodology for measuring federal and state judicial performance in constitutional cases would be to select some court systems and compare how they ruled in particular kinds of cases. Such a study, however, likely would be plagued by so many basic methodological problems as to render its conclusions—for or against parity—meaningless.

The Solimine-Walker Investigation

To demonstrate this, consider the one study that explicitly set out to quantitatively compare constitutional rulings by federal and state courts. In the early 1980s, Professors Michael Solimine and James Walker attempted to measure empirically whether state courts are less competent or more hostile toward constitutional rights than federal courts.[50] They compared the rulings of federal district courts with state courts of appeals and state supreme courts as to several particular constitutional issues. Specifically, they examined the number of times the selected courts ruled in favor of individual rights in cases involving the First Amendment, the Fourth Amendment, and the equal protection clause of the Fourteenth Amendment.[51]

The authors found that in their sample, overall, federal courts decided in favor of the constitutional claim 41 percent of the time, while state courts ruled in favor of the constitutional claim in 32 percent of the cases.[52] They concluded that this difference was not statistically significant, because taken together the state and federal courts in their study decided in favor of the constitutional claim 36 percent of the time, placing the state courts' 32 percent record only slightly below this benchmark. Thus, Professors Solimine and Walker contend that their study establishes "that state courts are no more 'hostile' to the vindication of federal rights than are their federal counterparts . . . and that 'parity' does exist between federal and state courts." [53]

As I've indicated, the Solimine-Walker investigation has severe methodological problems. Although some of the pitfalls might be corrected in future studies, many seem likely to plague any attempt to quantitatively compare federal and state courts. Because this is the one study that purports to empirically prove the existence of parity, it warrants detailed analysis. First, by focusing only on reported court decisions, the authors ignore cases that settle out of court or might not even be brought before a judge because of perceived judicial hostility. The investigation examines only those cases in which the federal district court, or the state court of appeals or supreme court, issued a written decision. Differences in the courts, however, might affect dispositions prior to decisions and might produce dissimilar cases for written rulings. For example, if litigants perceive the federal courts as more favorably disposed toward plaintiffs with constitutional claims than are state courts, then defendants in federal court and plaintiffs in state court are much more likely to settle. Parties always compare the costs of additional litigation with what they are likely to gain by trying or appealing the case as opposed to settling it. At the very least, this means that counting only those cases brought to trial does not fully reflect the actual differences between the two court systems.

Furthermore, settlements could mean that the federal and state courts in the study were not confronted with similar cases. If, because of the parties' perceptions of likely outcomes, a higher percentage of defendants settle in federal court and a higher percentage of plaintiffs settle in state court, the remaining cases would not be identical. Federal courts would be left with comparatively weaker constitutional claims and state courts with comparatively stronger ones. Even if the courts ruled in favor of the constitutional claims in the same percentage of cases, the differences among the cases would prevent the study from proving anything about the actual quality of the courts. In fact, if federal courts had weaker cases for the party bringing the claim and the state courts had stronger cases, an identical percentage of rulings in favor of the constitutional claim would seem to disprove parity.

Similarly, by focusing on state courts of appeals and supreme courts (a problem more fully discussed below), the study ignores the fact that the perceived predisposition of the courts might keep appeals from ever being filed. For example, if the state courts of appeals and state supreme courts were likely to rule in favor of plaintiffs' constitutional claims, then in some instances, losing defendants might not appeal, figuring that their chances of prevailing on appeal did not justify the cost. As such, measuring only the cases brought to trial would underestimate the proclivity of the courts to uphold constitutional rights. Conversely, if the state courts of appeals and supreme courts were hostile to federal rights, then losing plaintiffs with constitutional claims might choose not to appeal. Again, leaving untried cases out of the sample and looking solely to decisions from tried cases would serve to underestimate the courts' hostility.

A second methodological problem with the investigation is that it does not account for possible differences in the content of the cases. For example, the study focused on both civil and criminal cases. Criminal cases involve instances in which individuals are prosecuted for violating criminal statutes and individuals raise constitutional claims by challenging the investigative or trial procedures, or by challenging the constitutionality of the statute they are prosecuted for violating. State criminal prosecutions cannot be removed to federal court, and federal courts cannot enjoin prosecutions under unconstitutional state statutes. Hence, federal courts are hearing criminal prosecutions under federal statutes, and state courts are deciding criminal cases brought under state statutes. The cases might not be comparable because Congress and the state legislatures might not be equally likely to enact unconstitutional statutes. If, for instance, state legislatures are more likely to produce constitutionally defective statutes than is Congress, even state courts more hostile to federal rights still might declare a greater number of statutes to be unconstitutional.

The civil cases also might vary so much in content as to invalidate a comparison between federal and state courts based on the decisions reached. It is quite possible that the federal courts were hearing civil cases in which the plaintiffs' complaints presented a constitutional claim, whereas the state courts were hearing constitutional claims raised as defenses. Currently, federal and state courts have concurrent jurisdiction over civil cases raising constitutional claims. That is, the plaintiff may file such a case in either federal or state court, and if it is filed in state court, the defendant may remove it to federal court. Therefore, the plaintiff may choose to litigate in federal court if that forum is perceived as more hospitable to constitutional claims. If the plaintiff believes he or she has a better chance of prevailing in state court, the case would be filed there, but the defendant would theoretically remove it to federal court. By this analysis, there would be far more civil cases raising constitutional claims in federal court than in state court because either the plaintiff or the defendant could bring a case to the federal forum. The data from Professors Solimine and Walker confirms this hypothesis.

However, the cases that cannot be removed from state to federal court are those in which the constitutional claim is not apparent on the face of the plaintiff's complaint, such as when it arises as a defense. Thus, federal courts would be hearing cases in which the plaintiff's complaint alleged a violation of a constitutional right, but the state course might be hearing a disproportionate number of cases in which the constitutional issue arose as a defense. This might mean that the substantive content of the claims could vary because different kinds of constitutional arguments might appear as defenses rather than as the basis for complaints. Additionally, there might be a difference in the way a court treats constitutional issues depending on whether it is raised by the plaintiff or as a defense. In other words, the results of the study might reflect variations unrelated to the quality of the courts.

A third methodological problem with the study is that it does not provide a measure of the quality of the federal versus state court completely independent of each other. For example, except for Fourth Amendment search and seizure claims, constitutional claims can be relitigated in federal court by state prisoners in criminal cases on habeas corpus. Therefore, the study's finding that state courts are disposed toward constitutional claims in criminal cases that raise the First Amendment might be explained by the state courts' awareness of federal habeas corpus review in such cases. As such, it would be wrong to use the study to support limiting federal court habeas corpus relitigation based on a conclusion of state court parity.

A fourth methodological problem with the study is that the aggregate data supporting parity hide differences between the courts and the types of cases they likely confronted. If one examines specific areas in the investigation, it becomes clear that Professors Solimine and Walker find substantial differences, in fact, between the state and federal courts. For example, in civil cases, the federal courts ruled in favor of First Amendment claims 54 percent of the time, while the state courts in such cases decided in favor of First Amendment claims 40 percent of the time.[54] In equal protection cases, federal courts were twice as likely to rule in favor of constitutional claims than were the state courts.[55] These statistics should give one pause before one concludes that federal and state courts are fungible.

Moreover, the area in which there was the least difference between federal and state courts involved Fourth Amendment claims raised in criminal cases.[56] This might indicate parity between federal and state courts on this issue, or again, it might reflect differences in the content of the cases. Fourth Amendment claims usually involve objections by defendants to the admissibility of evidence on the grounds that the evidence was unconstitutionally obtained. Assume that state and local police are more egregious in their violations of the Fourth Amendment than federal agents. Even when the federal courts are generally more likely than the state courts to rule in favor of a Fourth Amendment claim in any particular case, the overall data might still show a relatively high degree of state court pro-defendant rulings because of the extreme violations of the Fourth Amendment. Again, the failure to control for the content of the cases, especially in light of possible differences in behavior between state and local police and federal agents, makes comparisons in Fourth Amendment cases suspect.

The study's choice to compare federal district courts with state courts of appeals and supreme courts poses a final, particularly significant, methodological dilemma. At minimum, this is a curious basis for evaluation if the goal is comparing federal court systems with state courts. Logically, the comparison would either include the courts of appeals in both systems or it would focus only on federal district courts and state trial courts. The study thus is structured in a way that ignores any defects in state trial courts and any benefits of federal appellate review.

The failure to examine state trial courts is an especially serious flaw in the study. If state trial courts were hostile to federal claims, such an attitude might be reflected in fact-finding related to constitutional claims. Because appeals courts generally review only questions of law, substantial evidence of non-parity would be overlooked. A potentially large bias in the state system against federal claims would not be reflected in the data measuring appeals court decisions.

Also, if state trial courts disproportionately ruled against constitutional claims, a number of losing parties might not appeal—perhaps because of the cost or frustration or, as described above, because of the perceived improbability of reversal in the court of appeals. Again, with respect to cases not appealed, a bias in the state system against federal claims would not be revealed in a study examining the courts of appeals.

Furthermore, even if state courts of appeals corrected all errors of state trial courts so that the entire state court system was equal to federal district courts, it is questionable whether this would really establish parity. It would mean that an individual with a constitutional claim has as great a chance of prevailing after litigating through two or three tiers of the state courts as he or she does by going in the first instance to the federal district court. Because the additional litigation imposes extra costs on the individuals and the court system, and delays the vindication of rights, the federal district court would be preferred over a state system where vindication of constitutional rights required appeals.

Solimine and Walker attribute their failure to consider state trial courts, in part, to the almost complete absence of written state trial court opinions.[57] This illustrates one of the inherent problems in trying to compare the two court systems.

I have focused at length on the methodological problems with this study, not only to refute its claim of empirically establishing parity, but more critically, to illustrate the difficulties in any quantitative comparison of court systems. Most of the failings described above—failure to account for out-of-court dispositions, to control for the content of the cases, to assess the courts independent of each other, to separate out the data—likely would confound other efforts to compare empirically the state and federal courts.

Alternative Empirical Measures

Because of the difficulties in directly proving one court system to be better than or as good as another, some scholars have devised alternative empirical measures which they claim serve to establish or refute parity. One type of study involves surveys of attorney attitudes concerning differences between state and federal courts. For example, Thomas Marvell, in his 1984 investigation, contacted attorneys who litigated student rights cases and asked them their reasons for selecting one forum over another.[58] Over 50 percent of the attorneys said they believed federal courts were more likely than the state courts to rule in favor of constitutional claims. Thus, Marvell concludes that his survey "presents empirical research which shows that parity does not exist."[59]

For several reasons, this study, and other opinion surveys, are unlikely to be accepted as proving the superiority of federal courts. Nor would opinion polls demonstrating lawyer confidence in state courts prove parity. At most, such surveys only demonstrate what attorneys think about parity; they do not and cannot prove anything about the actual differences between the courts. Those who believe that state courts are as likely to protect rights as are federal courts would argue that the attorneys' judgments lack empirical support and should be given little weight in determining whether parity exists.

Also, the Marvell study could be criticized as establishing only that at one point in time federal courts were perceived as being more hospitable to one type of claim, not that federal courts are inherently more likely to protect rights than are state courts. As the composition of the federal judiciary changes, as a result of substantial appointments by conservative presidents, for example, then the preferences could shift. Attorneys litigating student rights cases might thus prefer, at certain points in time, to proceed in state courts.

For this reason, survey research is unhelpful as a basis for formulating jurisdictional rules. Opinions of attorneys about the respective court systems probably will vary over time. Jurisdictional rules, however, are not likely to change each time there is a shift in attorney attitudes.

I am not arguing that the attorneys were incorrect in their perceptions or that the survey did not accurately measure their attitudes. Rather, the study is simply not likely to be accepted as proving anything about the actual comparative quality of state and federal courts.

The final type of empirical study compares U.S. Supreme Court reversal rates of state supreme courts with reversal rates in the United States Court of Appeals.[60] If the Supreme Court reverses the federal courts of appeals as frequently, or more so, than it does the state courts, then it is claimed that parity is proven. Conversely, if the state supreme court decisions are overturned more often, then it is argued that federal court superiority is established.

Such studies suffer from many serious flaws. First, comparing reversal rates of decisions by federal courts of appeals and state supreme courts ignores differences between the trial courts. As explained earlier, if one system's trial courts are more hostile to constitutional rights than the other's courts, this hostility might be reflected in adverse fact-finding or discouraged litigants choosing not to appeal—factors that would not be reflected in a study of appeals courts decisions.

Second, by focusing only on those cases in which decisions were reached and by ignoring out-of-court dispositions, the study may not be measuring substantial differences between the state and federal appeals courts. If a state's supreme court was perceived as hostile to federal claims, then fewer appeals would be filed in the state courts by those with constitutional arguments than in a system where the state's appeals courts were perceived as more receptive. In other words, evidence of the state court's hostility would not be reflected in the study. Moreover, if state courts were perceived as more hostile and federal courts more hospitable, then appeals in state court would be filed only when there were relatively strong claims, but a greater number of somewhat weaker appeals might be filed in federal court.

Third, the percentage of reversals might merely reflect the Supreme Court's assumption of parity or its deference to state courts. For example, perhaps because of considerations of federalism and comity, the Supreme Court might use a different standard in reviewing decisions from state courts than decisions from federal courts. Thus, there could be a number of instances in which the Court might reverse a decision had it come from the federal court of appeals but might have chosen not to take the case at all had it been litigated in the state courts. Hence, there would be a lower rate of state court versus federal court reversals. This is not because of differences or similarities between the courts, but because of the Supreme Court's approach to review.

The flaws in these studies are more than the kind of minor methodological problems that can be identified in all quantitative research. They are basic difficulties that undermine the reliability of the conclusions and make it quite unlikely that the studies will be persuasive to any except those who already share the position "proven" by the research. Although parity is an empirical question, no empirical answer seems possible.

Judicial History and Observation in the Parity Debate

Recognizing the improbability of empirically establishing state court parity, or federal court superiority, several commentators have tried to prove their assertions by using other types of evidence. Those who argue that federal courts are preferable to state courts in vindicating constitutional rights most frequently focus on the institutional characteristics of the two court systems with respect to judicial history and observation.[61] Unfortunately, neither form of proof is likely to resolve the parity debate.

First, those who believe the federal courts should have the preeminent role in enforcing constitutional rights describe a history of state court hostility to federal claims. Professor Neuborne shows that before the Civil War, the federal forum was used to implement the fugitive slave laws, which enforced the rights of slave owners under the Constitution's fugitive slave clause.[62] In that instance, access to state courts was sought by the antislavery movement, which perceived the states as less likely to enforce federal laws that supported slavery. After the Civil War, the perception of the relative trustworthiness of the federal and state courts shifted and federal courts were turned to because of the great hostility in the Southern states to former slaves. During the Lochner era, when the Supreme Court was regularly invalidating economic regulations, Professor Neuborne argues, federal courts were more disposed than were the state courts to protecting the economic rights established by the Supreme Court. There, of course, is evidence of substantial state court hostility toward protecting the rights of blacks during the civil rights movement of the 1960s. Based on this history, some scholars maintain that federal courts should be available to safeguard constitutional liberties.[63]

However, others deny that there is a consistent pattern of state court hostility to federal rights. Professors Solimine and Walker argue: "Doubters of parity, however, can marshal no evidence to suggest that state courts continued to be systematically hostile to federal rights after Reconstruction. To the extent that the hostility was revived in some state courts during the 1950's and 1960's, it was an unfortunate aberration not reflected on a nationwide basis today." [64] In fact, Solimine and Walker argue that the Southern states' hostility toward civil rights during the 1960s was not, for the most part, reflected in their state courts.[65] Ultimately, resolving the historical dispute would require a comparison of the federal and state court decisions during that time period and would entail all of the empirical problems described above.

However, those who proclaim that there is parity between federal and state courts dismiss the past as irrelevant. They contend that even if state courts once were hostile to federal rights, times have changed. They argue, for example, that there has been a steady increase in the quality of state judiciaries.[66]

Additionally, there have been changes in the composition of the federal judiciary. Republicans have occupied the White House for twenty of the past twenty-eight years, and Presidents Ronald Reagan, George H. W. Bush, and George W. Bush have consistently appointed conservative judges. Studies demonstrate that judges appointed by Republicans are more likely to vote in a conservative manner and against individual liberties than their Democratic counterparts.[67] Thus, while the judges appointed by Presidents Franklin Roosevelt, Harry Truman, Robert Kennedy, and Lyndon Johnson, constituting most of the federal bench during the 1960s, might have been more disposed toward individual rights than the state courts during that time, there is no reason to believe the situation is the same today.

History will not resolve the parity debate. Those who defend state court parity often argue that the past is irrelevant in evaluating contemporary courts. They contend that "whatever the historical scorecard of state courts in enforcing federal rights, such a record has only a tangential relevance to the modern debate over parity."[68]

Institutional Characteristics of the Two Judicial Systems

A different explanation for why federal courts are more willing and able to protect constitutional rights involves a comparison of institutional characteristics of the two judicial systems. The contention is that the many differences between the federal and state courts make the federal judiciary more predisposed than the state courts to ruling in favor of constitutional claims.

One such difference is the political insulation of the federal judiciary. Federal judges have life tenure, whereas judges in over forty states face some form of electoral review. In constitutional cases, courts often are asked to act in a counter-majoritarian fashion, protecting minorities or individual rights from discrimination or infringement by elected officials. The claim is that federal judges, with their jobs and salaries assured by Article III of the Constitution, are more willing to defy political pressure and vindicate constitutional rights than are state judges, who must face the voters.[69]

Another alleged difference is that, overall, federal judges are of a higher quality than their state counterparts.[70] In part, this stems from the differences in the selection processes used for federal and state judges. The federal selection process, which generally includes bar association review, evaluation by senators, and scrutiny by the incumbent administration, is thought to yield more uniformly qualified judges than the state processes.[71] Moreover, the existence in most states of electoral selection or review of judges is thought to deter some highly qualified individuals who do not want to participate in such a political process.

Other factors, too, are believed responsible for a more uniformly well-qualified federal judiciary. The smaller number of federal judges enhances the prestige of serving on that bench and thus attracts the most qualified individuals to federal judgeships. Some believe that there is a strong relationship between exclusivity, prestige, and the quality of the judges. The generally larger salaries paid at the federal level as compared with those at the state also are thought to yield higher quality judges. Furthermore, it is argued that institutional factors, such as more and better law clerks, lower caseloads, and more frequent handling of constitutional issues, may produce more technical competence in federal courts than in the state judiciaries.[72]

Finally, it is claimed that the "psychological mind-set" of federal judges makes them more likely to rule in favor of constitutional claims.[73] Federal judges, it is suggested, are more likely to see their primary role as upholding the Constitution than are their state counterparts.

It is argued that these factors, taken together, make the federal courts superior to the state courts for the protection of constitutional rights. No less than the American Law Institute concluded in its study of the federal courts: "[I]t is difficult to avoid concluding that the federal courts are more likely to apply federal law sympathetically and understandingly than are state courts."[74]

Yet, despite all of these factors, the Supreme Court frequently has concluded that state judges are as able and willing to protect constitutional rights as are federal judges. Likewise, scholars arguing in favor of parity dispute the above factors and especially contest whether they cause federal courts to be superior to state courts in protecting rights. They contend that state systems as a whole are as likely to rule in favor of constitutional liberties as are federal systems. For example, they dispute claims about the superior quality of federal judges. Professor Bator writes: "State supreme court justices as a group are as well paid and have as much prestige as federal judges. Those that I have met seem to me to be as expert on issues of federal constitutional laws as are federal judges. . . . [T]he case for channeling cases to the federal courts on the ground that sufficiently competent and expert consideration of constitutional issues cannot be expected from the state appellate courts has simply not been made." [75]

Advocates of the parity position also deny that electoral accountability of state judges influences their rulings in constitutional cases. Professors Solimine and Walker write that "[i]t does not follow . . . that elections of state judges . . . will influence the subsequent decisions of elected judges. Recent scholarship indicates a weak linkage . . . between environmental variables such as public opinion, and court functions." [76]

Moreover, it is argued that even if there are differences between state and federal courts, these disparities do not necessarily translate into federal courts being more disposed to protecting federal constitutional rights. Even if federal judges are of a higher quality than state judges because of greater salary, more prestige, or better institutional support, that does not mean that there are differences in the way the judges handle constitutional cases. In fact, there is no reason to believe that better judges are necessarily more disposed toward safeguarding individual liberties.

Advocates who contend that there is parity between federal and state courts argue that other factors that are the same in the two systems— such as the oath to uphold the Constitution, the judicial role, and the transmission of information from attorneys—are more important in determining results than any differences between the courts. [77] Thus, defenders of parity argue that there are minimal variations between the state and federal benches, and those differences that do exist have little effect on the decision-making process.

The problem is that without empirical measurement, each side of the parity debate simply has an intuitive judgment about whether the institutional differences between federal and state courts matter in constitutional cases. Each side explains its position, but neither has any way to prove it or to refute the opposing claim. Justices and commentators have impressionistic judgments about the relative abilities and proclivities of federal and state courts, but there seems to be no way to confirm or dislodge those impressions. For this reason, one group continually asserts that there is no parity, while the other proclaims that parity exists, and the debate stagnates. Therefore, discussions about parity seem futile.

There are many possible directions for analysis in light of this conclusion. One possibility would be to try, again, to devise an empirical measure of federal and state court behavior in constitutional cases to try to prove or deny parity. Although it would be expensive, better studies can be undertaken. For example, surveys should not be limited to cases in which there were written opinions. Also, there should be careful "matching" of cases to assure similar content and data that accounts for possible differences between geographic areas.

Another possibility is simply to continue to have jurisdictional rules based on assumptions about parity. One might conclude that parity must remain the key question in determining the scope of federal jurisdiction. If federal courts are superior to state courts, jurisdictional rules should reflect this, but if state courts are as good, then federal jurisdiction is far less important. By this view, the issue of parity cannot be avoided even if the conclusion is based on intuition. After all, I have shown only that the parity debate is stalemated, not that parity is the wrong question.

Yet another alternative is to try to find an acceptable way to define a role for the federal courts without regard to parity. In the next section, I explain why these efforts have so far failed. In the final section of this chapter, I argue that looking at federalism as being about empowerment offers a way of defining federal court jurisdiction without regard to parity.

ATTEMPTS TO DEFINE A ROLE FOR THE FEDERAL COURTS WITHOUT REGARD TO PARITY

At least three principles attempt, in constitutional cases, to define a role for the federal courts irrespective of their comparative quality with state courts. The first, "comity," requires that federal courts respect the dignity of state courts as those of another sovereign and avoid friction with state judiciaries. The second is based on the principle of "legislative supremacy" and asks the Supreme Court to implement congressional decisions about federal jurisdiction and not make independent judgments about parity. Third, a presumption can be made either against or in favor of federal court jurisdiction; it can be argued that the structure and history of the Constitution gives state or federal courts the preeminent role in deciding constitutional issues.

The Three Principles and the Federal Role

None of the above perspectives actually succeeds in avoiding the question of parity, however. In fact, each makes implicit assumptions about the parity issue.

1. Comity

The Burger Court frequently stated that federal court jurisdiction must be exercised in a manner that does not insult the state courts or cause friction with them.[78] This concern has been captured in the term *comity*—the respect owed to a state's courts as those of another sovereign.

The principle of comity might be simply an outgrowth of an assumption of state court parity. That is, one could argue that assuming state courts are as good as federal courts, they deserve respect and jurisdictional principles that reflect their equal quality. However, if comity is based on an assumption of parity, analysis of comity would collapse immediately into the dispute over whether state courts are equal to federal courts in their ability and willingness to protect constitutional rights.

Alternatively, comity might be developed as a principle independent of any assumptions about parity. The argument would be that whatever their actual comparative quality, and perhaps especially because quality cannot be measured or known, federal jurisdictional principles must be based on respect for state courts.

I am not suggesting that the Burger or Rehnquist Court used comity irrespective of parity. On the contrary, as explained above, each Court's decisions restricting federal court jurisdiction were based on an assumption of state court parity. Neither the Burger nor the Rehnquist Court explicitly declared that comity was an alternative and independent argument; even without regard to parity, comity requires deference to the state courts. Nonetheless, in theory, the concept of comity articulated by the Burger Court can be used independently as a principle for defining federal court jurisdiction. Especially if one begins with the premise that the debate over parity is futile, one might turn to comity as a separate principle for defining federal jurisdiction. It is this possibility that I consider here.

The Burger and Rehnquist Courts often proclaimed the need to respect the dignity of the state courts, avoiding federal jurisdictional principles that might implicitly insult state judges or cause friction among them. For example, in *Younger v. Harris*, the Court held that federal courts may not enjoin pending state court criminal prosecutions because of comity in large part.[79] In *Younger*, and in its progeny extending its principles to civil cases, the Court emphasized that an injunction halting state court proceedings is a "negative reflection" on the competence of state courts and a disruption bound to cause friction between the court systems.[80]

The principle of comity articulated in *Younger* was extended to prevent federal courts from granting damages to remedy injuries suffered as a result of allegedly unconstitutional state tax systems. In *Fair Assessment in Real Estate Association Inc. v. McNary*, the Supreme Court refused to allow the federal court to decide a Section 1983 challenge to the constitutionality of a state's tax collection practices, because "such a determination would be fully as intrusive as the equitable actions that are barred by principles of comity."[81]

In *O'Shea v. Littleton*, the Supreme Court held that a complaint alleging a practice of racial discrimination by state courts in sentencing and setting bail had to be dismissed.[82] In part, the dismissal was because a "periodic reporting system that might be used to evaluate state court conduct would constitute a form of monitoring of the operation of state court functions that is antipathetic to established principles of comity."[83]

Likewise, in *Rizzo v. Goode*, the Supreme Court dismissed a class action suit alleging a practice of illegal and unconstitutional police mistreatment of minority citizens.[84] The Court stated that "these principles of comity and federalism likewise have applicability where injunctive relief is sought, not against the judicial branch of the state government, but against those in charge of an executive branch of an agency of state or local governments." [85]

Similarly, in holding that state court decisions should have preclusive effect in federal Section 1983 actions and prevent relitigation issues, the Court emphasized that "comity between state and federal courts is a bulwark of the federal system" and that the dignity of the state courts necessitates federal judicial respect for state court judgments.[86]

One of the most important areas where comity has been used as an argument is in decisions and congressional action limiting the scope of habeas corpus review. For example, the Court frequently emphasized that "federal habeas review creates friction between our state and federal courts, as state judges—however able and thorough—know that their judgments may be set aside by a single federal judge, years after it was entered and affirmed on direct appeal." [87]

Thus, comity has been emphasized by the Supreme Court and might be used to fashion jurisdictional rules. The principle would be that federal court jurisdiction should be defined in a way that does not offend or cause friction with state court judges.

I contend, however, that comity is an undesirable concept for defining federal jurisdiction and, as used by the Burger Court, it has been an often-invoked slogan without justification or adequate substantive content. First, it must be recognized that the very existence of federal courts and most federal jurisdiction is based on a distrust of state courts. Diversity jurisdiction, for instance, exists because of a fear that state courts will be parochial and protect their own citizens at the expense of out-of-staters. Removal jurisdiction, especially in the civil rights removal context, reflects a distrust of state courts.[88] General federal question jurisdiction was created in 1875 because of fear over state court hostility to federal claims. In fact, framers, such as James Madison, who argued for the existence of lower federal courts did so because of doubts about the state courts, especially in cases involving federal law and out-of-state citizens.

Therefore, because the existence of federal courts and federal jurisdiction is, in itself, an implicit insult to the state courts, it does not make sense to say that jurisdictional principles must be defined to avoid offending the dignity of state courts. In light of the insult to state courts represented by the very existence of federal jurisdiction, it is not clear how much additional affront there is in allowing federal courts to enjoin unconstitutional state court proceedings or in expanding habeas corpus jurisdiction.

Second, the concept of comity, reflecting a concern for the dignity of state courts and the need to avoid federal court friction with state judiciaries, is based on an unexplained and undefended theory about the psychology of state judges. For example, the claim that federal habeas corpus relief for state prisoners causes friction with state judiciaries assumes that state judges carefully follow the progress of their cases in federal court and hence are upset when their decisions are reversed. Yet, I have seen no evidence for this assertion, and given the case loads of state judges, it is questionable that they have the time to keep track of the ultimate disposition of most of their cases.

In fact, if it is assumed that state judges do follow federal habeas petitions, then an argument could be made that habeas review decreases friction between federal and state judges. In the vast majority of instances, federal courts deny habeas petitions. Habeas petitions are rarely granted; commentators agree that generally less than 1 percent of habeas petitions are granted.[89] Therefore, because federal courts side with state judges in over 95 percent of the cases, if state judges follow the disposition of their cases, habeas review should serve as positive reinforcement, not a source of friction.

More generally, it is not clear that state judges perceive federal court jurisdiction either as an insult or a source of friction. State judges might believe that just as state courts are the preeminent interpreter and enforcer of state law, so do federal courts occupy that role with regard to federal law. This view is one of mutual respect and role specialization; no insult, other than whatever is inherent to the existence of federal courts, is implied. Alternatively, state court judges might view the jurisdictional statutes as creating a choice of forum for constitutional litigants.

Professor Martin Redish explains that allowing federal courts to enjoin unconstitutional state court proceedings is not an insult from this perspective: "The extent of the insult [to state judges] caused by a federal injunction . . . is debatable. Allowing a defendant in a state criminal proceeding to obtain a federal determination of his constitutional claim might be viewed simply as offering a choice of forum for the adjudication of his constitutional rights, a choice traditionally considered a valuable element of modern federalism." [90]

I am not making any claim about the actual psychology and views of state court judges. Rather, the point is that there are many possible ways state courts can view federal jurisdiction. Arguments based on comity and avoiding friction make assumptions about this, but never justify them.

Finally, and most significantly, if federal courts are superior to state courts, then it should not matter whether expansive federal court jurisdiction would insult state judges. Insult would be deserved; correcting errors and protecting individuals who are wrongfully incarcerated are more important than harmony between levels of government. Surely, "jurisdictional doctrine should not translate into an empty display of respect or carefulness to avoid wounding the egos of state judges." [91] Federal court enforcement of constitutional rights, such as in desegregation and reapportionment cases, frequently causes friction between federal and state governments. Yet, such tensions are accepted as a part of constitutional governance.

In other words, comity cannot operate as a principle for defining federal jurisdiction independent of parity. If there is not parity, then federal jurisdiction is justified regardless of the insult or friction. Conversely, if there is parity between federal and state courts in constitutional cases, then arguably, federal jurisdiction is unnecessary and the principle of comity is superfluous.

Some, most notably Professor Paul Bator, argue that insults to state judges are to be avoided because they diminish the quality of state judicial performance. [92] Bator contends that open recognition of state court inferiority would create a self-fulfilling prophecy and further lessen the quality of state courts in deciding constitutional issues. According to this position, even if state courts are inferior, jurisdictional principles should not take this into account because it only would make state courts worse.

There are several problems with Bator's thesis. First, again, it is based on an unjustified theory of the psychology of state judges. Professor Bator assumes that federal court jurisdiction would demoralize state court judges and impair their performance. It is equally possible that the scope of federal jurisdiction would not matter to state judges, that they are now doing the best they can and would continue to do so; or that the implicit insult would motivate them to improve to meet the higher expectations. For example, if state judges follow the ultimate disposition of their cases in federal court and dislike being reversed, it seems quite possible that they might be careful to protect constitutional rights to minimize the chances of being overruled.

Second, Bator's theory presumes without explanation that the error corrections to be gained from more expansive federal jurisdiction are essentially lost by the decrease in state judicial performance. Professor Bator's concerns could be addressed by allowing all constitutional claims to be litigated de novo (anew) in federal court, thereby negating any effects of state court hostility or incompetence.

Finally, Bator does not explain whether there is a threshold after which federal court jurisdiction insults state courts and adversely influences their performance, or whether the insult is continual, with each additional increase in federal jurisdiction causing a new affront and a further decrease in performance. If it is the latter, then the very existence of federal courts, and all the prior statements by the Supreme Court about federal court superiority, already have demoralized state courts. If this is so, then Professor Bator's theory would establish that there is not parity between federal and state courts—which contradicts the very position he frequently has championed. The question then would become how much insult each additional expansion of federal court jurisdiction would add to state court judges, and how much would that insult hurt state court handling of constitutional cases. Alternatively, if the insult occurs only after a certain point, then that threshold would need to be identified.

In sum, comity—as the Supreme Court has defined the concept—

does not succeed in avoiding the issue of parity. Those who believe federal courts to be superior reject considerations of comity because, according to this argument, protecting dignity or lessening friction is less critical than safeguarding rights. Those who contend there is parity can defend a role for the federal courts without regard to comity; in fact, comity would merely be the respect owed to equally capable courts. Either way, discussions about comity cannot be independent of the debate about federal and state court parity.

2. Legislative Supremacy

Another way that the parity issue might be avoided is by according Congress plenary, or absolute, authority to determine federal court jurisdiction. By this principle, the federal courts should follow congressional direction—exercising and refusing jurisdiction only when instructed to do so by the legislature. The Supreme Court need not, and should not, fashion its own jurisdictional rules. It is for Congress to determine the scope of federal court jurisdiction and the relationship between federal and state courts. Hence, it is unnecessary and wrong for the Court to face the question of parity and define federal jurisdiction based on conclusions concerning the relative quality of federal and state courts.[93] According to the legislative supremacy view, "[V]irtually all the debate over the relative competence of federal and state courts as enforcers of federal rights becomes logically irrelevant, except to the extent it is directed exclusively to a call for legislative revision."[94]

There are strong arguments supporting this position. The Supreme Court has held that Congress has broad authority to determine the jurisdiction of the lower federal courts. The Court on several occasions concluded that because Congress has discretion as to whether to create lower federal courts, it also has discretion to determine their jurisdiction.[95] To the extent that Congress has enacted statutes defining federal jurisdiction, it would violate separation of powers for the courts to disregard them unless they were unconstitutional.[96]

The legislative supremacy approach, if followed, might cause a substantial change in many principles defining federal court jurisdiction. For example, legislative history clearly shows that Congress enacted

Section 1983 and the statute allowing federal habeas corpus review for state prisoners because of a grave distrust of state courts.[97] As the Supreme Court has recognized, the very purpose of these statutes "was to interpose the federal courts between the States and the people, as guardians of the people's federal rights."[98]

In light of Congress's desire to expansively open federal courts to constitutional claims, it is questionable whether the Supreme Court's narrowing of jurisdiction under the civil rights statutes can be squared with a model that gives Congress plenary authority to define federal court jurisdiction.

It is not my intent to challenge the principle that it is for Congress to define federal jurisdiction. My argument is only that this approach does not eliminate the need to address whether parity exists between federal and state courts in their handling of constitutional cases.

First, the principle of legislative supremacy in defining federal court jurisdiction simply shifts the question of parity from the courts to Congress. In deciding issues such as the breadth of federal court jurisdiction, when state court decisions should have preclusive effect in state courts, and whether federal courts can enjoin state court proceedings, Congress would still need to consider the comparative quality of federal and state courts in constitutional cases. All the arguments about parity would shift to the legislative forum. The absence of an empirical measurement of parity would mean that a majority of Congress would substitute its intuitive judgment about parity for the judgment now made by the Supreme Court. Put another way, this approach does not provide a way to define federal jurisdiction irrespective of parity; it merely changes who makes the judgment. Indeed, recent statutes modifying federal jurisdiction—such as the Antiterrorism and Effective Death Penalty Act and the Class Action Fairness Act—have been explicitly based on judgments about parity.

Second, even if the Supreme Court is committed to following Congress's determination of federal jurisdiction, the Court still would have a great deal of discretion in fashioning jurisdictional rules. The Court would need some principle for exercising this discretion and determining federal court jurisdiction where Congress is silent or its intent is unclear.

The Court would turn to considerations of parity unless there were an alternate principle for defining federal jurisdiction.

In part, the Court has discretion in determining federal court jurisdiction because of ambiguity in Congress's intent as expressed in the legislative history of the jurisdictional statutes. The problems and inherent uncertainties in relying on legislative histories are familiar.[99] There inevitably will be many jurisdictional issues where congressional intent is nonexistent or unclear, providing the Court with substantial discretion in defining federal court jurisdiction. As Professor Ann Althouse explains in her 1987 article: "Although Congress initially prescribes the jurisdiction of the federal courts, the courts themselves find extensive room for interpretation of these grants of jurisdiction." [100]

Admittedly, a principle of legislative supremacy might resolve many questions of federal jurisdiction without regard to parity. Nonetheless, this approach would not resolve all issues concerning the scope of federal jurisdiction. For many questions, the Court would have discretion and, absent an alternative principle, would rely, explicitly or implicitly, on considerations of parity. Thus, given the impasse in the parity debate, it remains desirable to identify an alternative principle to use in those circumstances in which legislative intent is uncertain or nonexistent.

Third, an underlying problem with legislative supremacy in defining federal jurisdiction is that the principle authorizes the complete elimination, or restriction in particular kinds of cases, of lower federal court jurisdiction. The principle accords Congress plenary power in establishing federal courts and determining their jurisdiction. Potential restrictions on federal court jurisdiction in constitutional cases are very troubling if state courts are not equal to federal courts in their ability and willingness to protect constitutional rights. For example, Professor Theodore Eisenberg argues that the existence of lower federal court jurisdiction is "constitutionally required" in order to assure the vindication of federal rights. He contends that, in light of the enormous proliferation of litigation, review by the Supreme Court is insufficient to assure adequate protection of federal interests.[101]

Thus, the desirability of according to Congress complete authority to define federal court jurisdiction turns, in part, on whether there is parity between federal and state courts. Arguments over Congress's power to determine federal court jurisdiction likely will become, in part, a debate over whether congressional restrictions on jurisdiction are acceptable in light of the parity or non-parity of federal and state courts. In short, although the legislative supremacy approach has many strengths, it will not avoid the need for facing the parity question.

Finally, there is the possibility of having to rely on presumptions to resolve the parity debate. Frequently, when there is empirical uncertainty, analysis turns to presumptions. Presumptions offer a basis for action in a world of incomplete information and of empirical questions for which there are not empirical answers. Both sides of the parity debate have attempted to defend their positions by creating and invoking presumptions.

3. Presumption for or against Federal Jurisdiction

Some commentators maintain that state courts should be presumed to be adequate and federal jurisdiction should exist only when state courts provide insufficient protection of federal rights. Professor Bator argues: "[The state court should be allowed] to adjudicate, and to do so dispositively, if—but only if—there was or will be a 'full and fair opportunity' to litigate the constitutional question in the state court. . . . [I]f it is shown that the state forum was or will be inhospitable, if corrective process is unavailable in the state court system, then the federal court will step in to adjudicate the federal claim." [102]

Similarity, Professor Althouse argues that federal jurisdiction should be reserved for when the "states either are failing to follow or are misapplying federal law." [103] According to Althouse, so long as states are performing adequately, federal jurisdiction is unnecessary. The effect is to create a presumption in favor of state court jurisdiction.

Alternatively, some argue that federal courts presumptively should be available to decide federal constitutional claims. For example, Professor Redish writes: "It seems intuitively appropriate to provide federal courts the primary responsibility for adjudicating federal law, and leave as the primary function of state courts the defining and expounding of state policies and principles." [104]

Consistent adherence to either presumption would bring about a marked change in many jurisdictional principles. For example, allowing state courts to decide federal questions, unless they are demonstrated to be inadequate, would lead to much broader abstention principles than now exist.[105] This allowance to the states then might, if followed by Congress, result in the complete elimination of the general federal question jurisdiction. Conversely, a presumption that federal courts should decide federal constitutional claims is incompatible with many jurisdictional doctrines created by the Burger and Rehnquist Courts, such as those preventing federal courts from enjoining unconstitutional state court proceedings, giving preclusive effect to state court decisions in constitutional cases, and precluding relitigation of Fourth Amendment search and seizure claims on habeas corpus.

However, such presumptions would not end the stalemate in the parity debate. Rather, arguments over the presumptions would simply replicate the existing impasse in determining whether state courts are equal to federal courts in protecting constitutional rights. Each side will assert its presumptions and deny those of the opposition. The presumptions are axioms; one either accepts or rejects them. Undoubtedly, those who believe in parity will choose the presumption that accords state courts responsibility for deciding constitutional claims, while those who deny parity will select the presumption that gives federal courts the preeminent role in constitutional cases. The debate over presumptions is at least as futile as that over parity.

In fact, the absence of empirical evidence for or against parity makes it likely that the presumptions would be virtually irrebuttable. It would be extremely difficult for a litigant to prove that a state court system was incompetent in dealing with constitutional claims or was hostile to federal rights. Advocates of such a presumption in favor of state courts have not explained what evidence of state inadequacy would be sufficient to justify access to the federal forum. Except in cases in which the state procedures were defective, there probably would not be a finding of state court inadequacy, even if the state courts were less able and willing to protect federal rights.

With respect to current Supreme Court cases requiring deference to state courts unless they are proven inadequate, instances in which the state courts are deemed insufficient are rare. Perhaps because of the empirical problems in proving inadequacy, and a commitment to avoiding friction with the state courts, federal courts are loath to find state courts incompetent. As Professor Donald Zeigler notes, "Virtually any theoretically available state remedy will be deemed adequate, even if it is futile in practice." [106] In other words, a presumption of state court competency and adequacy would be virtually irrebuttable.

Correspondingly, a presumption in favor of federal jurisdiction also would be irrebuttable. Defining federal courts as having the preeminent role in enforcing and applying federal law leaves no room for demonstrating the superiority of state courts. Those who advocate broader state court jurisdiction flatly reject a definition that accords the federal courts the primary responsibility for deciding constitutional claims.

Certainly, each side might try to justify its presumptions. For instance, both sides are likely to argue that their position is supported by the structure of the Constitution and the framers' intent. Professor Bator argues that the primacy of state courts runs "in an unbroken line from the Federalist Papers down to today's Supreme Court opinions." [107] He contends that the framers intended for state courts to be the primary protectors of federal rights, and thus his presumption in favor of state courts is justified historically.

But Professor Akhil Amar persuasively argues the opposite position in his 1985 article: that the framers distrusted state courts, and the structure of the Constitution gives federal courts the preeminent role in protecting federal rights.[108] Professor Amar writes that Article III affirms "the parity of all federal judges, and its equal and opposite recognition that non-Article III state court judges do not enjoy such constitutional parity. . . . It would have been grossly out of character for the Framers to have committed 'ultimate' trusteeship of the Constitution to state judges." [109]

This historical argument seems particularly difficult to resolve because the text and the framers' intent can be invoked to support either position. The Constitution accords Congress discretion as to whether to create lower federal courts; however, there is also a textual argument that

Article III compels the existence of a federal forum for federal claims. The structure of the Constitution does contemplate a federal judicial power, but it also contemplates federalism.

The framers' views don't resolve the issue, either. Some at the Constitutional Convention wanted to leave all cases to state courts, reviewed only by the Supreme Court; others, such as James Madison, insisted on the creation of lower federal courts. One's historical conclusions are likely to reflect one's preferences concerning federal jurisdiction. Finally, and most importantly, the relevance of the framers' intent for contemporary constitutional interpretation is, at the very least, debatable.

In sum, there is little difference between creating a presumption for or against federal jurisdiction and making an assumption about parity. Both judgments are largely intuitive and offer little probability of resolving the stalemated debate.

AN ALTERNATIVE TO PARITY: FEDERALISM AND LITIGANT CHOICE AS EMPOWERMENT

I believe that viewing federalism as empowerment provides an alternative principle for defining federal court jurisdiction that does not rely on assumptions of parity. Specifically, individuals with constitutional claims generally should be able to choose whether to litigate in federal or state court. This principle should guide Congress in enacting jurisdictional statutes and the Supreme Court in fashioning the common law of jurisdictional rules when congressional intent is nonexistent or uncertain. Under the litigant choice principle, the role of the federal courts in constitutional cases is to provide an alternative forum to the state courts, which, as argued below, maximizes the opportunity for the protection of individual liberty, increases litigant autonomy, and enhances federalism. It is based on the central idea of federalism as expanding, rather than limiting, power, because all levels of courts—state and federal— would be available to vindicate constitutional claims.

The litigant choice principle avoids the parity question, because jurisdictional rules implementing it allow the individual with a constitutional claim to choose the forum. The jurisdictional rules are not designed to channel cases to either federal or state courts; the litigant choice principle is not based on any overall evaluation of the comparative qualities of the state and federal court systems. Those who strongly believe in the importance of federalism can subscribe to this approach because it preserves a role for both federal and state courts. The premise of concurrent federal and state court jurisdiction is consistent with the Constitution and current federal jurisdictional statutes. At the same time, those who believe that federal courts are superior to state courts can agree to this principle because it provides litigants with constitutional claims complete access to the federal courts.

Several clarifications are useful at the outset. First, although I speak generally of constitutional claims, my primary concern is with cases involving individual rights and liberties. These include the Bill of Rights, other fundamental rights (such as privacy, the right to travel, the right to vote), the equal protection clause, the contracts clause, and the prohibitions against ex post facto (retroactive) laws and bills of attainder (legislation that imposes punishment without trial). Because, for the reasons discussed below, I prefer to be over-inclusive and allow litigant choice in greater rather than fewer cases, I speak generally of constitutional claims.

Second, I contend that the litigant choice principle is usually, but not always, a desirable basis for devising jurisdictional rules. There are circumstances in which countervailing reasons can be made for not allowing individuals with constitutional claims to select the forum. For instance, issues pertaining to questions of federal separation of powers should not be litigated in state courts. The federal government's interest in having disputes among its branches resolved in federal court seems greater than the values served by the litigant choice principle. Generally, though, the litigant choice principle is a desirable and useful basis for jurisdictional rules. Even if the litigant choice principle is rejected for some types of claims—for instance, it is not realistic to allow the federal government to be sued in state court—it should be followed for as many types of constitutional cases as possible.

This section of the chapter is divided into three parts. First, I present the advantages of allowing litigants a choice of forum in constitutional cases. In the second part, some of the practical implications of this principle for federal jurisdictional rules are noted. Finally, possible criticisms and problems are addressed.

1. Advantages of Allowing Litigants with Constitutional Claims to Choose between Federal and State Courts

The litigant choice principle has many advantages. First, permitting a party with a constitutional claim to choose whether to litigate in federal or state court maximizes the opportunity for protecting constitutional rights. As discussed above, there is enormous variation among the state and federal courts throughout the country. In a nation with fifty state court systems and ninety-one federal districts, it is likely that some state courts will be superior to the federal courts in protecting individual rights, while in other areas, the state courts will be inferior to the federal judiciary. In fact, in most areas, the courts probably vary depending on the particular issue; a state court might be better in upholding some constitutional rights, but worse at others.

The litigant choice principle allows an individual with a constitutional claim to choose between state or federal court, and thus to select the forum likely to provide the most sympathetic hearing. The litigant, and his or her attorney, are in the optimal position to assess in that geographic area which court offers the better chance of vindicating the particular constitutional claim.[110]

Some might argue, however, that without empirical evidence as to actual differences between the courts, attorneys cannot make reliable choices, and they might even misperceive the differences between the particular state and federal courts. Although these information problems exist, I believe that the litigant choice principle offers the greatest likelihood of channeling cases to the most sympathetic forum. Attorneys have access to the best possible information concerning differences in the courts in their area. They can research the state and federal courts' decisions in their locale as to the specific issues involved in their case and, from observation and conversations, they can gain knowledge about litigation resolved without written opinions. Also, lawyers formulate impressions about each court's general disposition toward constitutional claims. Moreover, attorneys have strong incentives to determine as accurately as possible which forum offers them the best chance of pre-vailing in any case. Although such information is imperfect, it offers the maximum opportunity for protecting constitutional rights. Ultimately, empirical proof is unlikely; however, if the goal is directing a case to the court most sympathetic to the particular constitutional claim, it is pref-erable to allow the litigant to choose the forum rather than use random assignment or a blanket rule for the entire country.

The argument that the litigant choice principle maximizes the op-portunity for the protection of constitutional rights assumes, of course, that it is desirable to maximize the likelihood of vindicating such claims. While some may challenge this premise, most of the participants on both sides of the parity debate already have conceded this goal. Those who maintain that federal courts are superior to state courts explicitly con-tend that the objective should be to maximize the opportunity for pro-tecting individual liberties.[111]

Those who argue that there is state court parity do not contest this objective; rather, they maintain that state courts are equally likely to rule in favor of the individual and against the government in constitutional litigation.[112] Their claim is not that state courts are superior because they would produce different, and by their view, better results. Instead, they contend that state courts are equally sympathetic to federal rights, thereby admitting the desirability of maximizing the opportunity for safeguarding individual liberties. For these defenders of parity to claim now that state courts are preferable because they offer less likelihood of protecting individual rights would be a shift of position.

Moreover, analytically, it makes sense to design court systems and jurisdictional rules so as to maximize the opportunity for protecting constitutional rights. Logically, the court system must strive toward one of the three following goals: maximization of the opportunity for the protection of rights, minimization of the opportunity for the protection of rights, or neutrality as to the opportunities for protecting rights.

The first, maximizing the opportunity for the protection of rights, is most consistent with this country's commitment to individual liber-ties and to upholding the Constitution. It would be strange to place the presumption *against* the protection of constitutional rights. In other words, in light of a clear and consistent social commitment to individual liberties—reflected by the liberties' enshrinement in the Constitution, their supremacy over all other government actions, and their place in the nation's consciousness—it would not make sense to design jurisdictional rules that were hostile or indifferent to this goals.[113]

To say that the system should maximize the opportunity for protecting constitutional rights obviously does not imply that the individual raising a constitutional claim always should win. Constitutional cases almost invariably involve some form of balancing of the individual's rights and the society's interests. The point is only that individuals alleging constitutional violations should have a chance to be heard in the forum, state court or federal court, that they perceive to be most sympathetic.

One response to this is that it risks the overprotection of constitutional rights. Yet, as Professors Howard Fink and Mark Tushnet observe, "[T]here is no such thing in constitutional terms, as overprotecting liberty. If there were, statutes going beyond constitutional minimum protections would be questionable, and they generally are not."[114] Furthermore, in light of the empirical uncertainty, a choice must be made as to what risk of error is most acceptable. It is better to risk overprotection of individual liberties by having very sympathetic courts than to permit underprotection in more hostile judiciaries.

Simply put, if the premise of maximizing the opportunity for protecting constitutional rights is accepted, then the litigant choice principle naturally follows. This is because individuals are in the best position to know which court offers the greatest opportunity for vindicating the claim. This position is based on a normative argument, that it is desirable to maximize the protection of rights; and an empirical argument, that parties and their attorneys are likely to choose the forum which is most sympathetic to their case.

A second benefit of allowing individuals with constitutional claims to choose between federal and state court is that it enhances litigants' autonomy. Professor Judith Resnik explains that "[w]hile we have procedural doctrines . . . that impose some constraints on litigants' choices, we have generally remained loyal to litigants' autonomy."[115] That is, unless there are compelling reasons to the contrary, litigants should be allowed to make as many choices as possible about the proceedings. Litigant autonomy is not absolute; however, nor is it the only value to be maximized in designing jurisdictional rules. Autonomy is simply one goal in situations in which there are not overriding interests. For instance, full adherence to allowing litigants a choice of forums might justify permitting the parties to proceed in the states of their choice; however, all of the values underlying the concepts of personal jurisdiction and venue explain why litigants' choices among states are restricted.

Furthering litigant autonomy enhances individual dignity. Professor Resnik continues: "Implicit in litigants' autonomy is concern about respect for individual dignity. To enhance dignity, government should provide individuals with choices about protection and assertion of their rights." [116] Litigant autonomy is also desirable as a way of maximizing satisfaction with the system; individuals are more likely to respect a decision when they had a choice as to the forum. Simply put, it is desirable to permit individuals to make choices that are likely to be determinative of important aspects of their lives. Allowing individuals with constitutional claims to select whether to litigate in federal or state court increases the choices individuals make, and thereby enhances litigant autonomy. Especially if people believe that where a case is heard makes a difference, the process will seem fairer.

Individual autonomy is not fostered under the current jurisdictional rules. Often neither side gets to select the forum; the case is consigned by the jurisdictional rules to state court. For example, in *Fair Assessment in Real Estate Association Inc. v. McNary*, the Supreme Court held that Section 1983 suits for damages to compensate for allegedly unconstitutional tax systems could not be brought in federal court because of considerations of comity.[117] Neither side had any choice as to the forum. Likewise, when a substantial constitutional issue arises as a defense, even when it will be the only matter in dispute, the federal courts are not allowed to hear the case.[118] The litigants with constitutional claims have no choice. In such instances, the litigant choice principle would expand choice and autonomy.

Also, constitutional claims usually arise in litigation between the government and individuals because of the state action requirement; the

Constitution limits government, not private citizens. Individual autonomy, therefore, is something possessed by the person alleging a constitutional violation; the government obviously cannot invoke a claim of personal autonomy. As in the typical constitutional case, the government is the opposing party. Allowing individuals with constitutional claims to choose the forum enhances their autonomy without decreasing anyone else's autonomy.

A third benefit of allowing individuals with constitutional claims to choose whether to proceed in federal or state court is that federalism is enhanced. The litigant choice principle creates concurrent jurisdiction in all constitutional cases. Both the federal and state courts have jurisdiction, and it is up to the party asserting a constitutional claim to choose where to proceed. The principle thus preserves a role for the state courts; it in no way denigrates them. As such, the litigant choice approach avoids the negative consequences that Paul Bator claims arise from casting aspersions on the ability or willingness of state courts to protect federal rights.

In fact, the litigant choice principle could exemplify federalism at its best as a technique for enhancing the protection of constitutional rights. The Supreme Court often has declared that a central goal of federalism is advancing the protection of individual liberties. The Court has declared: "Just as the separation and independence of the coordinate branches of the Federal Government serves to prevent the accumulation of excessive power in any one branch, a healthy balance of power between the States and the Federal Government will reduce the risk of tyranny and abuse from either front." [119] Scholars, too, have argued that federalism exists to safeguard individuals rights. For example, Professor Akhil Amar contends that the underlying objective of federalism is maximizing individual liberties.[120] Amar argues that federalism optimally serves this function when it creates competition between federal and state governments in the protection of liberty. He writes: "[A] healthy competition among limited governments for the hearts of the American people can protect popular sovereignty and spur a race to the high ground of constitutional remedies. Each government can act as a remedial cavalry of sorts, eager to win public honor by riding to the rescue of citizens victimized by another government's misconduct." [121]

Professor Amar argues that when the federal and state courts have concurrent jurisdiction, they compete with each other in the protection of individual liberties. Each court system acts to make its forum attractive for litigants asserting constitutional claims. Others express a similar view about the desirability of concurrent jurisdiction as a way to spur the vindication of constitutional rights. Professor Ann Althouse writes that competition enhances federalism and individual liberties because the "state makes a 'separate sphere' for itself by inducing plaintiffs who generally would prefer a federal forum to choose state court instead in order to claim state-created rights." [122]

Whether the courts actually would compete to attract litigants is questionable. Each court system undoubtedly has enough business that it might not want to try to acquire more. In fact, one might say, not completely facetiously, that in these days of overburdened judiciaries, the incentive may be to express hostility to constitutional claims to convince the litigants to take their cases elsewhere. This, of course, is an oversimplification because it ignores the desire judges have to possess a reputation for high quality decisions in constitutional cases and the incentive jurisdictions have to keep litigation affecting them in their courts.

At minimum, the litigant choice principle enhances federalism by creating a concurrent role for the federal and state governments. At best, it offers a chance for maximizing individual rights by creating a competition between forums.

These federalism advantages make it possible for both sides of the parity debate to subscribe to the litigant choice principle. Obviously, critics of state courts can support litigant choice because it allows individuals to litigate their constitutional claims in federal court whenever they wish. While access to the federal courts is assured, there is likewise access to state courts when the state judiciary is perceived to be more sympathetic to constitutional claims.

Proponents of parity can also endorse the litigant choice principle. Professor Bator, one of the preeminent opponents of federal court supremacy, writes that federalism is a "partnership," not a "federal monopoly." [123] He goes on to explain that the litigant choice principle avoids creating either a federal or a state monopoly over constitutional litigation. Furthermore, Professor Bator writes that it is an independent argument in favor of a jurisdictional rule if it can be shown to create such "an incentive . . . for hospitable reception of claims of federal rights in the state courts; whereas it is an argument against a jurisdictional rule if it removes pressure from the state courts to improve their processes for the litigation of federal constitutional issues." [124]

2. Doctrinal Implications of Allowing Litigants with Constitutional Claims to Choose between Federal and State Court

In enacting statutes that define federal court jurisdiction, Congress, as stated, generally should allow litigants with constitutional claims to choose between federal and state court. Furthermore, where congressional intent is unknowable, because of its nonexistence on a particular topic or because of its ambiguity, the Supreme Court should fashion the common law rules of federal jurisdiction so as to allow litigants with constitutional claims to choose their forum for the most part.

To a large extent, existing statutes already support such an approach. Federal law, U.S.C., Section 1331, already creates broad federal court jurisdiction over all issues arising under the Constitution of the United States. The state courts also can exercise jurisdiction in these cases because there are no statutes creating exclusive federal court jurisdiction in constitutional cases. Hence, the Supreme Court could immediately begin following the litigant choice principle in defining federal court jurisdiction.

In fact, there is compelling evidence that the litigant choice principle was intended by Congress when it defined federal court jurisdiction. The congressional creation of concurrent state and federal jurisdiction in constitutional cases, which allows the plaintiff to choose state or federal court, and removal jurisdiction, which permits the defendant to take a case from state to federal court, evidences Congress's desire to leave forum selection to the parties. More specifically, in enacting Section 1983, which is the basis for most constitutional litigation against state and local governments, Congress sought to allow litigants with constitutional claims to choose between state and federal court. As the Supreme Court explained, "[M]any legislators interpreted the bill [the Civil Rights Act of 1871] to provide dual or concurrent forums in the state and federal system, enabling the plaintiff to choose the forum in which to seek relief." [125]

What would federalism as empowerment in the form of litigant choice principle mean for civil and criminal cases? In civil cases, the party—plaintiff or defendant—raising a constitutional claim should get to choose whether to litigate the case in state or federal court. After the party raising a constitutional claim has selected the court, the matter should remain in that court system until there is a final judgment and all appeals within that system are exhausted. Recourse to the Supreme Court would be available after a final judgment from the highest state court or the federal court of appeals. The selected court's decision should have preclusive collateral estoppel and res judicata effect (a final ruling judged on merit) in all other courts, as is true today.

Before explaining how this would change jurisdictional rules, it is important to address the question about the circumstances in which both the plaintiff and the defendant raise constitutional issues in civil cases. Usually, only one side asserts a constitutional right. Because of the state action requirement, most cases containing constitutional issues involve an individual as one party and the government as the other. The Constitution bestows rights and liberties on individuals, not on the government. When there is a lawsuit between the government and an individual, it is the individual who should get to choose.

It might be argued that the government has an important interest in the selection of the forum because it can raise constitutional issues such as federalism and separation of powers, even though these do not take the form of constitutional rights. Yet, to a large extent, the underlying rationale for structuring government using separation of powers and federalism is the belief that these techniques will maximize the long-term protection of individual rights. Because the Constitution is designed to protect the individual from the government, in a suit between the individual and the government, the individual should be allowed to choose the forum.

Constitutional issues arise in litigation between two private parties relatively infrequently.[126] If only one of these parties asserts a constitutional claim, then that party determines the forum under the litigant choice principle. In the rare circumstance in which the litigation is between two private parties and each asserts a constitutional claim, the litigant choice principle provides no basis for forum selection. The current jurisdiction rules could remain unchanged. If the plaintiff's complaint alleges a federal question, the plaintiff can bring the case to federal court. If the plaintiff files a case in state court that might have been brought in federal court, the defendant may remove it to federal court. Otherwise, absent another basis for federal court jurisdiction, the case must be litigated in state court. Since situations where two private individuals assert constitutional claims will be rare, the litigant choice principle applies in the vast majority of instances.

The litigant choice principle would change current jurisdictional rules in civil cases in two important respects. First, it would allow federal court jurisdiction based on constitutional claims raised as a defense. Currently, constitutional issues and other federal questions may be litigated in federal court only if they are on the face of the plaintiff's well-pleaded complaint.[127] A case cannot be heard in federal court if the constitutional issue in the case arises only as a defense, even if it is the sole matter in dispute. This court-created rule should be changed; federal courts should be available to hear constitutional claims regardless of which party raises them.

The reason for having federal court jurisdiction in constitutional cases applies whether the plaintiff or the defendant raises the constitutional issue. Federal courts exist to provide an alternative forum for the vindication of rights, thereby maximizing the opportunity for the protection of liberties, increasing litigant autonomy, and enhancing federalism. All of these objectives are served just as effectively by allowing defendants with constitutional claims to choose the forum as they are by permitting plaintiffs with such claims to select the court.

The second way litigant choice would change the rules in civil cases pertains to removal jurisdiction. Under the litigant choice principle, if the plaintiff presents a constitutional claim, he or she can bring the case to either federal or state court. Therefore, if the plaintiff files a constitutional claim in federal court, it remains there; this is the current scenario when the plaintiff initiates such a suit in federal court. What happens if the plaintiff with a constitutional claim chooses state court? Currently, the defendant can remove the case to federal court, assuming that it is a matter that could have been brought to the federal forum in the first instance. Under the litigant choice principle, however, when the plaintiff has a constitutional claim and the defendant does not, the plaintiff can choose to have the matter heard in state court. The defendant should not be able to remove such a case to a federal forum. This is one place where adherence to the litigant choice principle would require modification of the jurisdictional statutes.

Also with respect to removal jurisdiction, a defendant should be able to remove a case to federal court by alleging that the outcome of the case likely will turn on a federal issue. Defendants now may remove cases to federal court only if the plaintiff's complaint supports federal jurisdiction. Under the litigant choice principle, where the plaintiff in a civil case does not raise a constitutional issue, but the defendant does, the defendant should be able to remove the matter to federal court.

Finally, perhaps the most significant change in removal jurisdiction is that defendants alleging constitutional claims should be able to remove cases from federal to state court. Again, if the plaintiff does not raise a constitutional issue, but the defendant does, the defendant chooses the forum. Therefore, if the plaintiff filed the action in federal court, perhaps based on a federal statutory question, the defendant with a constitutional claim should be able to exercise the right to determine the forum and move the case to state court. This illustrates that the litigant choice principle truly makes no assumptions concerning the inherent superiority of either forum, leaving it entirely to the party with a constitutional claim to determine where it should be litigated.

The litigant choice principle also has important implications for criminal cases. Criminal prosecutions virtually always occur in the forum of the prosecutor; actions for violations of state laws occur in state court and federal prosecutions occur in federal court. An individual prosecuted in state court must raise all constitutional objections in the state court and must exhaust all appeals within that system. Then if the convicted defendant claims that his or her conviction violated federal law, he or she may present a habeas corpus petition to the federal court. The federal court need not give preclusive effect to the state court's decision on constitutional issues, except for Fourth Amendment search and seizure claims if there was an opportunity for a full and fair hearing in state court.

These current jurisdictional rules are not in accord with the principle that litigants with constitutional claims should be able to choose the forum. For example, if an individual who is prosecuted in state court challenges the constitutionality of the statute that is the basis for the prosecution, the issue must be litigated in state court. The reverse, of course, also is true; if a person is prosecuted in federal court under an allegedly unconstitutional statute, he or she must raise the constitutional claim in federal court. Similarly, if a defendant raises constitutional challenges to the admissibility of evidence or court procedures, the claims must be litigated in the forum of the prosecution. Basically, the defendant is not permitted to select the forum in criminal cases.

Adhering to the litigant choice principle in criminal cases would change jurisdictional rules dramatically. In fact, the changes likely would be so radical that the principle could not be applied in criminal cases in the same manner as in civil cases. To demonstrate the difficulty in applying the litigant choice principle in criminal cases, consider three different ways in which this principle could be implemented in criminal cases.

The simplest way would be to allow criminal defendants raising constitutional issues to remove the case from state to federal court or from federal to state court. If the defendant could show at the outset of the proceedings that the outcome of the case likely would turn on a question of constitutional law, the defendant could select whether to have the prosecutorial proceedings in state or federal court. Such litigation would fit within the scope of federal jurisdiction under Article III, because long ago the Supreme Court declared that cases can be tried under federal law if a question of federal law is likely to be determinative of the outcome of the litigation.[128]

Allowing removal of criminal prosecutions would be a radical change.

Some prominent scholars have advocated the idea in the past. In 1925, Charles Warren stated that the "doctrine that no Court could enforce the penal laws of another Government seems to have been established as a judicial [pronouncement], without much reasoning." [129] Professor Warren believed federal courts should be available to hear state criminal cases and "the State Courts, if they are willing, may take concurrent jurisdiction of . . . certain Federal crimes." [130]

Allowing removal of criminal cases when the defendant raises a substantial constitutional issue would gain all of the advantages of the litigant choice principle. The defendant could choose the forum that offered the opportunity for maximizing the protection of rights. Enhancing litigant autonomy by allowing a choice of forum seems especially critical in criminal cases, where the coercive power of the state is brought to bear against an individual. Federalism is served because the courts of either jurisdiction would be available to provide a remedy against the other.

The likely objection to allowing removal of criminal cases is that states have an interest in having state law prosecutions in state court, and the federal government could claim a similar interest as to federal prosecutions. Interestingly, this argument implicitly assumes that there is a difference between federal and state courts and, in fact, that state courts are better for state law issues and federal courts are better for federal law issues. But most of those who believe in parity do not think that one court is better than the other. And those who argue against parity offer up as their objective the maximization of constitutional rights protection; for the reasons stated earlier, allowing criminal defendants with constitutional claims to choose the forum would accomplish this goal.

I recognize that allowing removal of criminal cases from one jurisdiction to another would be an enormous change. After two hundred years of generally allowing each jurisdiction to try its own criminal cases, revising the rules to allow for removal seems quite improbable.

An alternative approach to removal in criminal cases would be to allow parties with constitutional claims to interrupt the ongoing litigation and go to the other forum. For example, if a person prosecuted in state court challenged the constitutionality of a statute which was the basis for that prosecution, the individual could litigate the issue in either federal or state court before standing trial. If the defendant chose to litigate the issue in federal court, the state court proceedings would be stayed pending the resolution of the constitutional claim. In essence, the procedure would be identical to that now followed under the *Pullman* abstention, which requires that federal courts abstain and send cases to state court for a clarification of state law; likewise, federal proceedings are stayed pending the state court's decision of the state law issue.[131]

There are many disadvantages to such an approach. Unless there was a limit on the number of times a defendant could go to the other forum to raise constitutional issues, the case could conceivably shuttle back and forth endlessly between the courts. Undeniably, criminal defendants anxious to delay their possible conviction could use this technique to greatly protract the litigation and the ultimate resolution of their cases. Given the long delays of many years that are common in instances of *Pullman* abstentions, there likely would be substantial opposition to allowing a defendant to take a potentially determinative constitutional claim to either federal or state court.

A final alternative—and the one I advocate—would be to require the defendant to litigate initially in the jurisdiction of the prosecution, but then permit complete relitigation of constitutional claims. In other words, if a state court defendant indicated at the outset that he or she wanted to litigate constitutional claims in federal court, the defendant would later have the right to do so de novo. A convicted defendant denied a choice of forum would not be bound by the state court's decisions on constitutional issues.

Essentially, except for Fourth Amendment claims, this approach is now followed in criminal cases for state court prisoners. If the defendant raises a constitutional challenge in state court, the defendant, after exhausting all state appeals, may relitigate in federal court on habeas corpus. I believe, though, that many of the onerous restrictions imposed on habeas litigants by Congress and the Supreme Court in recent years—the prohibition of successive petitions, the strict statute of limitations, the requirement for complete exhaustion—would be reconsidered if the litigant choice principle were implemented. All of these obstruct the ability of state prisoners to relitigate their constitutional claims in federal court.

Following the litigant choice principle and federalism as empowerment would mean that those convicted in federal court could later relitigate their constitutional claims in state court. This, though, is not realistic. No mechanism for this ever has existed. Indeed, the case of *Tarble*
long has prevented state courts from granting such a remedy by prohibiting states from issuing habeas corpus against a federal officer.[132]

3. Potential Problems with the Litigant Choice Principle

Although many of the potential objections to the litigant choice principle
focus on the doctrinal implications discussed above, another likely criticism is that the litigant choice principle would increase federal court litigation. At the outset, it is important to note that it is unclear what effect
the litigant choice principle would have on federal court dockets. If there
truly is parity between federal and state courts, it is unlikely that the
litigant choice principle would spur the wholesale removal of constitutional cases from state to federal court. Actually, if state courts truly are
equal to the federal courts, even in constitutional cases, then some federal cases might be removed to state court. Professor Burt Neuborne—
previously quoted critic of state court parity—observes that "if we are
lucky, the healthy movement toward serious constitutional jurisprudence
in the state courts will continue to the point where civil rights—civil liberties lawyers in large numbers will be tempted to resort to them." [133]

Of course, federal court litigation will increase if federal courts are
more willing and able to vindicate constitutional claims than are the
state courts. Also, given variations among courts, it is possible that in
some areas of the country, federal court litigation will increase and in
other places, state court workloads will expand. The cumulative effect
on federal courts, however, is not predictable.

The litigant choice principle might not cause a substantial overall increase in the amount of litigation. Its largest effect would be to shift cases
from one court system to the other, with society's total expenditure on
courts and litigation realizing no substantial growth. Judicial economy is
not lessened if the only effect is to change the court that hears the case.

Moreover, even if there were an increase in the federal judicial workload, and even if it were established that this is an undesirable end, this is

not necessarily a reason to reject the litigant choice principle. An alternative solution would be to eliminate federal jurisdiction in some types of nonconstitutional cases, such as by abolishing diversity jurisdiction.

Finally, with a possible increase in the federal court workload would come benefits that likely would exceed the conceivable costs. There would be a marked growth in federal dockets only if litigants perceived the federal to be superior to the state forum. And if this were, indeed, the perception of litigants, this would provide a strong reason for expanding the federal courts.

The central idea of federalism as empowerment is that it is desirable to have multiple levels of government available to address society's problems; if one level fails, another is there. This is true with regard to court jurisdiction. There is inherent redundancy to having federal and state courts with concurrent jurisdiction.[134] But a crucial advantage of this redundancy is that if one level is inadequately enforcing constitutional rights, another exists.

For decades, discussions of federal jurisdiction among scholars and judges have explicitly or implicitly rested on judgments about whether there is parity between federal and state courts. Some vociferously contend that state judiciaries are equal to federal courts in their willingness and ability to protect federal rights. Others respond with comparable certainty that federal courts are superior to state courts in constitutional litigation. Yet, both sides face substantial problems in establishing their positions. For instance, if state courts are perceived to be truly as good as federal courts, then federal courts seem superfluous. Advocates of parity offer little explanation as to why the federal judiciary even need exist. By contrast, those who proclaim federal court superiority can be challenged to prove their assertion. Such proof is not likely forthcoming.

Allowing litigants with constitutional claims to choose the forum makes sense in terms of the underlying policies behind federal jurisdiction and, at the same time, has the potential of ending the impasse in the parity debate.

CHAPTER 6

Empowering States:
A Different Approach to Preemption

THUS FAR, I HAVE DISCUSSED federalism as empowerment in terms of what it would mean for the authority of the federal government, both for Congress and the federal judiciary. Equally important, though, is how this approach to federalism would empower state and local governments. Specifically, viewing federalism as empowerment should include a far narrower preemption doctrine. This would lessen the situations in which state and local laws are preempted and increase the powers of states and localities to govern as they choose. In other words, federalism as empowerment is not about aggrandizing power for the federal government; it is about equipping government at all levels with the authority to address key social issues.

When historians look back at the Rehnquist Court, undoubtedly they will say that its federalism decisions represented the most significant changes in the law. As described in Chapter 1 and analyzed in subsequent chapters, the past ten years of the Rehnquist Court has limited the scope of Congress's power under the commerce clause and Section 5 of the Fourteenth Amendment.[1] In addition, the Court has revived the Tenth Amendment as a constraint on federal authority[2] and has greatly expanded the scope of state sovereign immunity.[3]

One would expect that a Court concerned with federalism and states' rights also would be narrowing the scope of federal preemption of state laws. Narrowing the circumstances of federal preemption leaves more room for state and local governments to act. Quite the opposite, though, has occurred. Over the same time period in which the Rehnquist Court has revived federalism as a limit on Congress's power, the Court repeatedly has ruled for the preemption of important state laws, even when federal law was silent about preemption or explicitly preserved state laws.

For example, in *Geier v. American Honda Motor Co. Inc.*,[4] the Court preempted a state product liability lawsuit for an unsafe vehicle, even though a statutory provision expressly provided that "[c]ompliance with" a federal safety standard does "not exempt any person from any liability under the common law."[5] *Lorillard Tobacco Co. v. Reilly*[6] held that federal law preempted a state regulation governing the location of cigarette advertising with respect to children. *Crosby v. National Foreign Trade Council*[7] invalidated a Massachusetts law that prohibited the state from purchasing goods and services from companies that did business with Burma. In *American Insurance Association v. Garamendi*,[8] the Supreme Court preempted a California law requiring that insurance companies doing business in that state disclose Holocaust-era insurance policies. The Court invalidated the California statute, despite the absence of any federal law expressing an intent to preempt state law, based on the "dormant foreign affairs power of the president." Each of these cases is discussed in detail later in the chapter.

At the very least, these and other cases like them are inconsistent with the Supreme Court's often-stated presumption against preemption. For example, the Court declared:

[B]ecause the States are independent sovereigns in our federal system, we have long presumed that Congress does not cavalierly preempt state-law causes of action. In all preemption cases, and particularly in those in which Congress has legislated in a field which the States have traditionally occupied, we "start with the presumption" that "the historic police powers of the States were not to be superseded by the Federal Act unless that was the clear and manifest purpose of Congress."[9]

Yet, the recent Supreme Court preemption cases clearly presume to favor preemption.[10] In each case, the text of the federal law was silent about preemption and it so happened there was no conflict between the federal and state law. Nonetheless, in each, the Court found preemption, often with the justices who were counted among the majority being the most committed to using federalism as a limit on federal power. For example, in *Lorillard*, the decision to preempt state regulation of local cigarette advertising was 5–4, with the five justices in the majority being

Chief Justice William Rehnquist and Justices Sandra Day O'Connor, Antonin Scalia, Anthony Kennedy, and Clarence Thomas. These, of course, are the same five justices who were in the majority in the 5–4 decisions limiting the scope of Congress's commerce power, reviving the Tenth Amendment, and expanding the scope of sovereign immunity.

More profoundly, the Court's recent preemption decisions expose the political content of its federalism rulings. The Court has preempted state laws regulating such politically influential monoliths as big tobacco, the auto industry, and insurance. Interestingly, most of the Supreme Court's federalism decisions invalidating *federal* laws have struck down provisions in civil rights laws—such as the Violence Against Women Act, the Religious Freedom Restoration Act, the Age Discrimination in Employment Act, and the Americans with Disabilities Act. Comparing the Court's preemption rulings with its decisions limiting Congress's authority under the commerce clause and Section 5 of the Fourteenth Amendment suggests that what animates the Rehnquist Court is less a real concern for states' rights and federalism and more a judgment about what laws are politically desirable.

If it is a federal law expanding civil rights protection, the Rehnquist Court is willing to use federalism to invalidate it, as it did in striking down the Violence Against Women Act and the Religious Freedom Restoration Act, and as the Court did in preventing enforcement against the states through Title I of the Americans with Disabilities Act and the Age Discrimination in Employment Act. But if it is a state regulation of business, the Rehnquist Court is quite willing to find it preempted by federal law, as it did in the cases mentioned above and that are described in detail later on. This indicates that the Court was hiding its value choices to limit civil rights laws and to protect business from regulation in decisions that seem to be about very specific doctrines of constitutional law, such as the scope of the commerce power and the circumstances of preemption.

This chapter begins by briefly describing the law of preemption. I then explain the broad view of preemption reflected in the Supreme Court's recent decisions. After this description, I turn to normative analysis and explain why these decisions are undesirable. I conclude by offering a different approach to preemption—one that is consistent with empowering government at all levels. Courts should find preemption only when a law expressly preempts state and local action, or if there is a direct conflict between federal and state law. From this perspective, the Supreme Court's recent preemption cases are wrong because they invalidate state and local laws that ensure desirable effects, such as creating liability for injured consumers, protecting children from tobacco advertisements, and requiring insurance companies to disclose their Holocaust-era policies. At the same time, this approach preserves the ability of Congress to preempt state and local regulation where national uniformity is necessary; Congress just must say that is what is desired. Preemption would remain unchanged under my approach when a provision of federal law expressly preempts state law, or when there is a direct conflict between federal and state law.

States' rights are not an end in themselves. They are a means to the crucial objectives of advancing freedom and enriching the lives of those in the United States. Unfortunately, the Supreme Court's decisions limiting federal power in the area of civil rights and invalidating desirable state laws based on preemption have had exactly the opposite effect.

PREEMPTION: AN OVERVIEW

Article VI of the Constitution contains the supremacy clause, which provides that the Constitution, and laws and treaties made pursuant to it, are the supreme law of the land. If there is a conflict between federal and state law, the federal law holds sway and the state law is invalidated because federal law is supreme.[11] As the Supreme Court declared: "[U]nder the Supremacy Clause, from which our pre-emption doctrine is derived, 'any state law, however clearly within a State's acknowledged power, which interferes with or is contrary to federal law, must yield.'"[12]

The difficulty, of course, comes with deciding whether a particular state or local law is preempted by a specific federal statute or regulation.[13] As in so many other areas of constitutional law, there is no clear rule for determining whether a state or local law should be invalidated on preemption grounds. The Supreme Court once remarked that there is not "an infallible constitutional test or an exclusive constitutional yardstick. In the final analysis, there can be no one crystal clear distinctly marked formula." [14]

Traditionally, the Supreme Court has identified two major situations in which preemption occurs. One is when a federal law expressly preempts state or local law. Any time that Congress has the authority to legislate it can declare in the text of the statute that federal law is exclusive in the field.

The other situation is when preemption can be implied. The Court has identified three types of implied preemption. One is termed "field preemption"—in which the scheme of federal law and regulation is "so pervasive as to make reasonable the inference that Congress left no room for the States to supplement it." [15] Another type of implied preemption is when there is a conflict between federal and state law. Even if federal law does not expressly preempt state law, preemption will be ruling when "compliance with both federal and state regulations is a physical impossibility." [16]

Implied preemption also will be found if state law impedes the achievement of a federal objective. Even if federal and state law are not mutually exclusive and even if there is no congressional expression of a desire to preempt state law, preemption will be decided if state law "stands as an obstacle to the accomplishment and execution of the full purposes and objectives of Congress." [17] The Supreme Court summarized the tests for preemption in *Gade v. National Solid Waste Management Association*, the tests for preemption were summarized by the Supreme Court:

Preemption may be either express or implied, and is compelled whether Congress' command is explicitly stated in the statute's language or implicitly contained in its structure and purpose. Absent explicit preemptive language, we have recognized at least two types of implied preemption: field preemption, where the scheme of federal regulation is so pervasive as to make reasonable the inference that Congress left no room for the States to supplement it, and conflict preemption, where compliance with both federal and state regulations is a physical impossibility, or where state law stands as an obstacle to the accomplishment and execution of the full purposes and objectives of Congress. [18]

Although these categories, or minor variations, are frequently used, they are not distinct. For example, even if there is statutory language expressly preempting state law, Congress rarely is clear about the scope of what is preempted or how particular situations should be handled. Courts must decide what is preempted, and this inevitably involves an inquiry into congressional intent.[19] Conversely, implied preemption is often a function of both perceived congressional intent and the language used in the statute or regulation.

Indeed, the Supreme Court has recognized that in both express and implied preemption, the issue becomes discerning congressional intent. The Court has said that "[t]he question of whether a certain state action is preempted by federal law is one of congressional intent." [20] It has remarked that " '[t]he purpose of Congress is the ultimate touchstone' in every preemption case." [21] The problem, of course, is that Congress's intent, especially as to the scope of preemption, is rarely expressed or clear. Therefore, although the Court purports to be finding congressional intent, it often is left to make guesses about purpose based on fragments of statutory language, random statements in the legislative history, and the degree of detail of the federal regulation.

The Supreme Court frequently has said that congressional intent must be clear to find preemption because of a desire, stemming from federalism concerns, to minimize invalidation of state and local laws. Thus, the Court has observed: "Congress . . . should manifest its intention [to preempt state and local laws] clearly. . . . The exercise of federal supremacy is not lightly to be presumed." [22]

Over recent years, there has been a dramatic increase in preemption decisions by the United States Supreme Court.[23] Preemption issues arise in literally every area of federal law and regulation.

Ultimately, preemption doctrines are entirely about federalism; they concern allocating governing authority between the federal and state governments. A broad view of preemption leaves less room for governance at the state and local levels. It is for this reason that, at times, the Court has declared that the preemption analysis "start[s] with the assumption that the historic powers of the States [are] not to be superseded by . . . [a] Federal Act unless that [is] the clear and manifest purpose of Congress." [24] But a very narrow preemption doctrine minimizes the reach of federal law and risks undermining the federal objectives. Therefore, it is somewhat surprising that, as described below, the Rehnquist Court, with its commitment to federalism and protecting states' rights, was willing to find federal preemption. [25] One way to empower states is to narrow the reach of federal preemption, but this has not occurred.

The basic question is how willing courts should be to decide in favor of preemption. Should there be a strong presumption against a court concluding that there is preemption? If so, what should be sufficient to overcome this preemption? Or should courts be willing to find preemption whenever doing so would effectuate the purposes of federal law?

The Court's Recent Preemption Decisions: Putting a Presumption against the States

The Supreme Court's recent preemption decisions are striking because they are so at odds with deference to the states. To illustrate, I briefly describe in this section several recent cases and how they put the presumption in favor of preemption. The normative criticism of this approach and these rulings is in the following section. It is important to note that all of these cases came during the same period when the Rehnquist Court was emphasizing the importance of protecting state power from federal regulation.

Geier v. American Honda Motor Co. Inc. [26]

Alexis Geier bought a 1987 model Honda Accord. She was seriously injured when the car crashed into a tree. She sued saying that the absence of airbags was a design defect that was responsible for her injuries. The Department of Transportation had promulgated rules pursuant to the National Traffic and Motor Vehicle Safety Act for 1987 automobiles. The regulations required that some but not all of an auto manufacturer's 1987 vehicles be equipped with passive restraints such as airbags. Geier's Honda was outfitted only with seatbelts. The defendant argued that Geier's suit was preempted by federal law because her Honda was built in compliance with the federal safety requirements.

The problem with this is that National Traffic and Motor Vehicle Safety Act, which was the basis for the Department of Transportation regulations, had a savings clause that nothing within the law was meant to preempt any other cause of action that might exist. The law expressly said that "[c]ompliance with" a federal safety standard does "not exempt any person from any liability under the common law." [27] Geier argued that this provision prevented a finding of federal preemption.

The Supreme Court rejected Geier's argument and found federal preemption notwithstanding the savings clause. Justice Stephen Breyer, writing for the majority, said that this was not a situation of express preemption, but instead conflicts preemption. [28] Allowing state liability for cars made in compliance with the federal safety standard was deemed to conflict with the federal law. Justice Breyer declared that the savings clause did not foreclose preemption because there was no indication that Congress wanted to permit lawsuits when cars were made in compliance with the Department of Transportation's safety regulations. [29]

The only way to make sense of the case is to see it as putting a presumption in favor of preemption. [30] The federal statute expressly indicated that it did not preempt state law tort suits. There was no conflict between allowing Geier to sue and any provision of federal law. The Court nonetheless ruled in favor Honda and deemed a state tort action to be preempted. The decision obviously favored business over the consumer, but more generally, it limited states in an area—that is, tort law—traditionally governed by state regulation without an express preemption provision or any conflict between federal law and state law.

Lorillard Tobacco Co. v. Reilly[31]

In this case, the Court invalidated a Massachusetts regulation that prohibited outdoor cigarette advertisements, such as billboards, within one thousand feet of a playground or school. [32] The state's obvious goal was to decrease children's exposure to cigarette advertising. The Supreme Court relied on the language of a federal law adopted in 1969 that proscribes any "requirement or prohibition based on smoking and health . . . imposed under State law with respect to the advertising or promotion" of cigarettes. [33] The Court reviewed the history of federal regulation of cigarette advertising and concluded, "In the 1969 amendments, Congress not only enhanced its scheme to warn the public about the hazards of cigarette smoking, but also sought to protect the public, including youth, from being inundated with images of cigarette smoking in advertising. In pursuit of the latter goal, Congress banned electronic media advertising of cigarettes. And to the extent that Congress contemplated additional targeted regulation of cigarette advertising, it vested that authority in the FTC."[34] The Court decided that the preemption provision applied to all attempts by state and local governments to regulate cigarette advertising in any way.

Justice John Paul Stevens, in a dissenting opinion, argued that the state law was not preempted because it regulated the location and not the content of cigarette advertisements.[35] The majority, however, rejected this distinction and declared: "But the content/location distinction cannot be squared with the language of the pre-emption provision, which reaches all 'requirements' and 'prohibitions' 'imposed under State law.' A distinction between the content of advertising and the location of advertising in the [act] also cannot be reconciled with Congress' own location-based restriction, which bans advertising in electronic media, but not elsewhere."[36]

Again, this case can be understood only if it is seen as putting a presumption in favor of preemption.[37] The federal law was designed to limit cigarette advertising so as to protect children. The statutory provision was about the content of the warning labels on cigarette packages. The federal preemption provision was meant to keep states from adopting conflicting requirements for these labels that could interfere with marketing the product at the national level. There is nothing in the law which says or implies that *any* regulation of cigarette advertising is preempted by federal law. Indeed, the Massachusetts law advances the goals of the federal statute by protecting children from tobacco ads. The federal statute has nothing to do with the *location* of cigarette ads, such as whether there can be billboards near schools or whether ads in stores need to be a certain level above the floor. These issues, as the dissent points out, go entirely to placement, which is not addressed by the federal law.

Nonetheless, the Court protected the tobacco industry and invalidated the Massachusetts statute. As mentioned earlier, the case was 5–4, with the five justices—Rehnquist, O'Connor, Scalia, Kennedy, and Thomas—in the majority being the ones most committed to protecting states' rights. At the very least, the preemption provision is ambiguous as to whether it addresses location of advertising. A presumption against preemption would find that the statute does not apply to this. Congress, of course, if it disagreed, could then adopt a statutory provision providing preemption.

Crosby v. National Foreign Trade Council[38]

Massachusetts adopted a law that prohibited the state and its agencies from purchasing goods and services from companies that do business with Burma (Myanmar). The state adopted this regulation because of human rights violations in that nation. The Supreme Court unanimously found that the state law was preempted by federal law. Justice David Souter, writing for the Court, explained that Congress had enacted a sanctions regulation against Burma. He found that this preempted states from imposing their own sanctions.

Justice Souter rejected the state's argument that its policy furthered the federal objective of imposing sanctions on a nation that violated basic norms of human rights. Justice Souter wrote: "The conflicts are not rendered irrelevant by the State's argument that there is no real conflict between the statutes because they share the same goals and because some companies may comply with both sets of restrictions. The fact of a common end hardly neutralizes conflicting means." [39] Justice Souter went on to say that the existence of the state law "undermines the President's capacity . . . for effective diplomacy. It is not merely that the differences between the state and federal Acts in scope and type of sanctions threaten to complicate discussions; they compromise the very capacity of the President to speak for the nation with one voice in dealing with other governments." [40]

The decision, though unanimous, again must be seen as putting a presumption in favor of preemption. Congress had not expressed or implied any intent to preempt states from imposing sanctions, and the state law was not inconsistent with the federal law. There was no conflict between the Massachusetts regulation and matters of national diplomacy. The state was simply choosing how it would spend its taxpayers' money and who it would do business with. Many state and local governments adopted similar laws refusing to contract with companies doing business in South Africa at the time of apartheid. Nonetheless, the Court found preemption in *Crosby*.

American Insurance Association v. Garamendi[41]

California's Holocaust Victim Insurance Relief Act of 1999 (HVIRA) requires any insurer doing business in the state to disclose information about all insurance policies sold in Europe between 1920 and 1945. As Justice Ruth Bader Ginsburg noted in her dissent:

For insurance policies issued in Germany and other countries under Nazi control, historical evidence bears out, the combined forces of the German Government and the insurance industry engaged in larcenous takings of gigantic proportions. For example, insurance policies covered many of the Jewish homes and businesses destroyed in the state-sponsored pogrom known as Kristallnacht. By order of the Nazi regime, claims arising out of the officially enabled destruction were made payable not to the insured parties, but to the State. In what one historian called a "charade concocted by insurers and ministerial officials," insurers satisfied property loss claims by paying the State only a fraction of their full value.[42]

Despite some efforts by the federal government, insurance companies had been largely successful at stonewalling with regard to their Holocaust-era policies. To remedy this, and to protect its many residents who are Holocaust survivors and descendants of survivors, California enacted the HVIRA, which declares that "[i]nsurance companies doing business in the State of California have a responsibility to ensure that any involvement they or their related companies may have had with insurance policies of Holocaust victims [is] disclosed to the state."[43] The Relief Act requires insurance companies doing business in California to disclose information concerning insurance policies they or their affiliates sold in Europe between 1920 and 1945, and directs California's insurance commissioner to store the information in a publicly accessible "Holocaust Era Insurance Registry."[44] The commissioner is further directed to suspend the license of any insurer that fails to comply with the act's reporting requirements.[45] These measures, the act declares, are "necessary to protect the claims and interests of California residents, as well as to encourage the development of a resolution to these issues through the international process or through direct action by the State of California, as necessary."[46]

The Supreme Court, in a 5–4 decision, found that the California law was preempted by federal law. The Court said that the statute interfered with the president's conduct of the nation's foreign policy and was therefore preempted. The Court focused on executive agreements that the president had negotiated with Germany, France, and Austria.[47] However, the problem with this argument is that the California law does not conflict with any executive agreement, and as Justice Souter, writing for the majority, admitted, "[P]etitioners and the United States as amicus curiae [not a party to the litigation but an accepted adviser nevertheless] both have to acknowledge that the agreements include no preemption clause."[48] In other words, the Court found preemption despite the absence of any preemption clause and even though there was no conflict between federal law and the California statute.

In this case, the Court also relied on its prior decision in *Zschernig v. Miller* from 1968, which created a dormant foreign affairs power of the president.[49] In *Zschernig*, the Court declared unconstitutional an Oregon probate statute that prohibited inheritance by a nonresident alien, absent showings that the foreign heir would take the property "without confiscation" by his home country, and that American citizens would enjoy reciprocal rights of inheritance there. As Justice Souter explained in his majority opinion in *Garamendi*, the Court in *Zschernig* found "that state action with more than incidental effect on foreign affairs is preempted, even absent any affirmative federal activity in the subject area of the state law, and hence without any showing of conflict."[50] Even though no decision since *Zschernig* had relied on that case, the Court said that the case nevertheless provided a basis for invalidating California's law. The Court stressed that the California disclosure statute limited what the president might do in some hypothetical future negotiations. Moreover, Justice Souter said, "If any doubt about the clarity of the conflict remained, however, it would have to be resolved in the National Government's favor, given the weakness of the State's interest, against the backdrop of traditional state legislative subject matter, in regulating disclosure of European Holocaust-era insurance policies in the manner of HVIRA." [51]

At the very least, *American Insurance Association v. Garamendi* can be understood as creating an enormous presumption in favor of federal preemption of state law. In the absence of any express preemption or any conflict with federal law, the Court nonetheless found preemption simply because the California statute was seen as touching on an issue of foreign policy. The California law, of course, regulated businesses operating within its borders and did not directly deal with foreign nations. Nonetheless, the Court ruled that a broad "dormant foreign affairs power" of the president was sufficient to preclude the state law protecting California residents. It is hard to imagine a stronger presumption in favor of preemption.

WHAT'S WRONG WITH THE COURT'S APPROACH TO PREEMPTION?

The previous section attempted to show that many key preemption cases of the recent past are inconsistent with the Supreme Court's often-stated principle that federalism requires a presumption against preemption. The decisions, of course, also seem inconsistent with a Court committed to protecting states' rights and federalism. In each example, a significant choice of a state government was invalidated. One would imagine that a Court committed to protecting states would want to narrow the scope of federal preemption so as to leave more choices to state governments. But that was not at all the situation in the last ten years of the Rehnquist Court.

Yet, this does not go far enough from a normative perspective in explaining why the Court was wrong in these cases. The underlying question must be, Why have a presumption against preemption?[52] For justices committed to federalism and states' rights, the answer to this question should be easy. All the reasons they extol for protecting state governance by limiting federal power are justifications for a strong presumption against preemption.

In Chapter 3, I argued that the ultimate goals for the structure of government are providing effective governance and enhancing liberty. A broad preemption doctrine frustrates both of these objectives by invalidating desirable state laws and striking down state statutes that advance freedom. The four preemption cases described above are illustrative. I would argue, and I recognize others might disagree, that it is good to provide remediation for avoidable injury, to limit cigarette advertising directed at children, to forbid companies from doing business with human-rights indifferent nations, and to make information available to Holocaust-era victims and their descendants.

Moreover, even from the perspective of the values of federalism that the Supreme Court has identified, a broad approach to preemption is undesirable. For example, as discussed in Chapter 3, the Court often has emphasized that states are closer to the people and thus more likely to be responsive to public needs and concerns. This would justify a narrower approach to preemption so as to leave more governing authority to state and local governments.

Also, the Court has frequently spoken of the need to protect federalism for the sake of state-level experimentation. Justice Lewis Powell, in 1985, in dissenting from a case that upheld a federal law requiring state and local governments to pay their employees the minimum wage, lamented that "the Court does not explain how leaving the States, virtually at the mercy of the federal government, without recourse to judicial review will enhance their opportunities to experiment and serve as laboratories." [53] Likewise, Justice O'Connor, a couple of years previously, said that one of "the most valuable aspects of our federalism [is] . . . that the 50 states serve as laboratories for the development of new social, economic, and political ideas." [54]

Again, though, if the Court were to take seriously the desire to use states as laboratories for experimentation, it should apply a strong presumption against preemption. In each of the four recent preemption decisions described above, states were experimenting with ways of dealing with important social problems. But in none of these cases did the

Court give the slightest weight to the value of states as laboratories, which it is so fond of extolling when it comes to limiting congressional power.

Although, in Chapter 3, I questioned the relationship between these values and the Supreme Court's decisions invalidating federal laws, these considerations offer clear reasons for having a presumption against preemption. In addition to constraining experimentation, preempting state laws limits the ability of states to make choices as to how best to help their residents and limits the ability of states to advance liberty and freedom within their boundaries. Simply put, desirable state laws are invalidated when preemption is broadly inferred.

This can be seen by looking at the cases described above. In *Geier*, a state choice to grant remediation to injured citizens was preempted, notwithstanding a federal law preserving state causes of action. The benefits of liability, in terms of compensating injured people and deterring harmful products, are lost.

In *Lorillard*, the Court preempted a state law intended to protect children from tobacco advertising. Putting aside the First Amendment issue and focusing just on preemption, there can be no doubt that discouraging children from smoking is a compelling state interest. The Supreme Court frustrated the ability of states to respond to the desire of their residents to restrict cigarette advertising to children and stopped states from experimenting with new ways of accomplishing this.

In *Crosby*, the Court denied Massachusetts the ability to decide how it wanted to spend its taxpayers' money. The state law in *Crosby* forbade companies from doing business in Burma. The state was not making foreign policy for the United States but making a choice as to how Massachusetts dollars would be spent.

In *Garamendi*, the Court denied California the ability to help its many residents who were survivors of the Holocaust and descendants of survivors. The state was frustrated in its regulation of businesses within California, a traditional prerogative of state governments. Also, the country lost the benefit of seeing how California's experiment with this type of regulation would work.

To be clear, I am not arguing that Congress lacked the authority to preempt state laws in these areas. As I discuss in more detail later on,

Congress should be able to do so if it expressly declares that state and local regulations are preempted. Rather, my point is that in each of these cases, desirable state laws were lost because of the Court's abandoning the presumption against federalism. The laws were desirable because of what they sought to achieve. The state laws were desirable also in terms of the underlying values of federalism that were compromised by the presumption in favor of preemption in these cases.

It is striking that in each of these four recent decisions the Supreme Court ruled in favor of business interests and against state regulations. The four cases decided in favor of the automobile industry, cigarette manufacturers, companies doing business in Burma, and insurance firms. When these cases are juxtaposed with the Supreme Court's federalism decisions limiting federal power from the past decade, a clear hierarchy of the Rehnquist Court's values becomes clear. Two principles explain the majority of these rulings:[55]

1. If there is a state challenge to a federal civil rights law, the state wins and the federal interests lose.[56]
2. If there is a business challenge to a state regulatory law, the state loses.

This comparison undermines the view that the Rehnquist Court's decisions limiting federal power are animated by a concern over states' rights or by a neutral methodology. Instead, they reflect traditional conservative value choices to limit civil rights and to protect business. The preemption cases are thus illuminating in showing that this emperor really has no clothes; federalism is used, as it has been so often throughout American history, to cloak conservative substantive value choices in a seemingly more neutral and palatable garb.

A DIFFERENT VIEW OF FEDERALISM
AND PREEMPTION

As described throughout this book, for much of American history, and especially in recent years, federalism has been discussed primarily in terms of limiting federal power so as to protect state sovereignty. For example, during the first third of this century, dual federalism was entirely

about restricting the authority of Congress by narrowly defining its powers under Article I and by reserving a zone of activities to the states.[57]
Under the Warren Burger Court, federalism was used to restrict federal
court authority, such as the invocation of "Our Federalism" in *Younger
v. Harris*, which held that federal courts must abstain from decisions that
would interfere with on-going state court proceedings.[58] Most recently,
in the 1990s, in cases such as *New York v. United States*,[59] *United States
v. Lopez*,[60] and *Seminole Tribe of Florida v. Florida*,[61] the Court has invoked federalism to protect states from federal laws and federal courts.

But in this book, I argue for a dramatically different way of looking
at federalism: seeing it as empowerment, not limits. The key challenge
for the twenty-first century is government dealing with the enormous
problems facing American society. In this regard, federalism can make
a tremendous difference. My central thesis is that the value of having
multiple levels of government is having many institutions capable of acting to solve social problems. From this perspective, federalism should
be viewed as not being about limits on any level of government, but
about empowering each to act to solve difficult social issues.[62] In earlier
chapters, I have explained what this would mean in terms of Congress's
power and federal court authority.

My focus here is on what federalism as empowerment would mean in
terms of preemption. A key way of empowering state and local governments is by lessening the circumstances under which there is preemption by federal law. I propose preemption be found only in two circumstances: where a federal law expressly preempts state law, and where
there is an actual conflict between federal and state law. If a federal
statute contains a provision which declares that federal law is exclusive
in an area, courts would find state and local laws in that field to be preempted. Also, if federal law and state law were mutually exclusive, if it
were not possible to comply with both, then state and local laws would
be deemed preempted.

In other words, no longer would preemption be found based on a
state or local law interfering with a federal objective if there was not an
express preemption provision and if there was not a conflict between
federal and state law. Likewise, no longer would preemption be found

based on an inference from legislative history, or because of an inference that Congress wanted federal law to wholly occupy a field. Preemption would be limited to instances in which Congress, in the text of a statute, preempted state and local law, or in which there was a direct conflict between federal and state law.

This would preserve the ability of Congress to preempt state law whenever it deemed that to be in the nation's interest. It also would preserve the supremacy of federal law by ensuring that any conflict between the levels of government would be resolved in favor of federal power. But it would dramatically limit the ability of federal courts to find preemption based on inferences concerning congressional intent or because of a dormant power of the federal government. This approach to preemption would have produced the opposite results in *Geier*, *Lorillard*, *Crosby*, and *Garamendi*. As explained earlier, in none of these cases was preemption based either on an express statutory provision or on a conflict between federal and state law.

This, of course, would not resolve all preemption issues. As evidenced by the countless cases concerning ERISA (Employee Retirement Income Security Act) preemption, even explicit preemption provisions require interpretation as to their scope and application. Similarly, deciding whether there is a conflict between a federal and a state law often is disputed and depends on how the purpose of each is conceptualized. But limiting preemption in this way would go far toward empowering state and local governments to have more authority to reflect the choices of their residents, to experiment, and most importantly, to provide effective government and to advance liberty and freedom.

What are the objections to this approach to preemption? The most important is the same objection to empowering the federal government discussed previously: this could lead to more undesirable state and local laws. Power, of course, can be used for good or for ill. States might use their greater authority, rather than to protect consumers and advance individual freedom, to advance more pernicious objectives.[63] Empowering government can be bad.

There, of course, is an irony if this argument is made by those who urge limits on federal power in the name of states' rights and federalism.

In that context, there is a proclaimed need to trust state and local governments. I return to Justice Kennedy's very significant words in *Alden v. Maine*,[64] which held that state governments have sovereign immunity and cannot be sued in federal court, even to enforce federal statutes. In response to an argument that this would undermine the supremacy of federal law, Justice Kennedy declared that "trust in the good faith of state governments provides an adequate assurance" of state compliance with federal mandates. It is ironic that in the area of preemption, trust in the good faith of state governments seems to vanish.

But there is a more critical response to those who rightly object that state and local governments might act in an undesirable way: Congress could preempt state actions, and courts, of course, could invalidate laws that conflict with the Constitution and federal law. Any time that Congress has the authority to act, it can enact a law expressly preempting state and local regulation. If Congress did not like the Massachusetts law regulating the placement of cigarette advertisements, it could adopt a federal statute prohibiting states from regulating the location of these ads. If Congress did not like the Massachusetts law refusing to do business with companies engaged in business in Burma, the legislature, under its power to regulate commerce with foreign nations, could adopt a statute forbidding such state actions. If Congress did not want states such as California requiring insurance companies to disclose their Holocaust-era policies, it could adopt a federal statute forbidding such state regulations.

In other words, I am not arguing for eliminating preemption. Quite the contrary, I believe that preemption is essential to ensure the supremacy of federal law. But I do argue for a dramatically reduced preemption doctrine so as to empower state and local governments.

A more nuanced argument against my position would be that there are many situations in which preemption would be desirable but for which Congress cannot or will not adopt preemption provisions and for which there is not a conflict between federal and state law. In these instances, the reduced preemption doctrine would mean that undesirable state and local laws remain. This is not unlike the argument made in favor of having a dormant commerce clause, which provides that the courts have the power to strike down state and local laws that place an undue burden on interstate commerce. The concern animating the dormant commerce clause is that there are too many instances in which state and local governments will excessively burden interstate commerce and in which Congress cannot or will not act. It is thought necessary to have courts strike down such state and local laws, rather than rely solely on Congress to preempt them.

The problem with this argument is that it requires an impossible comparative assessment. The comparison would need to be between the number and effect of the bad state laws that remain with narrower preemption as opposed to the number and effect of good laws that are struck down with a broader approach to preemption. There is no way that such a comparison ever could be attempted. Even if there could be agreement as to what are good and bad laws, there is not a way to count or to make a qualitative assessment of their impact. The choice between these perspectives must be resolved in another way.

One is the assumption of this book, that society faces enormous problems, and empowering government to deal with them is desirable. But I realize that this argument will not persuade those who do not share this assumption and who prefer a broader preemption doctrine out of concern for undesirable state and local laws remaining in force because of congressional inability or unwillingness to enact express preemption provisions.

Especially for these critics, there is another, more important, response. The approach to preemption that I urge would mean a reduced role for the judiciary and a greater role for the legislature. This has the virtue of leaving more governance to the democratic process. There would be fewer situations in which courts would find preemption, and more of the burden would be placed on Congress to decide whether state and local laws should be preempted. Again, of course, it must be recognized that federalism as empowerment would not eliminate the judicial role. Courts would still need to decide whether there was express preemption or a conflict between federal and state law. A significant number of preemption cases involve just these issues. The federal judiciary still would play a crucial role in invalidating state and local laws where there is an applicable express preemption provision or where there is a conflict between federal and state law. But cutting back on preemption, by definition, would lessen the situations in which federal courts would invalidate state and local laws.

An advantage of this, of course, is that more governance is left to the political process and less to the unelected judiciary. Indeed, that is the virtue of federalism as empowerment in all areas. Broadly defining the scope of Congress's power and eliminating the Tenth Amendment as a constraint would reduce the situations in which federal courts strike down federal laws.

Conservative justices are quick to extol the merits of the democratic process when opposing judicial protection of individual rights. But they seem to give little weight to the democratic process when preempting state and local laws or when striking down federal statutes in the name of federalism. Federalism as empowerment would mean more deference to federal, state, and local governments, and far fewer situations in which courts strike down laws that are the product of the democratic process.

Lest I be accused of hypocrisy, I do not want to overstate the need for judicial deference to the political process. I believe in robust judicial protection of individual liberties and civil rights, even when it displaces the choices of popularly elected legislatures. My point is simply that federalism as empowerment, by limiting situations in which courts will strike down federal, state, and local laws, has the appeal of greater judicial deference to the democratic process.

Under the approach I urge in this book, as described most pointedly in Chapter 5, the role of the federal courts in protecting individual liberties and civil rights would be enhanced. Also, as discussed in Chapter 3, I would eliminate sovereign immunity as a limit on the ability of the federal government to provide relief against state governments. But federal courts would play much less of a role in enforcing the structure of government.[65] Congress would be empowered with much broader authority under the commerce clause and under the enforcement provisions of the post–Civil War amendments. No longer would the Tenth Amendment be a limit on federal power. At the same time, a reduced preemption doctrine would mean that state and local governments would have more authority to legislate. Simply put, government at all levels would be more empowered to solve society's problems.

Conclusion

FEDERALISM AS EMPOWERMENT SEEMS far removed from what the United States Supreme Court is willing to embrace today or in the foreseeable future. I realize that some may shrug at this endeavor and ask, Why bother?

In responding, I would begin by pointing out that much of what I am urging is within the realm of the possible. The broad definition of federal legislative power that I advocate was the law throughout the nineteenth century and for almost sixty years from 1937 until the 1990s. Moreover, if John Kerry had won the United States presidential election in 2004, rather than George W. Bush, we likely already would be seeing a return to these principles. Virtually all the decisions protecting states' rights during the Rehnquist Court were 5–4 rulings, with Chief Justice William Rehnquist and Justices Sandra Day O'Connor, Antonin Scalia, Anthony Kennedy, and Clarence Thomas in the majority. Justices John Paul Stevens, David Souter, Ruth Bader Ginsburg, and Stephen Breyer dissented.

If, rather than President Bush, President Kerry had appointed justices to replace the outgoing Rehnquist and O'Connor, there likely would be six votes today to overrule the past fifteen years of federalism decisions limiting Congress's powers, reviving the Tenth Amendment as a limit on federal authority, and expanding state sovereign immunity. These new justices, together with Stevens, Souter, Ginsburg, and Breyer, likely would have gone a long way toward what I advocate in this book.

Now, though, with Chief Justice John Roberts and Justice Samuel Alito joining Justices Scalia, Kennedy, and Thomas, there are five votes to continue and increase the use of federalism as a limit on federal power. To me, that makes it even more important to criticize this effort and to propose an alternative vision.

Federalism is a unique area in constitutional law because the Supreme Court has not followed a consistent path. It instead has swung back and forth between two alternative perspectives. As described throughout this book, for the first one hundred years of American history, the Court took a very nationalist view, broadly defining federal power and rejecting the need for judicial protection of state governments. For the first third of the twentieth century, until 1936, the Court shifted to a federalist perspective. It narrowly defined Congress's power and used the Tenth Amendment to restrict federal authority for the express purpose of protecting state governments. Then the pendulum swung back sharply toward the nationalist viewpoint, and from 1937 to the 1990s, the Court returned to a very expansive interpretation of Congress's power. But the addition of conservative justices, especially in the appointments by Presidents Ronald Reagan and George H. W. Bush, meant that by the 1990s, the Court would shift back to enforcing federalism and states' rights as a limit on federal power.

This history leaves no doubt that some day the pendulum will swing back again toward the nationalist view and away from judicial use of federalism to constrain federal authority. I obviously hope that day comes very soon. But whenever the shift occurs, there will be a need for an intellectual foundation for the new approach to federalism. That is my ultimate aim for this book. I have tried to articulate a very different view of federalism than the ones that have been debated and discussed for so long.

Throughout American history, the focus has been on the extent to which federalism should be a limit on federal power. I urge courts to look at federalism as empowerment to ensure that all levels of government have the authority needed to deal with society's most grave problems. America in the twenty-first century faces global warming, woefully inadequate health care, a growing gulf between rich and poor, and the seemingly intractable racial divide. These, and others, are issues that require the attention of governing agencies at all levels. In this book, I have sought to describe how we can best equip and empower government with the tools to tackle these problems.

Notes

INTRODUCTION

1. New York v. United States, 550 U.S. 144 (1992).
2. Printz v. United States, 521 U.S. 898 (1997).
3. United States v. Lopez, 514 U.S. 549 (1995).
4. United States v. Morrison, 529 U.S. 598 (2000).
5. By "formalism," I simply mean that the Court was reasoning deductively from assumed premises and did not consider the functional benefits or disadvantages of its decisions. I discuss the formalistic nature of the decisions in detail in Chapter 2.
6. City of Boerne v. Flores, 521 U.S. 507 (1997).
7. Florida Prepaid Postsecondary Education Expense Board v. College Savings Bank, 527 U.S. 627 (1999) (federal law authorizing suits against states for patent violations deemed unconstitutional; Eleventh Amendment bars such suits); Kimel v. Florida Board of Regents, 528 U.S. 62 (2000) (state governments cannot be sued for violating the Age Discrimination in Employment Act because the law does not fit within the scope of Congress's power under Section 5 of the Fourteenth Amendment); University of Alabama v. Garrett, 531 U.S. 356 (2001) (state governments cannot be sued for violating Title I of the Americans with Disabilities Act, which prohibits employment discrimination against the disabled).
8. Geier v. American Honda Motor Co. Inc., 529 U.S. 861 (2000).
9. Crosby v. National Foreign Trade Council, 530 U.S. 363 (2000).
10. Lorillard Tobacco Co. v. Reilly, 533 U.S. 525 (2001).
11. The commerce clause refers, of course, to Congress's power to regulate commerce with foreign nations and Indian tribes as well as among the states. Section 5 of the Fourteenth Amendment authorizes Congress to enact laws to enforce the Fourteenth Amendment, which includes the due process, equal protection, and citizenship clauses.
12. The Tenth Amendment provides that all powers not granted to the United States, or prohibited to the states, are reserved to the states and the people, respectively. Its meaning has been in dispute throughout American history, especially as to whether it reserves a zone of activities for exclusive state control.
13. See, e.g., City of Los Angeles v. Lyons, 461 U.S. 95 (1983) (relying on federalism, in part, to hold that plaintiffs seeking injunctive or declaratory relief must show a likelihood of future harm and denied standing to a plaintiff to challenge the police use of a chokehold).
14. See, e.g., Seminole Tribe of Florida v. Florida, 517 U.S. 44 (1996) (holding that Congress can authorize suits against states only when acting pursuant to Section 5 of the Fourteenth Amendment and not pursuant to any other congressional power).
15. See, e.g., Younger v. Harris, 401 U.S. 37 (federal courts must abstain and may not enjoin pending state court proceedings).

16. See, e.g., McCleskey v. Zant, 499 U.S. 467 (1991) (federal courts may not hear successive habeas corpus petitions unless there is a showing of cause and prejudice, or actual innocence); Teague v. Lane, 489 U.S. 288 (1989) (federal courts may not hear habeas corpus petitions asserting new constitutional rights unless they are rights that would have retroactive application).

17. In my criticism of the Supreme Court's decisions, I am very much in agreement with Judge John Noonan's book, *Narrowing the Nation's Power: The Supreme Court Sides with the States* (2002). Although I agree with many of Judge Noonan's criticisms of the Supreme Court's recent federalism decisions, my approach is quite different from Judge Noonan's. My focus is on justifying a new conception of federalism as empowerment of government at all levels.

18. United States v. Lopez, 514 U.S. 549 (1995) (invalidating the Gun-Free School Zone Act, which prohibits possessing a firearm within one thousand feet of a school).

19. Printz v. United States, 521 U.S. 898 (1997); New York v. United States, 550 U.S. 144 (1992). The earlier decision was National League of Cities v. Usery, 426 U.S. 833 (1976), which was overruled in Garcia v. San Antonio Metropolitan Transit Authority, 469 U.S. 528 (1985).

20. See, e.g., Federal Maritime Commission v. South Carolina Port Authority, 535 U.S. 743 (2002) (state governments cannot be sued in agency adjudicatory proceedings); Alden v. Maine, 527 U.S. 706 (1999) (state governments cannot be sued in state court, even on federal claims, without their consent).

21. See generally *Contract with America: The Bold Plan by Rep. Newt Gingrich, Rep. Dick Armey, and the House Republicans to Change the Nation* (E. Gillespie & B. Schelihas eds. 1994).

22. Unfunded Mandates Reform Act of 1995, 2 U.S.C. §1501 (West Supp. 1997).

23. 28 U.S.C. §§2249–66 (Supp. 1997).

24. For example, Federal Maritime Commission v. South Carolina Port Authority; University of Alabama v. Garrett; Kimel v. Florida Board of Regents; Alden v. Maine; Florida Prepaid v. College Savings Bank; Printz v. United States; Seminole Tribe of Florida v. Florida; and United States v. Lopez all have been 5–4 decisions, with these justices in the majority and Justices John Paul Stevens, David Souter, Ruth Bader Ginsburg, and Stephen Breyer dissenting.

25. Personal Responsibility and Work Opportunity Reconciliation Act of 1996, Public Law No. 104-193, 110 Stat. 2105.

26. In October Term 2006, Chief Justice Roberts and Justice Alito voted in the conservative direction in every ideologically divided case. See, e.g., Gonzales v. Carhart, 127 S. Ct. 1610 (2007) (the federal Partial Birth Abortion Ban Act of 2003 is constitutional); Parents Involved in Community Schools v. Seattle School District No. 1, 127 S. Ct. 2738 (2007) (school systems violated equal protection in using race in assigning students to public schools so as to achieve desegregation).

27. See, e.g., Samuel H. Beer, *To Make a Nation: The Rediscovery of American Federalism*, 224 (1993).

28. See, e.g., Carter v. Carter Coal Co., 298 U.S. 238 (1936) (invalidating federal regulation of employment, including a minimum wage); Hammer v. Dagenhart, 247 U.S. 251 (1918) (invalidating the federal regulation of child labor); United States v. E. C. Knight, 156 U.S. 1 (1895) (holding that the Sherman Antitrust Act could not be applied to businesses engaged in production).

29. See Forrest McDonald, *A Constitutional History of the United States*, 193 (1982); William Manchester, *The Glory and the Dream*, 164–66 (1974).
30. Beer, *supra* note 27, at 19–20.
31. Id. at 2.
32. William Brennan, *State Constitutions and the Protection of Individual Rights*, 90 Harv. L. Rev. 489 (1977).
33. Others have noted this as well. See, e.g., H. Geoffrey Moulton Jr., *The Quixotic Search for a Judicially Enforceable Federalism*, 83 Minn. L. Rev. 849, 921 (1999).
34. For an excellent argument that the Supreme Court's federalism decision in *Printz v. United States* was highly formalistic, see Evan Caminker, Printz, *State Sovereignty, and the Limits of Federalism*, 199 Sup. Ct. Rev. (1997).
35. 426 U.S. 833 (1976).
36. My approach shares many characteristics with Robert Schapiro's excellent writings on interactive federalism. See, e.g., Robert A. Schapiro, *Toward a Theory of Interactive Federalism*, 91 Iowa L. Rev. 243 (2005).
37. In this regard, in Chapter 4, I expressly challenge the reasoning of scholars who argue that judicial protection of federalism is needed to uphold the rule of law and to safeguard the federalist structure of American government. See Vicki C. Jackson, *Federalism and the Uses and Limits of Law:* Printz *and Principle?* 111 Harv. L. Rev. 2180 (1998).

CHAPTER I

1. 312 U.S. 657 (1941).
2. 469 U.S. 528 (1985).
3. 401 U.S. 37, 44–45 (1971).
4. Surprisingly few commentators have discussed the seeming inconsistency between the Supreme Court's Tenth and Eleventh Amendment decisions. An exception is George Brown, *State Sovereignty under the Burger Court—How the Eleventh Amendment Survived the Death of the Tenth: Some Broader Implications of* Atascadero State Hospital v. Scanlon, 74 Geo. L. J. 363 (1985).
5. See, e.g., United States v. Georgia, 126 S. Ct. 877 (2006) (state governments may be sued pursuant to Title II of the Americans with Disabilities Act, 42 U.S.C. §12131, which prohibits state and local governments from discriminating against people with disabilities in government programs, services, and activities, and from violating the constitutional rights of prisoners in terms of cruel and unusual punishment); Central Virginia Community College v. Katz, 126 S. Ct. 990 (2006) (sovereign immunity does not apply in Bankruptcy Court proceedings); Gonzales v. Raich, 125 S. Ct. 2195 (2005) (the federal Controlled Substances Act does not exceed the scope of Congress's authority under the commerce clause when it is applied to marijuana grown within a state for personal medicinal use or distribution without charge); Tennessee v. Lane, 541 U.S. 509 (2004) (state governments may be sued for violating the family leave provisions of the Family and Medical Leave Act); Nevada Department of Human Resources v. Katz, 538 U.S. 721 (2003) (state governments may be sued for violating the family leave provisions of the Family and Medical Leave Act).
6. Bruce Ackerman has written extensively as to why 1937 should be considered a "constitutional moment" that effectively changed the nature of the Constitution. See

Bruce Ackerman, *We the People: Foundations* (1992); Bruce Ackerman, *The Storrs Lecture: Discovering the Constitution*, 93 Yale L. J. 1013 (1984).

7. 301 U.S. 1 (1937).

8. 312 U.S. 667 (1941).

9. 317 U.S. 111 (1942).

10. Indeed, the very phrase "dual federalism" vanished from the Supreme Court reports until reinvoked by Justice Scalia's majority opinion in Printz v. United States, 521 U.S. 898, 918 (1997). Now it is frequently used by the Court. See, e.g., Federal Maritime Commission v. South Carolina State Port Authority, 535 U.S. 743, 751 (2002).

11. See, e.g., E. C. Knight Co. v. United States, 156 U.S. 1 (1895) (precluding application of federal antitrust laws to production).

12. Hammer v. Dagenhart, 247 U.S. 251 (1918).

13. United States v. Butler, 297 U.S. 1 (1936).

14. Carter v. Carter Coal Co., 298 U.S. 238 (1936).

15. 312 U.S. at 462.

16. 304 U.S. 64, 78–80 (1938).

17. Id. at 78–80.

18. 304 U.S. at 73 n.5, citing Charles Warren, *New Light on the History of the Federal Judiciary Act of 1789*, 37 Harv. L. Rev. 49 (1923).

19. Warren said that the original draft of the Rules of Decision Act provided "[t]hat the Statute law of the several States in force for the time being and their unwritten or common law now in use, whether by adoption from the common law of England, the ancient statutes of the same or otherwise, except where the constitution, Treaties or Statutes of the United States shall otherwise require or provide shall be regarded as the rules of decision in the trials at common law in the courts of the United States in cases where they apply." Warren, *supra* note 18, at 51–52, 81–88, 108. Warren contended that the drafters of the Judiciary Act intended for state common law to be followed and that the modification in this law was only stylistic.

20. It should be noted that some contend that Warren misinterpreted the language that was deleted; the original phrasing simply provided that the states' common law would control only until federal courts developed the federal common law to replace it. William Crosskey, *Politics and the Constitution in the History of the United States*, vol. 1, 626–28; vol. 2, 866–71 (1953).

21. Henry Friendly, *In Praise of Erie: And of the New Federal Common Law*, 39 N.Y.U. L. Rev. 383, 390 (1964).

22. 304 U.S. at 74. Justice Brandeis phrased the argument in terms of discrimination. He wrote: "Swift v. Tyson introduced grave discrimination by noncitizens against citizens. It made rights enjoyed under the unwritten 'general law' vary according to whether enforcement was sought in the state or federal court. . . . Thus, the doctrine rendered impossible equal protection of the law." Id. at 74–75. This appears to be a rhetorical flourish rather than a constitutional argument because the Supreme Court had not yet applied the requirements of equal protection to the federal government. This did not expressly occur until Bolling v. Sharpe, 347 U.S. 497 (1954).

23. 304 U.S. at 77–78.

24. 304 U.S. at 79.

25. Id. at 78.

26. 301 U.S. 1 (1937).
27. Id. at 31 (quoting §2[7] of the act).
28. Id. at 26.
29. Id. at 40.
30. Id. at 37 (citations omitted).
31. Almost simultaneously, the Supreme Court abandoned its substantive due process doctrines that limited the ability of state and local governments to regulate the economy.
32. National Labor Relations Board v. Friedman-Harry Marks Clothing Co., 301 U.S. 58 (1937). See also United States v. Fainblatt, 306 U.S. 601 (1939) (upholding application of the act to a small New Jersey company that employed only sixty people).
33. 312 U.S. 100 (1941).
34. Id. at 113.
35. Id. at 115.
36. Id. at 124.
37. 317 U.S. 111 (1942).
38. Id. at 120.
39. Id. at 124.
40. Id. at 127.
41. Id. at 127–28. In 2005, the Supreme Court applied *Wickard* to hold that Congress could regulate the private cultivation and possession of marijuana for medicinal purposes. The Court held that this fit within the scope of Congress's commerce power because like the wheat in *Wickard*, marijuana is a commodity that is bought and sold in interstate commerce. Gonzalez v. Raich, 545 U.S. 1 (2005). *Raich* is discussed below at text accompanying note 148.
42. Laurence Tribe, *American Constitutional Law*, 378 (2d ed. 1987).
43. 426 U.S. 833 (1976).
44. In Hodel v. Virginia Surface Mining & Reclamation Association, 452 U.S. 264 (1981), the Court articulated a four-part test for when the Tenth Amendment limits Congress's power. In *Hodel*, the Court upheld a federal law that regulated strip mining and required reclamation of strip-mined land. The Court said that for a federal law to violate the Tenth Amendment, it needed to regulate "the States as States"; it must "address matters that are indisputably attribute[s] of state sovereignty"; it must directly impair the states' ability to "structure integral operations in areas of traditional governmental functions"; and it must not be such that "the nature of the federal interest . . . justifies state submission." The Court in *Hodel* found that the law, the Surface Mining Control and Reclamation Act of 1977, was constitutional because it did not regulate the states as states.
45. 469 U.S. 528 (1985).
46. Herbert Wechsler, *The Political Safeguards of Federalism: The Role of the States in the Composition and Selection of the National Government*, 54 Colum. L. Rev. 543 (1954).
47. 312 U.S. 496 (1941).
48. Id. at 500. Yet, commentators question whether this rationale justifies abstention. For example, Professor Martha Field challenges whether the *Pullman* abstention actually lessens friction between federal and state courts. There are, Professor Field

suggests, two possible outcomes when a federal court decides the state law issue instead of allowing the state court to rule. The federal court could come to the same conclusion as the state court would. For example, both might have invalidated the Texas law, or both might have upheld it. In such circumstances, friction is minimal or nonexistent because the result is identical regardless of which court decides the case. Alternatively, the federal court might reach a conclusion that differs from that of the state court. Under the *Pullman* abstention, this would occur if the state court upheld the regulation on state law grounds, but the federal court invalidated it on constitutional grounds when the matter returned to federal court. In this situation, abstention increases rather than decreases friction because the state court's decision is rendered superfluous and, in effect, is overruled.

49. 312 U.S. at 499–500.

50. But it should be noted that federal courts often are entrusted with resolving uncertain questions of state law. For example, under Erie Railroad Co. v. Tompkins, federal courts apply state law in all diversity cases. Frequently, this involves federal courts interpreting state laws that are unclear. See England v. Louisiana State Board of Medical Examiners, 375 U.S. 411, 426 (1964) (Douglas, J., concurring) (criticizing the *Pullman* abstention; under *Erie*, federal courts decide state law questions; the "fact that those questions are complex and difficult is no excuse for a refusal by the District Court to entertain the suit"). Moreover, the likelihood of error is uncertain. Federal district court judges sit in the same state as the state's judiciary. In most instances, the federal judges practiced law in that state and frequently decide cases under state law. Hence, it is questionable whether they are less capable of correctly interpreting state law than are state court judges.

51. See also Burford v. Sun Oil Co., 319 U.S. 315 (1943) (federal courts should abstain when there are challenges to complex state administrative procedures).

52. See, e.g., Fay v. Noia, 372 U.S. 391 (1963) (issues can be presented on federal habeas corpus that were not presented in state court unless there was a deliberate bypass of state court procedures).

53. For an excellent critique of these decisions restricting federal court jurisdiction, see Larry W. Yackle, *Reclaiming the Federal Courts* (1994).

54. Welch v. State Department of Highways and Public Transportation, 483 U.S. 468 (1987) (holding that states will not be found to have "constructively waived" their Eleventh Amendment immunity); Pennhurst State School and Hosp. v. Halderman, 465 U.S. 89 (1984) (holding that state officers may not be sued in federal court on pendent state law claims).

55. See, e.g., McCleskey v. Zant, 499 U.S. 467 (1991) (holding that prisoners may bring only one habeas corpus petition unless they can show cause and prejudice for not raising an issue in their initial petition); Teague v. Lane, 489 U.S. 288 (1989) (holding that habeas petitions may not assert new rights unless they are rights that would have retroactive application).

56. See, e.g., Younger v. Harris, 401 U.S. 37 (1971).

57. 423 U.S. 362 (1976).

58. 401 U.S. 37, 44–45 (1971).

59. 469 U.S. at 556.

60. Wechsler, *supra* note 46, at 543.

61. More recently, Professor Jesse Choper has advanced a similar thesis. See Jesse Choper, *Judicial Review and the National Political Process* (1980).

62. 401 U.S. at 41–45. See also Trainor v. Hernandez, 431 U.S. 434, 446 (1977); Judice v. Vail, 430 U.S. 327 (1977).

63. 454 U.S. 100, 113 (1981).

64. Migra v. Warren City School District Board of Education, 465 U.S. 75, 85 (1984); Allen v. McCurry, 449 U.S. 90, 96 (1980).

65. Kuhlmann v. Wilson, 477 U.S. 436, 453–54 n.16 (1986); Engle v. Isaac, 456 U.S. 107, 128 n.33 (1982). See also Paul Bator, *The States and Federal Constitutional Litigation*, 22 Wm. & Mary L. Rev. 605, 614–15 (1981).

66. I discuss this more fully in Erwin Chemerinsky, *Foreword: The Vanishing Constitution*, 103 Harv. L. Rev. 43, 102 (1989), and in Chapter 4.

67. Professor Larry Kramer makes a strong argument that the interests of the states are protected through mechanisms such as administrative bureaucracies and political parties. Larry Kramer, *Understanding Federalism*, 47 Vand. L. Rev. 1485 (1994). These are not the traditional types of political safeguards, but rather they offer a much more subtle account of the way in which the interests of the states are protected in the political process.

68. See Andrzej Rapaczynski, *From Sovereignty to Process: The Jurisprudence of Federalism after Garcia*, Sup. Ct. Rev. 341, 393 (1985).

69. Id. at 393.

70. See, e.g., David Ryden, *Representation in Crisis: The Constitution, Interest Groups, and Political Parties* (1996); Martin Shapiro, *Interest Groups and Supreme Court Appointments*, 84 Nw. U. L. Rev. 935, 938–39 (1990); Daniel R. Ortiz, *Federalism, Reapportionment, and Incumbency: Leading the Legislature to Police Itself*, 653 J. L. & Pol. 412 (1988).

71. See, e.g., Stone v. Powell, 428 U.S. 465, 494 n.35 (1976) (proclaiming that state courts are as willing and able to enforce federal rights as federal courts).

72. Jack H. Friedenthal et al., *Civil Procedure*, 24–25 (2d ed. 1992) (discussing the rationale for the existence of diversity jurisdiction).

73. William Wiecek, *The Reconstruction of Federal Judicial Power, 1863–1875*, 13 Am. J. Legal Hist. 333, 338 (1969) (describing distrust in state governments as the basis for the Civil Rights Removal law).

74. Id. at 338.

75. Max Farrand, 2 *The Records of the Federal Convention* 27–28 (1966) (quoting Madison, "Confidence cannot be put in the State Tribunals as guardians of national authority and national interests").

76. The concern for comity might reflect a related issue: a worry that "insulting" state court judges will adversely affect their performance. See Paul Bator, *The States*, supra note 65, at 625–26. But this is based on unsupported assumptions about the perceptions of state court judges and the behavior that follows from these perceptions. I respond in detail to this argument in Erwin Chemerinsky, *Parity Reconsidered: Defining a Role for the Federal Judiciary*, 36 U.C.L.A. L. Rev. 233, 288–89 (1988), and I discuss it in Chapter 5. Moreover, the same concern could be expressed that federal legislative action might be seen as an insult to state legislatures and could adversely affect their performance. Like the other arguments concerning federalism,

it seems questionable and not a basis for distinguishing between federal legislative and judicial power.

77. See Erwin Chemerinsky, *Federal Jurisdiction* ch. 7 (5th ed. 2007) (reviewing the history of the adoption of the Eleventh Amendment).

78. See Quackenbush v. Allstate, 517 U.S. 706 (1996); Deakins v. Monaghan, 484 U.S. 193 (1988).

79. Unfunded mandates now are restricted both by federal statute, see Unfunded Mandates Reform Act of 1995, 2 U.S.C.A. §1501 (West Supp. 1997), and by the Supreme Court, see Printz v. United States (1997).

80. One answer could be that states need protection from the federal courts, but not Congress, because there is the possibility of political influence and control of Congress, but not of the courts. However, this argument depends on the Wechsler thesis, discussed above, which says that states as entities have significant political power in Congress, especially as compared with other interest groups. Ultimately, it assumes that Congress will be more sensitive to the interests of states than will be the judiciary—a questionable premise.

81. See, e.g., Erwin Chemerinsky, *The Vanishing Constitution, supra* note 66, at 57.

82. Burt Neuborne, *The Myth of Parity*, 90 Harv. L. Rev. 1105–6 (1977).

83. In this chapter, I describe the cases and show how individually and collectively they establish a limit on Congress's power. In Chapter 2, I criticize each of these decisions for its formalist approach to federalism.

84. 469 U.S. at 580 (Rehnquist, J., dissenting).

85. 501 U.S. 452 (1991).

86. 505 U.S. 144 (1992).

87. 42 U.S.C. §2021e(d)(2)(C)(I).

88. 505 U.S. at 188.

89. Id. at 160.

90. Id. at 177.

91. 505 U.S. at 159–60.

92. See, e.g., Alden v. Maine, 527 U.S. 706 (1999) (states cannot be sued in state court even on federal claims).

93. 514 U.S. 549 (1995).

94. 18 U.S.C. §922(q)(1)(A); §921(a)(25).

95. Id. at 1626.

96. Id. at 1629.

97. 379 U.S. 241 (1964).

98. Id. at 1629.

99. See, e.g., Shreveport Rate Cases, 234 U.S. 342 (1914).

100. Id. at 1630.

101. Id.

102. Id. at 1659.

103. Another important opinion by Justice Thomas was his dissent in United States Term Limits v. Thornton, 514 U.S. 779 (1995). The majority declared unconstitutional a state law that limited essentially created term limits for members of Congress elected from that state. Justice Thomas wrote a dissenting opinion, joined by Rehnquist, O'Connor, and Scalia, that argued that federalism requires upholding the state law.

Justice Thomas emphasized that states retain ultimate sovereignty except in those areas where there is an express grant of power to the federal government. The opinion, though one vote short of a majority, is an important statement of four justices as to their deep commitment to using federalism to protect state governments.

104. As discussed in Gonzales v. Raich, 545 U.S. 1 (2005), the Court held that the federal law prohibiting cultivation and possession of marijuana for medicinal purposes was within the scope of Congress's commerce clause power.

105. In the years since *Lopez*, a number of federal statutes were challenged in the lower federal courts based on the case. Most of these challenges were unsuccessful. See, e.g., United States v. Guerra, 164 F.3d 1358 (11th Cir. 1999) (upholding Hobbs Act, 18 U.S.C. §1951); United States v. Owens, 159 F.3d 221 (6th Cir. 1998) (upholding federal money laundering statute, 18 U.S.C. §1956); (upholding Clean Water Act); Cheffer v. Reno, 55 F.3d 1517 (11th Cir. 1995) (upholding 18 U.S.C. §248, Freedom of Access to Clinic Entrances Act); United States v. Hanna, 55 F.3d 1456 (9th Cir. 1995) (upholding 18 U.S.C. §922(g)(1), Possession of a Firearm by a Convicted Felon); United States v. Wilks, 58 F.3d 1518 (10th Cir. 1995) (upholding 18 U.S.C. §922[o], Possession of a Machine Gun); United States v. Bishop, 66 F.3d 569 (3d Cir. 1995) (upholding 18 U.S.C. §2119, Carjacking); United States v. Hallmark Construction Co., 14 F. Supp. 2d 1069 (N.D. Ill. 1998). However, a few challenges based on Lopez have been successful (same); but see United States v. Murphy, 893 F. Supp. 614 (D.Va. 1995) (upholding same); United States v. Hampshire, 892 F. Supp. 1327 (D.Kan. 1995) (upholding same).

106. 517 U.S. 44 (1996).

107. 491 U.S. 1 (1989).

108. 517 U.S. at 45.

109. Id. at 66.

110. 521 U.S. 898 (1997).

111. 18 U.S.C. §922.

112. 521 U.S. at 918.

113. Id.

114. Id. at 922.

115. Id.

116. Id. at 935.

117. 521 U.S. 507 (1997).

118. 494 U.S. 872 (1990).

119. 42 U.S.C. §2000b(b).

120. Id. at 519–20 (emphasis added).

121. 529 U.S. 598 (2000).

122. 529 U.S. at 598, 613.

123. Id. at 615.

124. Id.

125. Id.

126. Id. at 617–18.

127. Id. at 627 (Thomas, J., concurring).

128. Id.

129. Id. at 634.

130. 527 U.S. 627 (1999).

131. 528 U.S. 62 (2000).

132. 531 U.S. 356 (2001).

133. 527 U.S. 706 (1999).

134. 527 U.S. at 711.

135. 535 U.S. 743 (2002).

136. Id. at 760 ("The preeminent purpose of state sovereign immunity is to accord States the dignity that is consistent with their status as sovereign entities.").

137. See, e.g., Laurence Tribe, *Unraveling National League of Cities: The New Federalism and Affirmative Rights to Essential Government Services*, 90 Harv. L. Rev. 1065 (1977); Frank Michelman, *States' Rights and States' Roles: The Permutations of "Sovereignty" in* National League of Cities v. Usery, 86 Yale L. J. 1165 (1977) (forecasting major implications from the decision, including it being used to create an affirmative right to government services).

138. See, e.g., Hammer v. Dagenhart, 247 U.S. 251 (1918).

139. 483 U.S. 203 (1987).

140. Indeed, some scholars have urged that federalism limits be imposed on Congress's spending power. See, e.g., Lynn Baker, *Conditional Federal Spending and States' Rights*, 574 Annals 104 (2001). For an excellent discussion of this, see Neil S. Siegel, *Commandeering and Its Alternatives: A Federalism Perspective*, 59 Vand. L. Rev. 1629 (2006).

141. See, e.g., Lawrence v. Florida, 127 S. Ct. 1079 (2007) (statute of limitations for the Antiterrorism and Effective Death Penalty Act is not tolled while petition for certiorari is pending in the Supreme Court for review of state collateral proceedings); Schriro v. Landrigan, 127 S. Ct. 1933 (2007) (under AEDPA, whether to grant an evidentiary hearing in a habeas corpus proceeding is within the discretion of the district court. The district court did not abuse its discretion in denying an evidentiary hearing in a circumstance where the defendant ordered the defense counsel to not present mitigating evidence in a capital case).

142. See Arizonans for Official English v. Arizona, 528 U.S. 43 (1997) (where possible federal courts should certify unclear questions of state law to state courts).

143. See, e.g., University of Alabama v. Garrett, 531 U.S. 356 (2001); Kimel v. Florida Board of Regents, 528 U.S. 62 (2000); Florida Prepaid Postsecondary Education Expense Board v. College Savings Bank, 527 U.S. 627 (1999).

144. 537 U.S. 129 (2003).

145. Id. at 146–47.

146. 125 S. Ct. 2195 (2005).

147. 541 U.S. 600 (2004).

148. 18 U.S.C. §622(a)(2).

149. 541 U.S. at 606.

150. Id. at 608.

151. 538 U.S. 721 (2003).

152. 541 U.S. 509 (2004).

153. 126 S. Ct. 877 (2006).

154. 126 S. Ct. 990 (2006).

155. United States v. Rybar, 103 F.3d 273 (3d Cir. 1996), *cert. denied*, 522 U.S. 807 (1997).

156. Chittister v. Department of Community and Economic Development, 226 F.3d 223 (3d Cir. 2000).
157. 126 S. Ct. at 2208.

CHAPTER 2

1. 462 U.S. 919 (1983).
2. 458 U.S. 50 (1982).
3. 478 U.S. 714 (1986).
4. See, e.g., Peter Strauss, *Formal and Functional Approaches to Separation of Powers—a Foolish Consistency?* 72 Cornell L. Rev. 488 (1987).
5. This chapter focuses on criticizing the decisions because of their formalism. In Chapter 3, I appraise the decisions from a functional perspective and argue that the cases do not serve the underlying values of federalism.
6. Herbert Wechsler, *The Political Safeguards of Federalism: The Role of the States in the Composition and Selection of the National Government,* 54 Colum. L. Rev. 543 (1954).
7. Jesse Choper, *Judicial Review and the National Political Process* (1980).
8. 469 U.S. 528 (1985).
9. 426 U.S. 833 (1976) (holding that it violates the Tenth Amendment to apply the Fair Labor Standards Act to state and local governments).
10. Id. at 553–54 (emphasis added; citations omitted).
11. 505 U.S. 144 (1992) (declaring unconstitutional the federal statute requiring states to clean up nuclear waste as impermissible commandeering of state governments).
12. 521 U.S. 898 (1997) (declaring unconstitutional the federal statute requiring state and local governments to do background checks before issuing permits for firearms as impermissible commandeering).
13. See, e.g., Seminole Tribe of Florida v. Florida, 512 U.S. 44 (1997) (Congress may authorize suits against state governments only when acting pursuant to Section 5 of the Fourteenth Amendment).
14. See Saikrishna B. Prakash & John C. Yoo, *The Puzzling Persistence of Process-Based Federalism Theories,* 79 Texas L. Rev. 1459 (2001); Larry Kramer, *Putting the Politics into the Political Safeguards of Federalism,* 100 Colum. L. Rev. 215 (2000).
15. See Andrzej Rapaczynski, *From Sovereignty to Process: The Jurisprudence of Federalism after Garcia,* 1985 Sup. Ct. Rev. 341, 393.
16. Id. at 393.
17. 529 U.S. 598 (2000).
18. Id. at 615.
19. Id. at 617–18.
20. 125 S. Ct. 2195 (2005).
21. 317 U.S. 111 (1942).
22. See Wickard v. Filburn, 317 U.S. at 124 ("nor can consideration of economic effects be foreclosed by calling them indirect"); A.L.A. Schecter Poultry Corp. v. United States, 295 U.S. 495 (1935) (drawing distinction between direct and indirect effects).
23. 505 U.S. 144 (1992).
24. Id. at 188.
25. For an excellent analysis of the commandeering principle and its implications, see Vicki C. Jackson, *Federalism and the Uses and Limits of Law: Printz and Principle?*

111 Harv. L. Rev. 2180 (1998); Evan H. Caminker, *State Sovereignty and Subordinancy: May Congress Commandeer State Officers to Implement Federal Laws?* 95 Colum. L. Rev. 1001 (1995).

26. 527 U.S. at 712.

27. 535 U.S. 743 (2002).

28. Id. at 760.

29. Id.

30. 527 U.S. at 728.

31. 134 U.S. 1 (1890).

32. See, e.g., Joseph D. Grano, *Judicial Review and a Written Constitution in a Democratic Society*, 28 Wayne L. Rev. 1, 7 (1981) (articulating the originalist philosophy); see also Robert H. Bork, *The Tempting of America* (1990) (defending originalist constitutional interpretation).

33. Seminole Tribe of Florida v. Florida, 517 U.S. at 100 (Souter, J., dissenting).

34. 527 U.S. at 754–55.

35. I develop this argument more fully in Chapter 6 of this book.

36. 529 U.S. 861 (2000).

37. 15 U.S.C. §1397(k).

38. 533 U.S. 525 (2001).

39. 530 U.S. 363 (2000).

40. 539 U.S. 396 (2003).

41. Medtronic Inc. v. Lohr, 518 U.S. 470, 472 (1996), quoting Hillsborough County v. Automated Medical Laboratories Inc., 471 U.S. 707, 715 (1985).

42. For an argument against the presumption against preemption, see Viet D. Dinh, *Reassessing the Law of Preemption*, 88 Geo. L. J. 2085 (2000).

43. 505 U.S. at 178.

44. 505 U.S. 144 (1992).

45. Id. at 173.

46. Id. at 188.

47. Id. at 175.

48. Id. at 161.

49. Id. at 169.

50. 514 U.S. 549 (1995). For a discussion of *Lopez*, See, e.g., Symposium, *Reflections on United States v. Lopez*, 94 Mich. L. Rev. 533 (1995); Lawrence Lessig, *Translating Federalism: United States v. Lopez*, Sup. Ct. Rev. 125 (1995).

51. 18 U.S.C. §922(q)(2)(A); §921(a)(25).

52. 458 U.S. 50 (1982).

53. 517 U.S. 44 (1996).

54. 5 U.S.C. §2710(d)(1)(C).

55. 5 U.S.C. §2710(d)(7).

56. See, e.g., John J. Gibbons, *The Eleventh Amendment and State Sovereign Immunity: A Reinterpretation*, 83 Colum. L. Rev. 1889 (1983); William Fletcher, *A Historical Reinterpretation of the Eleventh Amendment: A Narrow Construction of an Affirmative Grant of Jurisdiction Rather Than a Prohibition against Jurisdiction*, 35 Stan. L. Rev. 1033 (1983).

57. 491 U.S. 1 (1989).

58. Id. at 72.

59. Id. at 65.
60. 521 U.S. 261 (1997).
61. Id. at 236–37.
62. 521 U.S. 898 (1997).
63. 18 U.S.C. §922.
64. 521 U.S. at 905.
65. Id. at 898.
66. Id. at 970 (Souter, J., dissenting).
67. 521 U.S. at 918.
68. 521 U.S. at 922.
69. Justice Scalia cites to Calabresi & Prakas, *The President's Power to Execute the Laws*, 104 Yale L. J. 541 (1994).
70. See Lawrence Lessig & Cass R. Sunstein, *The President and the Administration*, 94 Colum. L. Rev. 1 (1994).
71. Evan H. Caminker, Printz, *State Sovereignty, and the Limits of Federalism*, 1997 Sup. Ct. Rev. 199, 200–201.
72. 521 U.S. at 519–20 (emphasis added).
73. *The Concise Oxford Dictionary of Current English*, 375 (1929).
74. *Merriam-Webster's Eleventh Collegiate Dictionary*, 413 (2003).
75. See, e.g., Erwin Chemerinsky, *Interpreting the Constitution* (1987) (arguing against originalism as a method of constitutional interpretation).
76. 521 U.S. at 520.
77. Id. at 520–21.
78. Id. at 520.
79. 521 U.S. at 520.
80. Id.
81. Id. at 522.
82. Id. at 519.
83. 384 U.S. 641 (1966).
84. 360 U.S. 45 (1959).
85. 384 U.S. at 646–47.
86. Id. at 652–53.
87. This also was the position taken by Justice John Marshall Harlan in a dissenting opinion, joined by Justice Potter Stewart. Justice Harlan wrote: "When recognized state violations of federal constitutional standards have occurred, Congress is of course empowered by §5 to take appropriate remedial measures to redress and prevent the wrongs. But it is a judicial question whether the condition with which Congress has thus sought to deal is in truth an infringement of the Constitution, something that is the necessary prerequisite to bringing the §5 power into play at all." 384 U.S. at 666 (Harlan, J., dissenting).
88. Id. at 649.
89. Id. at 650.
90. 384 U.S. at 667 (Harlan, J., dissenting).
91. Id.
92. 521 U.S. at 528.
93. 384 U.S. at 651 n.10.
94. Oregon v. Mitchell, 400 U.S. 112 (1970). Another major case that weighs Congress's

authority under Section 5 is *Oregon v. Mitchell*; however, it does not add much because of the absence of a majority opinion. The 1970 amendment to the Voting Rights Act prohibited all literacy tests and required that those age eighteen and older be entitled to vote. The Court unanimously upheld the prohibition of literacy tests on the grounds that this was necessary to remedy a historical form of discrimination. But by a 5–4 decision, the Court declared the eighteen-year-old vote unconstitutional. Unfortunately, there was no majority opinion. Justice Hugo LaFayette Black took the position that Congress could set the age for voting in federal elections but not in state elections because of federalism concerns. Justices William Orville Douglas, William Brennan, Byron White, and Thurgood Marshall concluded that Congress could set the age for federal and state elections because of its power under Section 5 to determine the meaning of equal protection. Finally, Chief Justice Warren Burger and Justices Potter Stewart, Harry Blackmun, and John Marshall Harlan argued that Congress has no authority to decide the meaning of the Fourteenth Amendment. Indeed, Justice Harlan explained that "Congress' expression of [its] view . . . cannot displace the duty of this Court to make an independent determination whether Congress has exceeded its powers." Id. at 204 (Harlan, J., concurring and dissenting). However, Justice Harlan's position here was a dissenting view rejected by the majority.

95. 446 U.S. 156 (1980).
96. 446 U.S. 55 (1980).
97. 446 U.S. at 177.
98. 538 U.S. 721 (2003).
99. 29 U.S.C. §2612(a)(1)(C).
100. Florida Prepaid Postsecondary Education Expense Board v. College Savings Bank, 527 U.S. 627 (1999).
101. Kimel v. Florida Board of Regents, 528 U.S. 62 (2000).
102. University of Alabama v. Garrett, 531 U.S. 356 (2001).
103. 541 U.S. 509 (2004).
104. 531 U.S. at 368.
105. Appendix C at 531 U.S. at 398 (Breyer, J., dissenting).
106. 531 U.S. at 370.
107. 538 U.S. at 736.
108. For an excellent summary of the legal realists critique of formalism, see Morton J. Horwitz, *The Transformation of American Law: 1870–1970*, 183–230 (1990).
109. Benjamin Cardozo, *The Nature of the Judicial Process*, 66–67 (1921), quoted in Horwitz, *supra* note 108, at 190.
110. An excellent article arguing for a functional approach to federalism is Edward L. Rubin & Malcolm Feeley, *Federalism: Some Notes on a National Neurosis*, 41 U.C.L.A. L. Rev. 903 (1994).
111. 521 U.S. at 907.
112. See, e.g., John J. Gibbons, *The Eleventh Amendment and State Sovereign Immunity: A Reinterpretation*, 83 Colum. L. Rev. 1889 (1983); William Fletcher, *A Historical Reinterpretation of the Eleventh Amendment: A Narrow Construction of an Affirmative Grant of Jurisdiction Rather Than a Prohibition against Jurisdiction*, 35 Stan. L. Rev. 1033 (1983).
113. 22 U.S. 1 (1824).

114. 426 U.S. 833 (1976).
115. Garcia v. San Antonio Metropolitan Transit Authority, 469 U.S. 528 (1985).
116. Hammer v. Dagenhart, 247 U.S. 251 (1918).
117. Carter v. Carter Coal Co., 298 U.S. 238 (1936).
118. Caminker, *supra* note 71, at 202.
119. See Rubin & Feeley, *supra* note 110 (arguing that the ongoing debate over federalism is really an argument about decentralization, which should be concerned with what tasks are handled best at which level of government).
120. See, e.g., Gregory v. Ashcroft, 501 U.S. 452, 458 (1991) (articulating the values served by federalism). These, and other values of federalism, are examined in Chapter 3.
121. For an excellent exploration of these values, see David L. Shapiro, *Federalism: A Dialogue* (1995).
122. Neil S. Siegel, *Commandeering and Its Alternatives: A Federalism Perspective*, 59 Vand. L. Rev. 629 (2006).
123. Caminker, *supra* note 71, at 207.
124. An argument could be made based on *New York v. United States*, and especially *Printz v. United States*, that such compulsion of states violates the Tenth Amendment.
125. 209 U.S. 123 (1908).
126. Charles Alan Wright, *Law of Federal Courts*, 292 (4th ed. 1983).

CHAPTER 3

1. Andrzej Rapaczynski, *From Sovereignty to Process: The Jurisprudence of Federalism after Garcia*, 1985 Sup. Ct. Rev. 341, 380.
2. Alexander Hamilton, Federalist No. 32, *The Federalist Papers* 199 (J. Cooke ed. 1988).
3. Rapaczynski, *supra* note 1, at 388.
4. This is also discussed below, where I consider in more detail whether the decisions have advanced liberty, and I argue that the rulings have been very regressive in terms of rights.
5. David Shapiro, *Federalism: A Dialogue* 92 (1995).
6. James Madison, Federalist No. 10, *The Federalist Papers*.
7. 488 U.S. 469 (1989).
8. Id. at 529, distinguishing Fullilove v. Klutznick, 448 U.S. 448 (1980) (Scalia, J., concurring in the judgment). In Adarand Constructors v. Pena, 515 U.S. 200 (1995), the Court overturned a distinction between state and federal authority to use affirmative action, holding that both must meet strict scrutiny.
9. Shapiro, *supra* note 5, at 93.
10. Id.
11. Edward L. Rubin & Malcolm Feeley, *Federalism: Some Notes on a National Neurosis*, 41 U.C.L.A. L. Rev. 903, 919 (1994). There is one Supreme Court decision, *Printz v. United States*, that mentions protection of local governments as part of safeguarding federalism. *Printz* invalidated a federal law that required state and local governments to do background checks before issuing permits for firearms. The other federalist Supreme Court decisions have all been about safeguarding state governments.
12. See Mount Healthy School District v. Doyle, 424 U.S. 729 (1977) (sovereign immunity does not apply to local governments).

13. New State Ice Co. v. Liebman, 285 U.S. 262, 311 (1932) (Brandeis, J., dissenting).
14. 469 U.S. at 567–68 n.13 (Powell, J., dissenting).
15. Federal Energy Regulatory Commission v. Mississippi, 456 U.S. 741, 787–88 (1982) (O'Connor, J., dissenting).
16. Rubin & Feeley, *supra* note 11, at 925.
17. Id.
18. United States v. Lopez, 514 U.S. 549, 552 (1995).
19. Printz v. United States, 521 U.S. 898, 921 (1997).
20. Gregory v. Ashcroft, 501 U.S. 452, 458 (1991).
21. Scholars, too, have made this claim. See Martin A. Feigenbaum, *The Preservation of Individual Liberty through the Separation of Powers and Federalism: Reflections on the Shaping of Constitutional Immorality*, 37 Emory L. Rev. 613 (1998).
22. I recognize, of course, that in many instances there could be debate over what is "rights progressive" as opposed to "rights regressive." For example, supporters and opponents of affirmative action would disagree as to whether it is rights progressive or rights regressive. But, as I explain in the chapter, the Court's decisions do not raise hard questions as to what is rights progressive versus rights regressive. The invalidation of laws, such as the Religious Freedom Restoration Act and the civil damages provision of the Violence Against Women Act, seem unquestionably rights regressive.
23. 521 U.S. 507 (1997).
24. 42 U.S.C. §2000b(b)-1
25. 494 U.S. 872 (1990).
26. 42 U.S.C. §2000b(b)-1.
27. Id. at 529, quoting Marbury v. Madison, 5 U.S. (1 Cranch) 137, 177 (1803).
28. 521 U.S. at 529.
29. Id. at 532.
30. 527 U.S. 627 (1999).
31. 528 U.S. 62 (2000).
32. 531 U.S. 356 (2001).
33. 383 U.S. 745 (1966).
34. 18 U.S.C. §241.
35. 383 U.S. at 762 (Clark, J., concurring).
36. Id. at 777 (Brennan, J., concurring in part and dissenting in part).
37. 529 U.S. 598 (2000).
38. 42 U.S.C. §13981.
39. This aspect of the case is described in Chapter 1 and criticized for its formalism in Chapter 2.
40. 529 U.S. at 621.
41. Id. at 623.
42. Id. at 626.
43. 517 U.S. 44 (1996).
44. 527 U.S. 706 (1999).
45. John Hart Ely, *Democracy and Distrust* 3 (1980).
46. Id.
47. I summarized and developed these criticisms in Erwin Chemerinsky, *Interpreting the Constitution* (1987).

48. See, e.g., Paul Brest, *The Misconceived Quest for the Original Understanding*, 60 B.U. L. Rev. 204 (1980).
49. H. Jefferson Powell, *The Original Understanding of Original Intent*, 98 Harv. L. Rev. 885 (1985).
50. The last section of this chapter considers sovereign immunity in detail, including whether it can be justified based on originalism.
51. See, e.g., John J. Gibbons, *The Eleventh Amendment and State Sovereign Immunity: A Reinterpretation*, 83 Colum. L. Rev. 1889 (1983); William Fletcher, *A Historical Reinterpretation of the Eleventh Amendment: A Narrow Construction of an Affirmative Grant of Jurisdiction Rather Than a Prohibition against Jurisdiction*, 35 Stan. L. Rev. 1033 (1983).
52. Younger v. Harris, 401 U.S. 37, 41 (1971).
53. See, e.g., Stone v. Powell, 428 U.S. 465, 493–94 (1976) (justifying restriction on habeas corpus based on parity between federal and state courts); see Paul Bator, *The State Courts and Federal Constitutional Litigation*, 22 Wm. & Mary L. Rev. 605 (1981) (arguing for restrictions on habeas corpus based on parity between federal and state courts).
54. See, e.g., John S. Baker Jr., *State Police Powers and the Federalization of Local Crime*, 72 Temp. L. Rev. 673 (1999); Kathleen F. Brickey, *Criminal Mischief: The Federalization of American Criminal Law*, 46 Hastings L. J. 1135 (1995); Sara Sun Beale, *Too Many and Yet Too Few: New Principles to Define the Proper Limits for Federal Criminal Jurisdiction*, 46 Hastings L. J. 979 (1995) (describing the federalization of traditionally local crimes).
55. See Forest McDonald, *A Constitutional History of the United States* (1982) (describing events leading to the Constitutional Convention).
56. Stephen M. Griffin, *Stop Federalism Before It Kills Again: Reflections on Hurricane Katrina*, 21 St. John's J. Legal Comment. 527 (2007).
57. Hammer v. Dagenhart, 247 U.S. 251, 274 (1918) ("There is no power vested in Congress to require the states to exercise their police power so as to prevent possible unfair competition").
58. Sara Sun Beale, *Too Many and Yet Too Few: New Principles to Define the Proper Limits for Federal Criminal Jurisdiction*, 46 Hastings L. J. 979, 993–94 (1995) ("A decentralized federal system is efficient; it permits criminal justice policy to be tailored to local conditions and policy preferences, and it furthers political accountability").
59. See, e.g., Miller v. California, 413 U.S. 15 (1973) (using contemporary community standards in defining what is obscene).
60. See, e.g., Euclid v. Amber, 272 U.S. 365 (1926) (expressing deference to local zoning regulation).
61. New York Times v. Sullivan, 376 U.S. 254, 273 (1964).
62. See Chapter 2, text accompanying notes 121–22.
63. 505 U.S. 144 (1992).
64. Id. at 188.
65. See Morton J. Horwitz, *The Transformation of American Law, 1870–1960: The Crisis of Legal Orthodoxy* (1992); see also Gabriel Kolko, *The Triumph of Conservatism: A Reinterpretation of American History, 1900–1916*, at 112, 129 (1963) (arguing that railroads favored national regulation as a way of protection from conflicting state laws).

66. See, e.g., Elk Grove Unified School District v. Newdow, 542 U.S. 1, 46 (2004) (Thomas, J., concurring in the judgment); Zelman v. Simmons-Harris, 536 U.S. 639, 679 (2002) (Thomas, J., concurring).

67. See Kenneth Davis, 5 *Administrative Law Treatise* 6–7 (2d ed. 1984) (quoting Blackstone); Charles H. Koch Jr., 2 *Administrative Law and Practice* 210 (1985).

68. United States v. Lee, 106 U.S. 196, 205 (1882).

69. Id. at 207 ("The principle has never been discussed or the reasons for it given, but it has always been treated as an established doctrine") (citations omitted).

70. See, e.g., Article I, §9 ("No Title of Nobility shall be granted by the United States").

71. John E. H. Sherry, *The Myth That the King Can Do No Wrong: A Comparative Study of the Sovereign Immunity Doctrine in the United States and the New York Court of Claims*, 22 Admin. L. Rev. 39, 56 (1969).

72. Marbury v. Madison, 5 U.S. (1 Cranch) 137, 163 (1803).

73. 527 U.S. 706 (1999).

74. 517 U.S. 44 (1996) (Congress may authorize suits against states only when acting pursuant to Section 5 of the Fourteenth Amendment and not pursuant to any other federal power).

75. Florida Prepaid Postsecondary Education Expense Board v. College Savings Bank, 527 U.S. 627 (1999).

76. Kimel v. Florida Board of Regents, 528 U.S. 62 (2000).

77. 527 U.S. at 712.

78. 517 U.S. at 69.

79. Cohens v. Virginia, 19 U.S. (6 Wheat.) 264, 411–12 (1821).

80. United States v. Lee, 106 U.S. 196, 205 (1882); see also Kennecott Copper Corp. v. State Tax Commission, 327 U.S. 573, 580 (1946) (Frankfurter, J., dissenting); Hill v. United States, 50 U.S. (9 How.) 386, 389 (1850); United States v. Clarke, 33 U.S. (8 Pet.) 436 (1834).

81. See, e.g., Antonin Scalia, *A Matter of Interpretation* (1998) (expressing adherence to a philosophy of original meaning).

82. 527 U.S. at 728.

83. 134 U.S. 1 (1890).

84. 527 U.S. at 713.

85. See, e.g., Joseph D. Grano, *Judicial Review and a Written Constitution in a Democratic Society*, 28 Wayne L. Rev. 1, 7 (1981) (articulating the originalist philosophy); see also Robert H. Bork, *The Tempting of America* (1990) (defending originalist constitutional interpretation).

86. Seminole Tribe of Florida v. Florida, 517 U.S. at 100 (Souter, J., dissenting).

87. See, e.g., John J. Gibbons, *The Eleventh Amendment and State Sovereign Immunity: A Reinterpretation*, 83 Colum. L. Rev. 1889, 1902–1914 (1983).

88. 3 *The Debates in the Several States Conventions on the Adoption of the Federal Constitution*, 526–27 (J. Elliot ed. 1937).

89. 473 U.S. at 265 (Brennan, J., dissenting) (describing Mason's opposition to Article III).

90. Elliot ed., *supra* note 88, at 543.

91. Id.

92. Gibbons, *supra* note 87, at 1902–1914.

93. Elliot ed., *supra* note 88, at 575.

94. 14 John P. Kaminsky & Gaspare J. Saladino, *The Documentary History of the Ratification of the Constitution*, 204 (1983).
95. Alexander Hamilton, Federalist Paper No. 81, *The Federalist Papers* at 487–88 (C. Rossiter ed. 1961) (emphasis in original).
96. Elliot ed., *supra* note 88, at 533.
97. Id.
98. Seminole Tribe of Florida v. Florida, 517 U.S. at 142–43 (Souter, J., dissenting).
99. Welch v. Texas Department of Highways & Public Transportation, 483 U.S. 468 (1987).
100. 527 U.S. at 764 (Souter, J., dissenting).
101. Elsewhere, I have questioned whether contemporary practices should matter in constitutional interpretation. See Erwin Chemerinsky, *The Jurisprudence of Antonin Scalia: A Critical Appraisal*, 22 Hawaii L. Rev. 385 (2000).
102. 527 U.S. at 764 (Souter, J., dissenting) (quoting 1 J. Story, *Commentaries on the Constitution*, Section 207, p. 149 [5th ed. 1891]).
103. See John J. Gibbons, *The Eleventh Amendment and State Sovereign Immunity: A Reinterpretation*, 83 Colum. L. Rev. 1889 (1983); William Fletcher, *A Historical Interpretation of the Eleventh Amendment: A Narrow Construction of an Affirmative Grant of Jurisdiction Rather Than a Prohibition against Jurisdiction*, 35 Stan. L. Rev. 1033 (1983).
104. 2 U.S. (Dall.) 419 (1798).
105. 57 U.S. at 741.
106. 5 U.S. at 180.
107. 17 U.S. at 431.
108. Id.
109. 527 U.S. at 724.
110. James Madison, The Federalist No. 51, *The Federalist Papers* at 322 (C. Rossiter ed. 1961).
111. 5 U.S. at 176.
112. Id. at 163.
113. Id.
114. Akhil Amar, *Of Sovereignty and Federalism*, 96 Yale L. J. 1425 (1987).
115. See Calvin R. Massey, *Sovereign Immunity in America: A Brief History*, 56 U. Chi. L. Rev. 61 (1989).
116. James E. Pfander, *Sovereign Immunity and the Right to Petition: Toward a First Amendment Right to Pursue Judicial Claims against the Government*, 91 Nw. U. L. Rev. 899 (1997).
117. Id. at 905.
118. Id. at 981.
119. See, e.g., Oestereich v. Selective Service Local Board No. 11, 393 U.S. 233, 243 n.6 (1968) (Harlan, J., concurring). See also Richard H. Fallon Jr., *Some Confusions about Due Process, Judicial Review, and Constitutional Remedies*, 93 Colum. L. Rev. 309 (1993) (arguing that the issue of whether there is a constitutional right to judicial review depends on the underlying substantive law).
120. Johnson v. Robison, 415 U.S. 361 (1974). See also Webster v. Doe, 486 U.S. 592 (1988) (refusing to find statute to preclude review of a claim by an employee of the CIA who alleged that he was fired because he was a homosexual).

121. See, e.g., United States v. Mendoza-Lopez, 481 U.S. 828 (1987); McNary v. Haitian Refugee Center Inc., 498 U.S. 479 (1991).

122. See Roth v. Board of Regents, 408 U.S. 564 (1972) (property interest exists if law creates a reasonable expectation to a benefit).

123. 445 U.S. 622 (1980).

124. 445 U.S. at 651.

125. See Clark Byse, *Proposed Reforms in Federal "Nonstatutory" Judicial Review: Sovereign Immunity, Indispensable Parties, Mandamus,* 75 Harv. L. Rev. 1479, 1526 (1962); Noel Fox, *The King Must Do No Wrong: A Critique of the Current Status of Sovereign and Official Immunity,* 25 Wayne L. Rev. 177, 187 (1979).

126. See, e.g., Ex parte Young, 209 U.S. 123 (1908) (ability to sue state officers for injunctive relief not barred by the Eleventh Amendment).

127. 527 U.S. at 749.

128. See The Siren, 74 U.S. (7 Wall.) 152, 154 (1868) ("The public service would be hindered, and the public safety endangered if the supreme authority could be subjected to suit at the instance of every citizen").

129. James S. Sable, *Comment: Sovereign Immunity; A Battleground of Competing Considerations,* 12 Sw. U. L. Rev. 457, 465 (1981); Littell v. Morton, 445 F.2d 1207, 1214 (4th Cir. 1971) ("The rationale for sovereign immunity essentially boils down to substantial bothersome interference with the operation of government").

130. Larson v. Domestic & Foreign Commerce Corp., 337 U.S. 682, 704 (1949).

131. See, e.g., Mount Healthy City School District Board of Education v. Doyle, 429 U.S. 274 (1977); Lincoln County v. Luning, 133 U.S. 529 (1890). Some criticize these decisions on the grounds that states should be able to transfer their immunity to local governments, which are created by the state and through which the states govern. See, e.g., Margaret Barrett, *Comment: The Denial of Eleventh Amendment Immunity to Political Subdivisions of the States; An Unjustified Strain on Federalism,* 1979 Duke L. J. 1042.

132. Monell v. Department of Social Services, 436 U.S. 656 (1978) (holding that local governments are persons within the meaning of Section 1983).

133. Schneider v. Smith, 390 U.S. 17 (1968); Larson v. Domestic & Foreign Commerce Corp., 337 U.S. 682 (1949); Land v. Dollar, 330 U.S. 731 (1947); see also Ex parte Young, 209 U.S. 123 (1908).

134. If the monetary relief, in reality, would be against the government, the suit is barred, even though the individual officer is named as the defendant. Larson v. Domestic & Foreign Commerce Corp., 337 U.S. at 687 ("the crucial question is whether the relief sought in a suit nominally addressed to the officer is relief against the sovereign"). See also Hawaii v. Gordon, 373 U.S. 57, 98 (1963).

135. See Kenneth Davis, *supra* note 67, at 22–24; Peter H. Schuck, *Suing Government,* 90–91 (1983).

136. Kawananakoa v. Polyblank, 205 U.S. 349, 353 (1907).

137. Id.

138. 491 U.S. 1 (1989) (holding that Congress could override the Eleventh Amendment if the statute was explicit in its text in doing so).

139. See Erwin Chemerinsky, *Federal Jurisdiction* (4th ed. 2003) 516–28 (describing officers protected by absolute immunity).

140. O'Shea v. Littleton, 414 U.S. 488 (1974) (declaring nonjusticiable a suit contending that the defendants, a magistrate and a judge, discriminated against blacks in setting bail and imposing sentences).

141. Federal Courts Improvement Act of 1996, Public Law No. 104-317, (b)-(c), 110 Stat. 3847.

142. Harlow v. Fitzgerald, 457 U.S. 800 (1982).

143. McCulloch v. Maryland, 17 U.S. (4 Wheat.) 316, 427 (1819).

144. 478 U.S. 186, 199 (1986), quoting Oliver Wendell Holmes, *The Path of the Law*, 10 Harv. L. Rev. 457, 469 (1897).

145. Alden v. Maine, 527 U.S. at 760 (Souter, J., dissenting).

146. 7 James D. Richardson, *A Compilation of Messages and Papers of the Presidents*, 3245, 3252 (quoted in Kennecott Copper Corp. v. State Tax Commission, 327 U.S. 573, 580 [1946]) (Frankfurter, J., dissenting).

CHAPTER 4

1. Richard H. Fallon Jr., *The Ideologies of Federal Courts Law*, 74 Virginia L. Rev. 1181 (1988). Richard Fallon has written a superb article describing competing ideologies of federal courts law and contrasting nationalist and federalist approaches. Although I use the nationalist and federalist labels, I do so more broadly than just within the context of federal jurisdictions. Although my content is different from Fallon's, the underlying concepts are very much the same: a nationalist approach, which broadly defines national powers (including federal courts authority), as opposed to a federalist approach, which narrowly defines the powers of the national government (including federal courts authority). As explained below, my intent is not to defend either of these visions but instead to offer an alternative that in some ways is nationalistic (e.g., defining Congress's power and federal court jurisdiction) and in other ways is federalistic (e.g., limiting the scope of federal preemption).

2. 22 U.S. 1 (1824) (broadly defining the scope of Congress's commerce power).

3. See, e.g., Carter v. Carter Coal Co., 298 U.S. 238 (1936) (limiting the commerce power); United States v. Butler, 297 U.S. 1 (1936) (invalidating spending law for violating the Tenth Amendment).

4. National League of Cities v. Usery, 426 U.S. 833 (1976) (holding it unconstitutional to require state and local governments to pay their employees a minimum wage).

5. Garcia v. San Antonio Metropolitan Transit Authority, 469 U.S. 528 (1985).

6. 505 U.S. 144 (1992).

7. These cases are described in detail in Chapters 1 and 2.

8. This, of course, was the issue in New York v. United States.

9. This is exactly what Congress did in the Violence Against Women Act, which the Court declared unconstitutional in United States v. Morrison, 529 U.S. 598 (2000).

10. American Insurance Association v. Garamendi, 539 U.S. 396 (2003).

11. Herbert Wechsler, *The Political Safeguards of Federalism: The Role of the States in the Composition and Selection of the National Government*, 54 Colum. L. Rev. 543 (1954).

12. 514 U.S. 549, 558 (1995).

13. 529 U.S. 598 (2000).

14. 297 U.S. 1 (1936).

15. See, e.g., Sabri v. United States, 541 U.S. 600 (2004) (affirming a broad definition of the spending power and upholding a federal law that made it a crime to bribe any person working for a government entity receiving more than $10,000 in federal money).

16. 483 U.S. 203 (1987).

17. I thus very much disagree with those who would impose limits on Congress's ability to put strings on grants to state and local governments. See Lynn Baker, *Conditional Federal Spending and States' Rights*, 574 Annals 104 (2001) (urging restrictions on congressional power to put strings on grants to state and local governments). The limit on conditional spending must assume an anti-commandeering principle within the Tenth Amendment, something I criticize in Chapters 2 and 3.

18. 109 U.S. 3 (1883).

19. Id. at 24–25.

20. Id. at 22.

21. Id. at 25.

22. Id. at 10–11.

23. Id. at 11.

24. 203 U.S. 1 (1906).

25. Id. at 20. Similarly, in Corrigan v. Buckley, 271 U.S. 323 (1926), and Hurd v. Hodge, 334 U.S. 24 (1948), the Court held that federal laws could not prohibit racially restrictive covenants; that is, contracts among residents of a neighborhood that they would not sell their property to blacks or Jews. In Shelley v. Kramer, 334 U.S. 1 (1948), the Court held that court enforcement of racially restrictive covenants would violate the Fourteenth Amendment.

26. 392 U.S. 409 (1968).

27. The dissent especially focused on whether Section 1982 was meant to apply to private conduct. 392 U.S. at 454 (Harlan, J., dissenting).

28. 392 U.S. at 440.

29. The Court also has broadened the interpretation of Section 1982 as applying to personal as well as real property. See Sullivan v. Little Hunting Park Inc., 396 U.S. 229 (1969) (discrimination in rental of property violates Section 1982).

30. 427 U.S. 160 (1976).

31. Id. at 173 (citation omitted).

32. 491 U.S. 164 (1989).

33. Section 1985(3) provides for liability "if two or more persons . . . conspire, or go in disguise on the highway . . . for the purpose of depriving, either directly or indirectly, any person or class of persons of the equal protection of the laws, or of equal privileges and immunities under the laws."

34. 403 U.S. 88 (1971).

35. Id. at 97.

36. 413 U.S. 455 (1973).

37. Id. at 470.

38. 383 U.S. 745 (1966).

39. 529 U.S. 598 (2000).

40. 394 U.S. 641 (1966).

41. 384 U.S. at 651 n.10.

42. 312 U.S. 100, 124 (1941).
43. See Hammer v. Dagenhart, 247 U.S. 251 (1918) (invalidating federal law prohibiting the shipment in interstate commerce of goods made by child labor).
44. 505 U.S. 144 (1992).
45. 521 U.S. 898 (1997).
46. Alden v. Maine, 527 U.S. 706 (1999).
47. Id.
48. See John J. Gibbons, *The Eleventh Amendment and State Sovereign Immunity: A Reinterpretation*, 83 Colum. L. Rev. 1889 (1983); William Fletcher, *A Historical Interpretation of the Eleventh Amendment: A Narrow Construction of an Affirmative Grant of Jurisdiction Rather Than a Prohibition against Jurisdiction*, 35 Stan. L. Rev. 1033 (1983).
49. There are alternative versions of the diversity theory. Professor William Fletcher argues that the amendment prohibits only those suits founded solely on diversity jurisdiction; federal question suits against states are allowed. William Fletcher, *The Diversity Explanation of the Eleventh Amendment: A Reply to Critics*, 56 U. Chi. L. Rev. 1261 (1989). In contrast, Professor Larry Marshall contends that states may not be sued by citizens of other states in federal court under either diversity or federal question jurisdiction. Lawrence C. Marshall, *Fighting the Words of the Eleventh Amendment*, 102 Harv. L. Rev. 1342 (1989).
50. Hammer v. Dagenhart, 247 U.S. 251 (1918).
51. United States v. E. C. Knight, 136 U.S. 1 (1895).
52. Carter v. Carter Coal Co., 298 U.S. 238 (1936).
53. Railroad Retirement Board v. Alton R.R. Co., 295 U.S. 330 (1935).
54. United States v. Butler, 287 U.S. 1 (1936).
55. United States v. Lopez, 514 U.S. 549 (1995).
56. United States v. Morrison, 529 U.S. 598 (2000).
57. Solid Waste Agency of Northern Cook County v. United States Army Corps of Engineers, 531 U.S. 159 (2001).
58. New York v. United States, 505 U.S. 144 (1992).
59. Printz v. United States, 521 U.S. 898 (1997).
60. Lorillard Tobacco Co. v. Reilly, 533 U.S. 525 (2001).
61. American Insurance Association v. Garamendi, 539 U.S. 396 (2003).
62. Geier v. American Honda Motor Co. Inc., 529 U.S. 861 (2000).
63. United States v. Morrison, 529 U.S. 598 (2000).
64. City of Boerne v. Flores, 521 U.S. 507 (1997).
65. Kimel v. Florida Board of Regents, 528 U.S. 62 (2000) (state governments cannot be sued for violating the Age Discrimination in Employment Act); University of Alabama v. Garrett, 531 U.S. 356 (2001) (state governments cannot be sued for violating Title I of the Americans with Disabilities Act).
66. I develop my objections to originalism and my view of constitutional interpretation in Erwin Chemerinsky, *Interpreting the Constitution* (1987).
67. 22 U.S. 1 (1822).
68. 2 U.S. 419 (1793).
69. Carter v. Carter Coal Co., 298 U.S. 238, 303–4 (1936).
70. Hammer v. Dagenhart, 247 U.S. 251, 276 (1918).

CHAPTER 5

1. A seminal article on the subject, and one responsible for focusing the debate around the concept of parity, is Burt Neuborne, *The Myth of Parity*, 90 Harv. L. Rev. 1105 (1977). The discussion of parity has continued for decades. See, e.g., Timothy Kerr, *Cleaning Up One Mess to Create Another*, 29 Hamline L. Rev. 206 (2006); John Blume, *AEDPA: The Hype and the Bite*, 91 Cornell L. Rev. 259 (2006). As used in this chapter, the issue of "parity" is whether, overall, state courts are equal to federal courts in their ability and willingness to protect federal constitutional rights. The comparison might be between federal district courts and state trial courts; or it might be the entire state court system as compared with federal district courts and courts of appeals; or even the entire state court system compared with the federal district courts.

2. See, e.g., Burt Neuborne, *Toward Procedural Parity in Constitutional Litigation*, 22 Wm. & Mary L. Rev. 725, 727 (1981) (arguing that a court is qualitatively better if it is more likely to attach a high value to protecting individual liberties).

3. See generally Michael Solimine & James Walker, *Constitutional Litigation in Federal and State Courts: An Empirical Analysis of Judicial Parity*, 10 Hastings Constit. L. Q. 213 (1983) (arguing that state courts are as likely to rule in favor of constitutional claims as are federal courts).

4. Paul Bator, *Finality in Criminal Law and Federal Habeas Corpus for State Prisoners*, 76 Harv. L. Rev. 441 (1963) (arguing that no set of results is preferable to any other; so long as there is a full and fair opportunity for a hearing, no relitigation is necessary of constitutional issues raised in habeas corpus petitions).

5. See, e.g., Fay v. Noia, 372 U.S. 391, 438 (1963) (state court prisoners may raise matters on federal habeas corpus that were not raised in state court, unless they deliberately bypassed state procedures); Brown v. Allen, 344 U.S. 443, 469 (1953) (state court prisoners can relitigate federal constitutional claims on habeas corpus).

6. See, e.g., Monroe v. Pape, 365 U.S. 167 (1961) (state officers act under color of state law for purposes of 42 U.S.C., Section1983, even if they are violating state statutes and rules).

7. See, e.g., Dombrowski v. Pfister, 380 U.S. 479 (1965) (permitting the federal court to enjoin state court proceedings).

8. See, e.g., England v. Louisiana State Board of Medical Examiners, 375 U.S. 411 (1964) (after federal court abstention, state court decisions on state law matters do not have res judicata effect—a final ruling that's judged on merit—on federal courts as to federal issues).

9. See, e.g., McCleskey v. Zant, 499 U.S. 467 (1991); Wainwright v. Sykes, 433 U.S. 72 (1977); Stone v. Powell, 428 U.S. 465 (1976); see Larry Yackle, *Explaining Habeas Corpus*, 60 N.Y.U. L. Rev. 991, 1022–24 (1985).

10. See, e.g., Parratt v. Taylor, 451 U.S. 527 (1981) (section 1983 does not create a remedy when the plaintiff seeks only a post-deprivation remedy for loss of property and the state adequately provides this).

11. See, e.g., Younger v. Harris, 401 U.S. 37 (1971) (federal courts may not enjoin pending state court criminal proceedings).

12. See, e.g., Allen v. McCurry, 449 U.S. 90 (1980) (state court decisions have preclusive effect on federal courts deciding claims under 42 U.S.C., Section 1983).

13. Public Law No. 104-132, April 24, 1996.

14. Public Law No. 109-2, §5, 119 Stat. 4 , at 11 (2005).

15. Max Farrand, *The Framing of the Constitution* 79 (1913) ("That there should be a national judiciary was readily accepted by all").

16. 1 Max Farrand, *The Records of the Federal Convention* 123 (1966).

17. 2 Farrand, *supra* note 15, at 27–28.

18. Id.

19. 22 U.S. (9 Wheat.) 738, 811 (1824).

20. Neuborne, *supra* note 1, at 1111.

21. Anthony Amsterdam, *Criminal Prosecutions Affecting Federally Guaranteed Civil Rights: Federal Removal and Habeas Jurisdiction to Abort State Court Trial*, 113 U. Pa. L. Rev. 793, 818 (1965).

22. Cong. Globe, 42d Cong., 1st Sess. 321 (1871) (remarks of Rep. Stoughton); see also id. at 374 (remarks of Rep. Lowe); id. at 459 (remarks of Rep. Coburn); id. at 609 (remarks of Sen. Pool); id. at 687 (remarks of Sen. Surz); id. at 691 (remarks of Sen. Edmunds).

23. Id. at 376 (remarks of Rep. Lowe).

24. See, e.g., W. Duker, *A Constitutional History of Habeas Corpus*, 189–90 (1980) (purposes of habeas corpus statute); Don Doernberg, *There's No Reason for It; It's Just Our Policy: Why the Well-Pleaded Complaint Rule Sabotages the Purposes of Federal Question Jurisdiction*, 38 Hastings L. J. 597, 647 (1987) (distrust of state courts and the creation of federal question jurisdiction).

25. Murdock v. City of Memphis, 87 U.S. (20 Wall.) 590, 626 (1874).

26. Neuborne, *supra* note 1, at 1106–1112.

27. Barron v. Mayor of Baltimore, 32 U.S. (7 Pet.) 243 (1833).

28. See, e.g., Duncan v. Louisiana, 391 U.S. 145 (1968) (applying to states Sixth Amendment right to a jury trial); Klopfer v. North Carolina, 386 U.S. 213 (1967) (applying to states Sixth Amendment right to a speedy trial); Pointer v. Texas, 380 U.S. 400 (1965) (applying to states Sixth Amendment right to confront witnesses); Malloy v. Hogan, 378 U.S. 1 (1964) (applying to states Fifth Amendment right to be free of compelled self-incrimination); Gideon v. Wainwright, 372 U.S. 335 (1963) (applying to states Sixth Amendment right to counsel); Mapp v. Ohio, 367 U.S. 643 (1961) (applying to states Fourth Amendment right to be free from unreasonable search and seizure and exclusionary rule); In re Oliver, 333 U.S. 257 (1948) (applying to states Sixth Amendment right to a public trial).

29. Professor Martha Field expresses this well: "There is a long line of cases proclaiming the federal courts superior to the state courts and 'an equally long, equally well-respected list of cases maintaining the contradictory position: state courts have the same responsibility toward federal claims that federal courts have and state courts cannot be presumed to do a less competent job." Martha Field, *The Uncertain Nature of Federal Jurisdiction*, 22 Wm. & Mary L. Rev. 683, 685–86 (1981).

30. Owen Fiss, *Dombrowski*, 86 Yale L. J. 1103 (1977) (Warren Court viewed the federal courts as "the primary guardian of constitutional rights").

31. See, e.g., Neuborne, *supra* note 1, at 1105 (Burger Court decisions based on assumption of parity).

32. See, e.g., Patsy v. Board of Regents, 457 U.S. 496, 532–33 (1982) (Powell, J., dissenting) (arguing for exhaustion of state administrative remedies before federal court adjudication of Section 1983 claims); Wisconsin v. Constantineau, 400 U.S. 433, 440

(1971) (Burger, C. J., dissenting) (objecting to Supreme Court's refusal to order federal court abstention because "no one could reasonably think that the judges of Wisconsin have less fidelity to due process requirements of the Federal Constitution than we do"); Dombrowski v. Pfister, 380 U.S. 479, 499 (1965) (Harlan, J., dissenting) (challenging Court's assumption of state court inferiority in allowing federal court injunction of state court proceedings).

33. See, e.g., Allen v. McCurry, 449 U.S. 90, 110 (1980) (Blackmun, J., dissenting) (objecting to preclusive effect of state court judgments in Section 1983 cases because of "policy in favor of federal courts" acting as the primary and final arbiters of constitutional rights); Stone v. Powell, 428 U.S. 465 (1976) (Brennan, J., dissenting) (disagreeing with majority's holding that Fourth Amendment claims could not be relitigated on habeas corpus).

34. See, e.g., Dombrowski, 380 U.S. at 484–85 (1965) (expressing trust in state courts, although upholding federal court injunction of state court proceedings); Amalgamated Clothing Workers v. Richmond Bros. Co., 348 U.S. 511, 518–19 (1955) (refusing to allow injunction of state court proceedings).

35. See, e.g., Rose v. Mitchell, 443 U.S. 545, 563 (1979) (allowing federal court habeas corpus relitigation of challenges to state court grand jury selection procedure because federal court review is necessary to correct state court constitutional errors); Steffel v. Thompson, 415 U.S. 452, 463–64 (1974) (permitting federal court declaratory judgment when there are no pending state proceedings, because federal courts are the primary vindicators of federal rights); Mitchum v. Foster, 407 U.S. 225, 242–43 (1972) (holding that Section 1983 is an exception to the Anti-Injunction Act, 28 U.S.C. §2283, because of congressional assumption that federal courts were meant to be the primary protectors of federal constitutional rights).

36. 344 U.S. 443 (1953).

37. Id. at 511.

38. Henry Hart, *The Supreme Court: 1958 Term Forward; The Time Chart of the Justices*, 73 Harv. L. Rev. 84, 106 (1959).

39. 428 U.S. 465 (1976).

40. Id. at 494 n.35.

41. Id.

42. See, e.g., McCleskey v. Zant, 499 U.S. 467 (1991) (precluding successive habeas petitions); Teague v. Lane, 489 U.S. 288 (1989) (limiting the use of habeas corpus to recognize new constitutional rights).

43. Neuborne, *supra* note 2, at 727.

44. Paul Bator, *The States and Federal Constitutional Litigation*, 22 Wm. & Mary L. Rev. 605, 631 (1981).

45. Id. at 633.

46. See Bator, *supra* note 44, at 629 (potentially "tremendous variations in the quality of the bench from state to state"); Field, *supra* note 29, at 684 ("sympathy toward federal claims . . . differ[s] in the various regions of the country").

47. See William Brennan, *State Constitutions and the Protection of Individual Rights*, 90 Harv. L. Rev. 489, 495 (1977).

48. See, e.g., Committee to Defend Reproductive Rights v. Myers, 29 Cal. 3d 252, 625 P.2d 779 (1981) (decision declaring it a violation of the California Constitution to deny Medicaid funding for abortions, contrary to the result reached by the United

States Supreme Court in interpreting the United States Constitution); State v. Santiago, 53 Haw. 254, 492 P.2d 657 (1971) (Hawaii Supreme Court decision, relying on the Hawaii Constitution, expanding the scope of the protections created by Miranda v. Arizona, 384 U.S. 436 (1966); Robinson v. Cahill, 62 N.J. 473, 303 A.2d 273 (1973) (decision declaring inequalities in education spending because of reliance of the local property tax to violate the New Jersey Constitution, contrary to the result reached by the Supreme Court under the United States Constitution).

49. Martin Redish, *Federal Jurisdiction: Tensions in the Allocation of Judicial Power*, 274 (1980).

50. Solimine & Walker, *supra* note 3, at 214.

51. Id. at 236.

52. Id. at 240.

53. Id. at 214–15.

54. Solimine & Walker, *supra* note 3, at 283 (53.8 percent as compared with 40.3 percent).

55. Solimine & Walker, *supra* note 3, at 243 (53.8 percent as compared with 40.3 percent).

56. Id. at 243–44.

57. Id. at 235 ("[A] study of opinions of state trial courts is virtually impossible. Full written opinions . . . are a rarity, and even the full opinions are rarely reported").

58. Thomas Marvell, *The Rationales for Federal Question Jurisdiction: An Empirical Examination of Student Rights Litigation*, 1315 Wis. L. Rev. (1984).

59. Id. at 1338.

60. See, e.g., Lee Epstein & Karen O'Connor, *States Before the U.S. Supreme Court: Direct Representation in Cases Involving Criminal Rights, 1969–1984*, 70 Judicature 305 (1987); Solimine & Walker, *supra* note 3, at 225 n.62 (relying on Vines's data to argue that state courts are comparable to federal courts); Kenneth Vines, *Southern State Supreme Courts and Race Relations*, 18 W. Pol. Q. 5 (1965) (examining Supreme Court reversals of race relation decisions in Southern courts between 1954 and 1963).

61. See, e.g., Neuborne, *supra* note 2, at 726 (need for qualitative analysis on the question of parity); Neuborne, *supra* note 1, at 1111–15 (experience), 1115–30 (institutional characteristics).

62. Neuborne, *supra* note 1, at 1110–11.

63. See, e.g., Redish, *supra* note 49, at 299; Neuborne, *supra* note 1, at 1108.

64. Solimine & Walker, *supra* note 3, at 224–25.

65. Id. at 225 n.62.

66. Bator, *supra* note 44, at 630 ("There are many states where it is clear that, in the past ten years, there have been substantial improvements in the receptivity of state judges to federal constitutional claims").

67. See, e.g., Cass R. Sunstein et al., *Ideological Voting on Federal Courts of Appeals: A Preliminary Investigation*, 90 Va. L. Rev. 301, 352 (2004).

68. Solimine & Walker, *supra* note 3, at 225.

69. See Richard Posner, *The Federal Courts: Crisis and Reform*, 187–88 (1985) (state court hostility to rights of criminal defendants because of political accountability); Neuborne, *supra* note 1, at 1127–28.

70. See Posner, *supra* note 69, at 144 ("[I]t is widely believed that federal judges are, on

average [an important qualifier], of higher quality than their state counterparts"). Of course, such discussions about quality raise major problems in defining quality.

71. Id. at 146.

72. See, e.g., Neuborne, *supra* note 1, at 1121.

73. Id. at 1124.

74. American Law Institute, *Study of the Division of the Jurisdiction between the State and Federal Courts* 166 (1969). The 1969 date of this conclusion should be noted. The study was undertaken during the 1960s, when there was Southern resistance to civil rights, and before the selection of the Nixon, Ford, and Reagan nominees to the federal bench.

75. Bator, *supra* note 44, at 630–31.

76. Solimine & Walker, *supra* note 3, at 230–31.

77. Bator, *supra* note 44, at 509 (state judges use same process of decision making as federal judges); Solimine & Walker, *supra* note 3, at 248 (information flow to judges an important determinant of results).

78. See, e.g., Fair Assessment in Real Estate Association Inc. v. McNary, 454 U.S. 100 (1981) (federal courts may not enjoin allegedly unconstitutional state tax collection systems); Rizzo v. Goode, 423 U.S. 362 (1976) (dismissal of challenge to police department practices, in part, on federalism grounds); Younger v. Harris, 401 U.S. 37 (1971) (federal courts may not enjoin pending state court proceedings).

79. 401 U.S. at 41–45.

80. Trainor v. Hernandez, 431 U.S. 434, 446 (1977); Juidice v. Vail, 430 U.S. 327 (1977).

81. Fair Assessment in Real Estate Association Inc. v. McNary, 454 U.S. 100, 113 (1981).

82. 414 U.S. 488 (1974).

83. Id. at 501.

84. 423 U.S. 362 (1976).

85. Id. at 380.

86. Migra v. Warren City School District Board of Education, 465 U.S. 75, 85 (1984); Allen v. McCurry, 449 U.S. 90, 96 (1980).

87. Kuhlmann v. Wilson, 477 U.S. 436, 453–54 n.16 (1986); Engle v. Isaac, 456 U.S. 107, 128 n.33 (1982); Bator, supra note 44, at 614–15 (Habeas corpus "creates a peculiarly abrasive and intrusive relationship between the federal and state courts, since it subordinates the entire hierarchy of state tribunals to a single federal district judge even in cases where there is no showing that the state courts failed to provide a fully hospitable forum for the litigation of the federal claim").

88. The Civil Rights Removal Statute is 28 U.S.C. §1443(1) (1982) (removal from state court to federal court a person "who is denied or cannot enforce [his or her equal rights] in the courts of such state"). This statute was expressly motivated by distrust of state courts. William Wiecek, *The Reconstruction of Federal Judicial Power, 1863–1875*, 13 Am. J. Legal Hist. 333, 338 (1969).

89. John Blume, *AEDPA: The "Hype" and the "Bite,"* 91 Cornell L. Rev. 259, 284 (2006).

90. Redish, *supra* note 49, at 299.

91. Ann Althouse, *How to Build a Separate Sphere: Federal Courts and State Power*, 100 Harv. L. Rev. 1485, 1538 (1987).

92. Bator, *supra* note 44, at 625–26.
93. Redish, *supra* note 49, at 274 (under the principle that Congress should define federal court jurisdiction, "the focus of the policy argument [is] not . . . whether state courts do as good a job as the federal courts").
94. Id. at 77.
95. See, e.g., Lauf v. E. G. Shiner & Co., 303 U.S. 323 (1938); Sheldon v. Sill, 49 U.S. (8 How.) 441 (1850).
96. Redish, *supra* note 49, at 274.
97. See Haring v. Prosise, 462 U.S. 306, 323 (1983) (noting "grave" congressional concern about state courts' likely failure to adequately protect federal rights).
98. Mitchum v. Foster, 407 U.S. 225, 242 (1972) (speaking of 42 U.S.C. §1983).
99. See, e.g., Felix Frankfurter, *Some Reflections on the Reading of Statutes*, 47 Colum. L. Rev. 527 (1947); Robert Weisberg, *The Calabresian Judicial Artist: Statutes and the New Legal Process*, 35 Stan. L. Rev. 213 (1983).
100. Althouse, *supra* note 91, at 1486.
101. Theodore Eisenberg, *Congressional Authority to Restrict Lower Federal Court Jurisdiction*, 83 Yale L. J. 498, 513 (1974).
102. Bator, *supra* note 44, at 626.
103. Althouse, *supra* note 91, at 1489.
104. Redish, *supra* note 49, at 3.
105. In Wisconsin v. Constantineau, 400 U.S. 433, 440 (1971), Chief Justice Warren Burger, in dissent, took such a position. He argued that the federal court should not decide a constitutional challenge to a state statute until the state courts have considered it under the state constitution.
106. Donald Zeigler, *Rights Require Remedies: A New Approach to the Enforcement of Rights in the Federal Courts*, 38 Hastings L. J. 665, 686 (1987).
107. Bator, *supra* note 44, at 606.
108. Akhil Amar, *A Neo-Federalist View of Article III: Separating the Two Tiers of Federal Jurisdiction*, 65 B.U. L. Rev. 205, 230 (1985).
109. Id. at 230, 238.
110. Howard Fink & Mark Tushnet, *Federal Jurisdiction: Policy and Practice*, 17 (1984) ("The litigant choice rule would rest on the view that litigants are likely to do a better job in assessing which forum will protect federal interests than either Congress or the courts").
111. See, e.g., Neuborne, *supra* note 2, at 729.
112. See, e.g., Solimine & Walker, *supra* note 3.
113. There is ample jurisprudential literature defending the importance of protecting rights. Such arguments, obviously, can be used to justify the desirability of maximizing the opportunity for the protection of rights. See, e.g., Ronald Dworkin, *Taking Rights Seriously* (1977).
114. Fink & Tushnet, *supra* note 110, at 17.
115. Judith Resnik, *Tiers*, 57 S. Cal. L. Rev. 837, 846–47 (1984).
116. Id. at 847.
117. 454 U.S. 100 (1981).
118. Louisville & Nashville Rail Road v. Mottley, 211 U.S. 149 (1908) (federal issues must be presented on the face of a well-pleaded complaint for federal question jurisdiction to exist).

119. Gregory v. Ashcroft, 501 U.S. 452, 458 (1991).
120. Akhil Amar, *Of Sovereignty and Federalism*, 96 Yale L. J. 1425, 1426 (1987) (identification of federalism with attempts to dilute protections of constitutional rights).
121. Id. at 1428.
122. Althouse, *supra* note 91, at 1525–26.
123. Bator, *supra* note 44, at 634.
124. Id. at 626.
125. Patsy v. Board of Regents, 457 U.S. 496, 506 (1982); see also Monroe v. Pape, 365 U.S. 167, 180 (1961).
126. For example, in libel cases between private parties, First Amendment issues often arise. See, e.g., New York Times v. Sullivan, 376 U.S. 254 (1964).
127. Louisville & Nashville Rail Road v. Mottley, 211 U.S. 149 (1908).
128. Osborn v. Bank of the United States, 22 U.S. (9 Wheat.) 738, 822 (1824).
129. Charles Warren, *Federal Criminal Laws and the State Courts*, 38 Harv. L. Rev. 545, 584 (1925).
130. Id. at 594.
131. England v. Louisiana State Board of Medical Examiners, 375 U.S. 411 (1964) (procedure in instances of Pullman abstentions); Railroad Commission v. Pullman Co., 312 U.S. 496 (1941).
132. 80 U.S. (13 Wall.) 397, 408–9 (1872).
133. Neuborne, *supra* note 2, at 731.
134. For excellent discussions of the importance of such redundancy in jurisdiction, see Robert Cover, *The Uses of Jurisdictional Redundancy: Interest, Ideology and Innovation*, 22 Wm. & Mary L. Rev. 639 (1981); Robert Cover & Alexander Aleinikoff, *Dialectical Federalism: Habeas Corpus and the Court*, 86 Yale L. J. 1035, 1076–78 (1977).

CHAPTER 6

1. See, e.g., United States v. Lopez, 514 U.S. 548 (1995) (invalidating the Gun-Free School Zone Act as exceeding the scope of Congress's commerce power); United States v. Morrison, 120 S. Ct. 1740 (2000) (invalidating the civil damages provision in the Violence Against Women Act); City of Boerne v. Flores, 521 U.S. 507 (1997) (invalidating the Religious Freedom Restoration Act as exceeding the scope of Congress's Section 5 power).
2. See, e.g., New York v. United States, 505 U.S. 144 (1992) (invalidating provisions of the Low-Level Radioactive Waste Act as violating the Tenth Amendment); Printz v. United States, 521 U.S. 898 (1997) (invalidating the Brady Handgun Control Act as violating the Tenth Amendment).
3. See, e.g., Seminole Tribe of Florida v. Florida, 517 U.S. 44 (1996); Florida Prepaid Postsecondary Education Expense Board v. College Savings Bank, 527 U.S. 627 (1999) (limiting Congress's power to authorize suits against state governments).
4. 529 U.S. 861 (2000).
5. 15 U.S.C. §1397(k).
6. 533 U.S. 525 (2001).
7. 530 U.S. 363 (2000).

8. 539 U.S. 396 (2003).

9. Hillsborough County, Florida v. Automated Medical Laboratories Inc., 471 U.S. 707, 715 (1985).

10. For an argument that counters the presumption against preemption, see Viet D. Dinh, *Reassessing the Law of Preemption*, 88 Geo. L. J. 2085 (2000).

11. See Gade v. National Solid Waste Management Association, 505 U.S. 88, 108 (1992) (deriving preemption from the supremacy clause); but see Stephen A. Gardbaum, *The Nature of Preemption*, 79 Cornell L. Rev. 767 (1994); S. Candice Hoke, *Transcending Conventional Supremacy: A Reconstruction of the Supremacy Clause*, 24 Conn. L. Rev. 829 (1992) (arguing that only some preemption should be based on the supremacy clause).

12. Gade v. National Solid Waste Management Association, 505 U.S. at 1084 (citations omitted). In Gibbons v. Ogden, 22 U.S. (9 Wheat.) 1.211 (1824), Chief Justice John Marshall said: "[A]cts of the State Legislatures . . . [that] interfere with, or are contrary to the laws of Congress [are to be invalidated because] [i]n every such case, the act of congress . . . is supreme; and the law of State though enacted in the exercise of powers not controverted, must yield to it."

13. The preemption can be by a federal law or by a federal regulation adopted pursuant to a federal statute. The Supreme Court has said that "state laws can be pre-empted by federal regulations as well as by federal statutes." Hillsborough County, Florida v. Automated Medical Laboratories Inc., 471 U.S. 707, 713 (1985).

14. Hines v. Davidowitz, 312 U.S. 52, 67 (1941).

15. Rice v. Santa Fe Elevator Corporation, 331 U.S. 218, 230 (1947).

16. Florida Lime & Avocado Growers Inc. v. Paul, 373 U.S. 132, 142–43 (1963).

17. Hines v. Davidowitz, 312 U.S. 52, 67 (1941).

18. 505 U.S. at 98 (citations omitted). In an earlier case, Pennsylvania v. Nelson, 350 U.S. 497, 502–5 (1956), the Supreme Court identified three situations where preemption could be found: "First, the scheme of federal regulation is so pervasive as to make reasonable the inference that Congress left no room for the states to supplement it. . . . Second the federal statutes touch a field in which the federal interest is so dominant that the federal system must be assumed to preclude enforcement of state laws on the same subject. . . . Third, [where] enforcement of state . . . acts presents a serious danger of conflict with the administration of the federal program."

19. Lorillard Tobacco Co. v. Reilly, 121 S. Ct. 2404, 2414 (2001) ("Congressional purpose is the 'ultimate touchstone' of our inquiry.") See Catherine Fisk, *The Last Article about the Language of ERISA Preemption?: A Case Study of the Failure of Textualism*, 33 Harv. J. on Legis. 37 (1996) (arguing that the distinction between express and implied preemption is one without much difference).

20. Gade v. National Solid Waste Management, 505 U.S. at 96 (citations omitted).

21. See Medtronic Inc. v. Lohr, 518 U.S. 470, 485 (1996), quoting Retail Clerks v. Schermerhorn, 375 U.S. 96, 103 (1963).

22. New York State Department of Social Services v. Dublino, 413 U.S. 405, 413 (1973) (citation omitted).

23. See Hoke, *supra* note 11, at 830 n.5.

24. Rice v. Santa Fe Elevator Corporation, 331 U.S. 218, 230 (1947).

25. See, e.g., Lorillard Tobacco Co. v. Reilly, 533 U.S. 525 (2001); Buckman Co. v. Plain-

tiffs' Legal Committee, 531 U.S. 341 (2001); Crosby v. National Foreign Trade Council, 530 U.S. 363 (2000); Geier v. American Honda Motor Co. Inc., 529 U.S. 861 (2000) (all finding federal law to preempt state law).

26. 529 U.S. 861 (2000).

27. 15 U.S.C. §1397(k).

28. 529 U.S. at 869.

29. Id. at 868–75.

30. The dissent by Justice Stevens forcefully makes this point, see 539 U.S. at 907 (Stevens, J., dissenting); see also Susan Raeker-Jordan, *A Study in Judicial Sleight of Hand: Did Geier v. American Honda Motor Co. Eradicate the Presumption against Preemption?* 17 B.Y.U. J. Pub. L. 1 (2002).

31. 533 U.S. 525 (2001).

32. The Court found that the Massachusetts law was preempted in its regulation of cigarette advertising. As for the regulation of cigar and smokeless tobacco advertising, which are not the subject of federal regulation, the Court ruled that the law violated the First Amendment.

33. 15 U.S.C. §1333(b).

34. 533 U.S. at 547–48.

35. 533 U.S. at 591 (Stevens, J., dissenting).

36. 533 U.S. at 548–49.

37. My focus here is only the preemption issue and not whether the Massachusetts law violates the First Amendment. I think that there is a strong argument that the Massachusetts law is unconstitutional and, in fact, the Court struck down the regulations as applied to smokeless tobacco on that basis. But whether the law should be preempted is a distinct question, and my response would be to disagree with the Court.

38. 530 U.S. 363 (2000).

39. Id. at 379–80.

40. Id. at 381.

41. 539 U.S. 396 (2003).

42. 539 U.S. at 430–31 (Ginsburg, J., dissenting) (citations omitted).

43. §13801(e).

44. §13803.

45. §13806.

46. §13801(f).

47. Id. at 413–16.

48. Id. at 417.

49. 389 U.S. 429 (1968).

50. 539 U.S. at 418.

51. Id. at 425.

52. As cited previously, for an argument that counters the presumption against preemption, see Dinh, *supra* note 10.

53. Garcia v. San Antonio Metropolitan Transit Authority, 469 U.S. 528, 567–68 n.13 (1985) (Powell, J., dissenting).

54. Federal Energy Regulatory Commission v. Mississippi, 456 U.S. 741, 787–88 (1982) (O'Connor, J., dissenting).

55. For a similar argument, made relatively early in the Supreme Court tenure of William

Rehnquist, see David Shapiro, *Mr. Justice Rehnquist: A Preliminary View*, 90 Harv. L. Rev. 293 (1977).

56. See, e.g., Kimel v. Florida Board of Regents, 528 U.S. 62 (2000) (states cannot be sued for violating the Age Discrimination in Employment Act); United States v. Morrison, 529 U.S. 598 (2000); City of Boerne v. Flores, 521 U.S. 507 (1997) (invalidating the Religious Freedom Restoration Act as applied to state and local governments). All of these, of course, are instances in which federalism was used to strike down laws expanding civil rights protection.

57. See, e.g., Carter v. Carter Coal Co., 298 U.S. 238 (1936); Hammer v. Dagenhart (The Child Labor Case), 247 U.S. 251 (1918); United States v. E. C. Knight Co., 156 U.S. 1 (1895) (invalidating federal laws as exceeding the scope of Congress's commerce clause authority or as violating the Tenth Amendment).

58. 401 U.S. 37 (1971). See also Fair Assessment in Real Estate Association Inc. v. McNary, 454 U.S. 100 (1981) (using federalism as a basis for precluding federal court review of the constitutionality of state taxes); Rizzo v. Goode, 423 U.S. 362 (1976) (using federalism as a basis for precluding federal court review of systematic police abuse).

59. 505 U.S. 144 (1992) (declaring unconstitutional a federal law as violating the Tenth Amendment because it coerced state legislative and regulatory activity).

60. 514 U.S. 549 (1995) (declaring unconstitutional the federal Gun-Free School Zones Act as exceeding the scope of Congress's commerce clause authority).

61. 517 U.S. 44 (1996) (holding that Congress may not override the Eleventh Amendment except if acting under Section 5 of the Fourteenth Amendment, and that state officers may not be sued pursuant to federal laws that contain a comprehensive enforcement mechanism).

62. For an argument that this conception of federalism is in accord with the design of the Constitution and is historically supported, see Deborah J. Merritt, *Federalism as Empowerment*, 46 U. Fla. L. Rev. 541 (1995).

63. Of course, if the state or local law infringed the constitutional protections of individual liberties or civil rights, federal courts would strike it down on that basis.

64. 527 U.S. 706 (1999).

65. In this way, my approach is similar in result to that asserted by Professor Jesse Choper, who has argued that judicial review should be about individual liberties and not about enforcing separation of powers, or federalism. But unlike Professor Choper, I would not eliminate judicial review of the structure of government. I do not consider separation of powers in this book, and I would retain judicial review with regard to federalism, though in a much restricted way. Jesse Choper, *Judicial Review and the National Political Process* (1980).

Index

and, 175, 179–80, 190–91, 193,
208–24; courts of appeals, 171, 187;
empowering, 12–13; federal appellate
review, 187; federal district courts,
171, 254n50; federalism as a limit on,
23–31, 34, 145–46; federal judges,
192–95; federal question jurisdiction, 156, 173, 271n49; federal rights
and, 207–8; individual liberties and,
245; institutional characteristics of,
192–95; judicial limits to power of, 4,
5, 9–10, 15, 22–31, 116–17; jurisdiction of, 3, 7, 13, 34, 156, 162, 169,
171–77, 196, 198–99, 201–9, 216–17,
271n49; legislative supremacy and,
202–5, 207–8; litigant choice and,
208–24; lower federal courts, 171,
202, 207–8; money damages and, 30;
political insulation of, 192; post–
Civil War, 191; power of, 241–42;
pre–Civil War, 191; quality of,
179–80, 185–86; redefining the role
of the, 168–224; specialized federal
tribunals, 171; state courts and,
12–13, 31, 116, 168–224, 253–54n48,
277n105. *See also* comity; parity;
state governments and, 124; state
laws and, 18, 241, 254n50; states
and, 12–13, 18, 24–25, 28–31, 124,
256n80; subject-matter jurisdiction,
34; superiority of, 173–74, 211, 224,
273n29; variation among, 210
federal district courts, 171, 254n50
*Federal Energy Regulatory Commission
v. Mississippi*, 104
federal funds, 49–50
federal government, 161, 245. *See also*
Congress; preemption; presidential
power; tyranny; federal agencies,
47, 119–20, 124, 231–32. *See also
specific agencies*; interests of the, 96;
limitations on the, 180, 247; post–
Civil War scope of the, 173; power
of the, 10–11, 100–101, 117, 158–59,
164–65, 180; pre–Civil War scope of
the, 172–73; preemption of state laws
by the, 65–66; state government and

the, 91, 230–31; supremacy of the,
96, 97
federal grants, 49–50, 149, 270n17
federalism, 16, 138–39, 155–56, 209,
227, 231, 237–40, 242–43, 251n37,
256–57n103, 258n140, 263n8,
281n56, 281n65; of the 1990s, 48–50,
57–97; alternative vision of, 1, 8–12;
as a basis for limiting government,
7–8, 9–10, 12; benefits of, 11, 98, 99.
See also federalism: values of; conservative use of, 5–8; constitutionality
and, 35; definition of, 93; dual federalism, 17, 49, 240–41, 252n10; in
the early twenty-first century, 86–90;
as empowerment, 1–14, 145–67,
168–224, 240–47; enhancing, 171,
208, 214–15, 218; failure of, 10;
federalism revolution, 48–54; federalist perspective on, 145–46, 154, 157,
247, 269n1; formalistic approach
to, 1–2, 57–97; functional approach
to, 98–99; as a limit on Congress, 9,
23, 30–47, 93, 159–60; as a limit on
federal judicial power, 2–3, 23–25; as
limits, 166; litigant choice in forum
selection and, 208–24; nationalist
perspective on, 145–46, 154, 155,
157, 247, 269n1; "new federalism"
of Ronald Reagan, 6; objections to
federalism as empowerment, 162–67;
objectives of, 117, 154; originalist
objections to federalism as empowerment, 163–65; "Our Federalism",
15, 116, 241; political safeguards of,
58–59; post-1937, 9–10, 15–36, 98,
116–17; pre-1990s, 116–17; preemption and, 230–31, 240–45; protection of, 58–60; of the Rehnquist
court, 48–50, 54, 56, 101, 104–5,
107, 115, 116–17, 123, 160, 225–27,
231, 237–40, 246; revival of, 31–47;
tenets of federalism as empowerment,
147–58; traditionally stated values of,
99–116; two views of, 145; values of,
4, 7–8, 93–94, 98–144, 146, 238–39,
240